The Color of Night

The Color of Night

A Young Mother, a Missing Child and a Cold-Blooded Killer

By L.C. Timmerman and John H. Timmerman

New Horizon Press
Far Hills, NJ

Timmerman, L.C. and Timmerman, John H.
The Color of Night: A Young Mother, a Missing Child
and a Cold-Blooded Killer
Cover design: Wendy Bass
Interior design: Susan M. Sanderson

Library of Congress Control Number: 2010928515

ISBN 13: 978-0-88282-322-5
New Horizon Press

Manufactured in the U.S.A.

2015   2014   2013   2012   2011   /   5   4   3   2   1

Dedication

We gratefully acknowledge the help and support of our families and dedicate this work to the memory of others who have endured the oppression of loss. We hope, however, that you are able to enjoy the story and find some kindred feelings, despite the brutality out of which it arises.

Authors' Note

This book is based on the experiences of the authors and reflects their perception of the past, present and future. The personalities, events, actions and conversations portrayed within this story have been taken from interviews, research, court documents, letters, personal papers, press accounts and the memories of some participants.

In an effort to safeguard the privacy of certain people, some individuals' names and identifying characteristics have been changed. Some characters may be composites. Events involving the characters happened as described. Only minor details may have been altered.

Contents

Preface

Newaygo County, Michigan, is a strangely beautiful, yet almost fearful land. Its muscular forests flex around sodden lowlands. Jungle-like cattail and coiling brush grow tall along swamps as black as a dying breath. Stretches of county road, interspersed with two-lane blacktop, wind through overhanging hardwood. In autumn, the sun-dazzled colors take your breath away. Pine trees of every sort, some scorched black and gray by wildfires, crouch at the edge of the road.

Even these paved roads have surprises and deceptions. At one intersection, a road to the right is signposted as 2nd Street; the road to the left, 32 Mile. People here don't depend on maps much.

An arthritic tracery of gravel roads, woven all across the county, doesn't even make the maps. Nor do they have names. Often they end in muddy tracks leading to an algae encrusted pond or stream. Here the local high school students build campfires and drink beer.

Hunting and fishing are the primary industries, drawing others from neighboring states and southern counties to these nearly primeval forests. They come with money. The bars overflow. Traffic at the prostitutes' establishments, mostly cramped trailers, is nonstop.

People grow deer bait in the mucky fields, harvest acres of beets and cull carrots that are processed into fifty-pound bags stacked up at produce stands along the two-lane roads. A bag of gnarled carrots goes for $3.00. The deer don't care what they look like. The total harvest of bait crops in Michigan can run thirty to forty million dollars a year.

Every few years, a deer is found contaminated with Chronic Wasting Disease, a form of transmissible spongiform encephalopathies (TSE) found in the animal's central nervous system and rumored to affect humans who eat venison. Everything stops as Department of Natural Resources officials try to trace the fatal strain. When the hunt stops, so do the bait shops, the whores and the bars. Farmers backhoe their crops as landfill or simply plow it under. Some tourists fish in the streams and rivers instead, hitting the salmon run from Lake Michigan.

The houses along these curving, wooded roads change in the blink of an eye. Altogether, there are not many of them. You come across a pocket of small homes in a clearing or a scattered stand of hunters' cabins at the edge of a wood, a party store or gas station nearby to service them. Now and then you see larger "retreat" houses, expensive places set well back from the road and built by refugees from the city. They wear gates and landscaping like skirts. Further along the same road, a group of trailers, some holding themselves together with little more than hope, gather together and form a community.

Most of these places are inhabited by ordinary, hardworking folk. They like the space of these north woods, the cheap land cut out of pine and sedum and backfilled lowlands. They have steady jobs, picnics and parties. They are intelligent and by and large love the land they live on and respect it deeply.

In worn clearings, in trailers and houses neglected and weathered beyond belief, live a few of those men and women somehow damaged. They are the ruined remains of wars, of psychological battles, of illnesses of mind and soul—no longer at ease in cities or towns. They need freedom.

As much as anything, the unsettled land of Newaygo County— its swamps and streams, its hardscrabble farms, its primeval forests that darken the sky—shapes the characters and events of this story. It is an easy land to get lost in, an easy land in which to lose someone.

A few key facts say much about the place and people of Newaygo County. The county spreads over 861 square miles—nineteen of which are composed purely of water. It does, after all, have a count of 230 natural lakes—omitting a few hundred swamps and sinkholes too small with which to bother. Hardy Dam, which centers the tourist fishing industry, is the largest earthen dam east of the Mississippi.

The significant thing for the dark events that unfold here—true events—is that the entire population for all those square miles is 48,000. Of those, the four places optimistically labeled by the United States Census Bureau as "cities" comprise 8,184 of the total population. Fremont, the largest city by virtue of having a baby food factory, tops out at 4,234. Newaygo has to stretch to meet its claim of 1,639. White Cloud, the county seat, weighs in at 1,420 and the city of Grant comes in at a svelte 881. That leaves about 40,000 souls to find their places among all those misbegotten miles.

Especially the lost souls.

In some—or at least one—of these derelict houses, live moral monsters, those whose lives are so twisted by personal desires or hatreds they can never be straightened again. Those whose darkness seeps through every pore like some miasmic power that beclouds all they meet. If all humankind carries a spore of evil, these are the ones who have willingly coaxed it to life and let it possess their very being.

Part I

Discovery

"The Horror! The Horror!"

Joseph Conrad
Heart of Darkness

Chapter 1

The Turtle Hunter

Kenny Mochenrose was still hungover. He laughed. He couldn't remember the last time he wasn't hungover.

He remembered last night vaguely, playing darts down at the tavern. He couldn't even hit the damn target; the thing seemed to keep moving on the wall. Played for a dime a dart. His pocket money had run out the same time as his last beer. He staggered out to the parking lot, made it inside his truck and passed out with the door open.

The cold awakened him around six. He pulled the door shut and fell asleep again.

By ten o'clock the tavern owner was pounding on the door and telling him to haul his ass home.

Kenny looked unsteadily into the bed of the pickup. *Damn, how did that john boat get there?*

Kenny thought for a moment, his head pounding. He was going to set turtle traps today, up at Oxford Lake. He'd been talking about it last night, before the beer caught up with him.

"What do you do with damn turtles?" Fat Hank had asked. The guy drank twice the beer Kenny had and didn't even seem tipsy. It just went into one of those big rolls around his gut. Like storage tanks. Fat Hank sucked on a black cigar that smelled like a roomful of farts.

"Eat 'em," Kenny had replied. "What else?"

"I wouldn't eat no turtle if my life depended on it. Think of them things. Living in some shitty muck, eating every dead thing that comes their way. Disgusting. Purely disgusting. Might as well eat shit."

"Naw. You got it wrong, Hank. I got me recipes. All stored up here." He tapped his forehead, missed on the second tap and poked his eye.

"I got me turtle soup." He counted on his fingers. "Turtle casserole. Smoked turtle. Turtle on the grill with hot sauce. That's probably the best."

Yeah. Kenny thought as he scratched his neck. *That explains the john boat. Yes, sir.* The traps were in it. Kenny Mochenrose had traps for anything. Traps for fat autumn squirrels. Fox and coon traps for hides. Turtle traps. Fish traps. He didn't even own a gun, just an old wooden baseball bat, splattered with blood and gore, that he used on the larger animals.

Well, he thought, *let's see if I'm sober enough to drive.* Oxford Lake wasn't but ten or twelve miles away. *Nobody ever patrols there. They'll never find my traps.*

County maps of Newaygo County aren't likely to show Oxford Lake. United States government topographical surveys locate it at latitude and longitude coordinates of N 43.10696 and W 85.73339, which helps little. Surrounded by scrub forest in a maze of marshland, the heart-shaped body of water tends to fluctuate in area according to rainfall or drought. On this day, it was hot and dry. It had been a wet spring. The air would be full of mosquitoes, but it didn't bother Kenny much. *They'll get their first jab in and fall over drunk,* he chuckled to himself.

What never changes in the lake is the deep, cold bed of muck that in some areas rises within two feet of the surface and in others disappears into a ninety foot tomb of impenetrable darkness. Twenty-one acres of algae and organic marshland.

One isn't likely to find Oxford Lake by looking or by chance. Yet, those who live in Monroe Township (378 households in thirty-six square miles), Newaygo County, know these tricky side roads and hidden lakes well. They start learning about them in high school. At fifteen or sixteen they borrow a friend's four-by-four to find a place to drink.

Kenny Mochenrose knew the lakes, streams and forests of Monroe Township like the label on a bottle of his preferred beer. He knew where to turn off the two-lane: by the lightning-struck elm that angled to the south. The dirt tracks were hidden by brush. He drove right through, a bumping noise coming from the truck bed as the john boat shifted. Kenny shifted to first gear here. The truck was badly aged, bearing dents and bruises from many a foray on such roads. Rust drooled around the headlights, long since knocking them cock-eyed despite the liberal use of duct tape to hold them in place. He didn't much care about the rusted doors and rear quarter panels. He thought it gave the old truck a touch of derelict class. The engine was pretty good, the old six steady over the bumps.

Kenny could drive this road in the dark of a new moon. Maybe better if the hangover wasn't slamming against the back of his eyelids, though. He hardly needed to watch the road and hardly did. He veered off the two-track slightly and hit a beech sapling, snapping its trunk like an axe blow. He heard the branches scrape along the drive shaft. *Who tol' that thing to grow there?* he wondered. He made the rest of the dips and curves without incident and was proud of himself for it.

The two-track angled through axle-high weeds, slipped through a stand of trees and flattened into a turnaround. Kenny stopped the truck and looked. He had to make a decision, which was hard going through his muddled mind, about whether to continue in the truck or on foot.

A path sloped down from the turnaround to the lake. A low lying mist hung over the water. The sky was an occluded gray, a fog bank scumming the forests. Dismal. Kenny wanted to sleep. The water looked all silvery. He got out of the truck and walked down the path to the lake. Mud sucked at the heels of his boots. Limp sumac hung over the path, brushing now and then at his cap. Drops of fog water clung to the bill.

You can't hardly call it a shore, he thought. Dark water crept up into swamp plants like some kind of ooze. *There'd be good turtles in there, good big ones. Dumb old lunkers with heads the size of baseballs.*

At the end of the path someone had laid a couple of old pallets nailed to two-by-fours to serve as a primitive dock. It was old now, rotted and coated with slick, dark moss. It bounced into the black water when Kenny stepped on it. *Well,* he thought, *no backing the truck down here. Even a four-by-four couldn't get out of here.* Kenny trudged back up the path. He lowered the tailgate of the truck, but sat there a few minutes smoking a cigarette and studying the lake, trying to remember where he had set traps before.

A few out by that island, he thought. *Except they aren't really islands so much as patches of muck. Couldn't hardly get a stake to hold there.* No, he'd put some along the shore, maybe try the island, see if it would hold anything. He could just see some big snappers coming up there to sun themselves. That is, if the sun ever came out.

He stood up, pulled the john boat out of the bed of the truck and let it drop onto the pebbles of the path. The dented aluminum received a few more dings.

The hoop traps were homemade and a mess. Kenny was a scrapper. On garbage and recycling days he patrolled the streets of the villages before dawn, using his halogen flashlight to spot any metal or anything that might be usable along the curb. Whatever he found went on the back of the truck. There was a slag heap of rusted metal behind his trailer. If anyone came to haul it away, they'd probably also take his trailer by mistake. But Kenny could fix just about anything he wanted or needed out of that old pile. Like his turtle traps.

He unloaded them into the john boat. He remembered making one—two round ends from barbeque grills and chicken wire. And that one—the hoop ends out of box springs spliced together with chicken wire nets. They worked, all right. He loaded all eight in the boat. *Ain't making two trips,* he figured. *It's downhill.*

Next he loaded the stakes, eight foot metal rods cut from rebar. He would slip the traps down over them, rather than bothering to tie them. Then the bait, a cardboard box of chicken heads and necks that still seeped black stains. Smelled so awful he lit another cigarette. *Damn,* he thought. *Almost forgot the oars.* He laughed out loud. *Wouldn't that be a pretty sight?*

Cigarette hanging from the corner of his lip, he began tugging the boat down the hill. *They'll be hell to pay*, he thought, *getting this thing back up. Maybe I'll just leave it in the water, check on the traps in a day or two.* The noise he made startled two large, ungainly birds on the opposite shore. *Blue herons*, he noted.

Kenny laid three traps among the shoreline cattails. Two inches of water and five feet of muck. He had painted the end of each rod with orange spray paint, also found while scrapping. The paint made them easy to find. One rod sank nearly to the paint line. *What the hell*, he thought, *might as well try a couple along the island. Long way to row, though.*

Partway across the lake to the island, Kenny lit another cigarette. All that work was making him warm. He took off his jacket and laid it in front of him. *A good jacket for mosquitoes*, he thought. *They can't hardly get through the grease and oil; rainproof, too.* He squinted against the cigarette smoke, watching a blue heron taking flight from the eastern shore. A bit of light slanted through the clouds.

He saw it then. Couldn't figure out what it was or how it got there. Sort of gray, catching the sun's light. Gray but shiny, like some kid's big beach ball. Or like some dead animal, bloating away for the turtles. Kenny dipped the oars.

He pulled hard at the oars once and let the john boat feather in. Curious, he got closer, still unable to find a shape.

The bloated body oozed muck. Blonde hair was grimed with algae.Kenny Mochenrose started vomiting. He couldn't stop. He couldn't even get it over the gunwale. Just his luck to see something like *that*. The vomit exploded against his brown jacket, spattered all over the boat. Then he pulled frantically at the oars. He thought he may have hit something once, something mushy, but he didn't stop. He got the boat straightened, made wildly for the shore. He couldn't see the spot where he entered the cattails and began to panic. Then he spotted the high cab of his truck and rowed like the devil had one foot in his boat and was gaining on him fast.

As he slammed the john boat alongside the pallet-made dock, he gathered up his stinking jacket and flung it behind him into the lake. *Good jacket, too,* he thought. It'd be covered with muck in an hour. With strength he didn't know he had, he pulled the groaning boat up to the truck, lifted the bow in and pushed it in. He dared one glance over his shoulder. He saw nothing. He collapsed in his truck. It began to drizzle. *What now?* he thought. *What now?*

His first impulse, naturally, was to get out of there. Forget the bloated body oozing muck he'd seen. He could call the state troopers, their anonymous tip line.

Wait a minute. Weren't the Staties looking for some girl? Maybe a month or two ago? Seems he had read something about an award. Reward, whatever you call it. He couldn't remember how much, but it was more than he had right now.

Kenny Mochenrose started the truck then remembered he didn't even have change to make a phone call. *Well, hell's bells. Outpost six isn't but twelve miles away. I'll drive there.* He checked his gas. *Hell, yes, I can make it.* His hands were still shaking as he put the truck in gear and lurched out onto the two-track.

The truck ran out of gas halfway there. He cursed loudly then looked up in surprise as two sheriff department cars, then a third, screamed down the highway.

Kenny leaned back against the seat. *Damn,* he thought, *someone must of got killed.*

Chapter 2

Second Sighting

George Vande Velde looked around with the same awe he always felt. He was still. His face grew damp with the ground fog. The marshland was primeval. He could imagine the great beasts plodding through these same wastes after the last glaciers receded. The moraines and marsh their playground. Bending necks toward new growth to rip and chew. This was the primitive world, far from the concrete, glass and steel encapsulation of Chicago. He needed this. It was the best investment he had ever made, whether he ever built on the acres he had purchased or not. He was a developer, after all, but not here.

This was the still point, the primitive. A world without noise, without decisions, without other people in their power suits and shiny shoes.

He saw a doe and her fawn nibbling daintily at a copse of bushes. The doe must have caught his scent. She lifted her head and stared at him full on for ten seconds. Then she flitted away, the fawn bouncing behind.

Birdsong floated from a nearby stand of trees. He hadn't yet learned the names of all the trees and foliage. He was learning the animals first and knew where the two families of mink lived. One lived in a large hollow log near a stream. They weren't very careful. Small bones of rodents, frogs and fish lay near the stream, waiting for a good rain to wash them downstream. The other family lived a ways off, in a rise of ground. It was by luck he had found the small, four-inch entrance hole, neatly disguised under tufts of some kind of weed.

He had tracked them from the stream, actually, curious why one set of tracks veered off in this direction. He followed, spotting a track here or there in sand or mud. Then he hunkered down with his binoculars and waited.

George Vande Velde had come up to Michigan looking for some retreat property. Like everyone else wanting an escape from Chicago and who had the money to spend, he contacted a realtor about Lake Michigan shoreline property. The realtor showed him a shack caving in on itself for 1.2 million dollars. "It has eighty feet of frontage," she gushed. With all the plastic pumped into her, she did as well. He looked for birds and all he saw were seagulls. He listened for songbirds and heard the bitchy gulls screaming and cawing. It nearly drove him nuts.

He came for quiet, not seagulls. The kids were out of the big house in North Chicago, his son being groomed to take over the firm, his daughter in her last year of medical residency. Since his wife died of breast cancer eighteen months before, a bitter, gray January day, the house felt like a tomb. Only the longtime maid or the lawn crew broke the musty air. When he got together with the kids, he met them at a restaurant in Chicago. He had put the big house up for sale six months after his wife died.

In all those years with his wife, he had never felt the desire or the need for other women. Maybe his business was his mistress, a demanding enough whore. Now he felt that all need and desire had shorted out, the wire ends burned in one massive electrical meltdown.

In one year he had had only one offer on the house—$350,000 below his asking price. He turned it down. Let them earn a little more money, he reasoned, and try again. Now he just wanted a retreat. Away from Chicago and the never-ending phone calls. Let his son handle them. He wanted to breathe deep and recall the days when there was so much good to remember. In Chicago there was so little time.

The shoreline along Lake Michigan was built up, cottages squeezed helter-skelter on paved drives with names like Paradise Pines or Maple Villa Drive. Water access assured. It was more squeezed than

Chicago, if that were possible. Better view to be sure and Chicago didn't have those young females spilling out of bikinis while they paraded along the beach.

On the way back after looking at two more grossly overpriced cabins, he had turned inland on a whim. Entering thick forest, he got thoroughly lost on some unnamed roads and finally stopped his SUV. What he saw beyond the bend of the road, stretched out like a broad silverback in the sun was Hardy Dam Pond. He parked the truck on the shoulder and walked along the road. On top of the dam the road narrowed to a decrepit two-lane, choked by more potholes and cracks than he had ever seen on one stretch. The railings were like some mad study in rust by a deranged sculptor. He wondered if the bridge would hold the SUV. Then he looked to the right, down the steep flank of the earthen dam, looked down at the tops of trees spread over the river valley. In the distance he could see where the river coiled into another, smaller lake.

This is the raw land, Vande Velde thought. His knees felt shaky, his heart pounded. This is the coarse stuff out of which histories were made or where they simply trailed off into the shadowed heart of the forests. It was one of those instantaneous things. He fell in love with the land.

He drove the SUV onto the narrow road, praying that no other vehicles would approach. He let the big truck idle across. From the top of the dam he saw a man shoreline fishing on the lake. Vande Velde parked in the first turnoff, killed the engine and approached him. The man didn't move. He had a stringer of crappies and bluegill, pretty good size, and an open forty ounce in a paper bag, also pretty good size, at his side.

"Morning." Vande Velde said.

"You ain't from around here. Lost?"

"Sort of. Looks like good fishing."

"You're welcome to dip a line."

"Actually, I'm looking for a realtor. Know where I can find one?"

"Croton's got one. If you can find the realtor. Got an office on the Croton Highway. If she's not there, try Gloria's."

"Gloria's?"

"Her name. Also the name of her restaurant. If you can't find her there, you can drive on down to Newaygo."

"Any idea how to get there?"

"Easy. Turn right on 40th, keep going. Same into Newaygo."

Vande Velde found the office—Croton Realty—closed and walked up the street to the restaurant. A woman with bright purple hair, long, was at a table, chatting with some men digging into big plates of stew. The stew smelled sweet, not like anything he had smelled before. He walked over to the table.

"Is Gloria in?" he asked.

"I'm Gloria," said the purple-haired woman. "Who's asking?"

She was a pretty woman, Vande Velde decided. Small face, an impish nose, a smile that dazzled. And nicely put together, too. He fished his billfold out and handed her his gold-embossed card. "I'm looking for some property," he said politely. "Wondered if you could help."

She studied the card. "Vande Velde Developments," she read. He wondered if she might be a little slow, the way she stared at the card, as if deciphering a puzzle.

"Chicago," she read. "And Urbana. Well, you did come a long way to develop."

The men at the table laughed.

"Sorry. I've got nothing for you."

"I think you may have misunderstood, Ms…"

"Gloria's fine. Works for everyone around here. We're pretty well-developed."

George seemed to think about saying that he could see that, but bit his tongue. "Perhaps we could discuss this in private?" he asked.

"Not much to talk about, but I'm due to sit down for a bit. Annie!" she called. An older woman appeared in the kitchen doorway. She looked a lot like Gloria, but thicker in the waist, with short, dark hair.

"Take over for a few, please?"

"Gotcha, Glo."

"Follow me," she said. "Grab a cup of coffee if you like."

It took Vande Velde about ten minutes to convince Gloria Farnum that he had no intention of developing land up here. As they walked from the restaurant to the realty office, he filled her in on his day and the epiphany he felt when he saw Hardy Dam and the big pond.

"So you'd like to be on or near water," she said.

"Maybe. Maybe I just want to be here."

She nodded.

When Gloria admitted him to the office, she had to switch on the lights. Dusk was settling in. Vande Velde spotted framed diplomas on the wall. Surprised, he walked over and studied them: Her realtor's license, of course. B.A. University of Chicago. M. Div. Trinity Seminary. Gloria Farnum. Still, he had to ask. "All yours?"

She nodded.

"So you've lived in Chicago?"

"Yes."

"How did you like it?"

"Hated it. Understand, I was born and raised in Croton. It makes a difference."

"M. Div.?"

"Pastor of Croton Methodist Church. Now let me boot up the computer and I'll show you what I have, which is anything available in about thirty miles."

She had done a good job designing her Web site. Gloria brought up rural property and George pulled his chair closer to her. He caught the light scent of her perfume. He glanced at her, bathed in the blue light of the computer. Her skin was flawless, already lightly tanned. She felt his eyes, turned toward him and smiled.

"May I ask what price range you're looking in?"

"Whatever it's worth," George responded.

She laughed and pulled up pictures of some behemoth estate.

George groaned. "That's what I'm trying to get away from," he said.

"I see."

They looked through spreads of another half dozen properties. In each, George spotted nearby houses and rejected them. One was an eighty acre farm, also rejected.

Zilch.

"Is that it?"

"That's all I have. Sorry. I mean, there is empty land through here, but a lot of it is state or federal owned. Wait a minute, though. Last weekend I listed twenty acres. Really rough land. I know the old man and his daughters."

"Tell me about it."

"I don't even have the site set up on the Web. I can download my pictures, though, and give you some idea."

When she was done showing the pictures, Vande Velde asked, "When can we see it?" Something had stirred in him. Something he hadn't felt in a long time. Like a tingling in his loins that moved through his body.

"Not tonight," she said.

George looked outside. It was full dark. "When?"

"After I feed you breakfast at the restaurant."

"Okay. Is there a motel nearby?"

"You passed it coming in. It has a pink neon light that doesn't work. The beds are guaranteed…to have mice turds, bed bugs and who knows what else. You can sleep here. I've got an extra room upstairs."

"You live up there?"

"I'm a realtor, remember. I own the building."

"If it's no trouble."

It wasn't. Nor was it when she washed up and slipped into his bed. Desire and need hit him like a thunderstorm.

At breakfast, she smiled at him over a cup of coffee. He worked on eating a full stack of blueberry pancakes drowned in locally made maple syrup. He felt like he should feel guilty. He didn't. She had washed out the purple hair dye. Her hair was raven black, very full and hanging to her shoulders.

"Does this bother you?" he asked.

"How so?"

"I mean, you're a Methodist minister."

"I am. I'm even a believer. Rare thing in this age."

"Must be Free Methodist."

She laughed. "Finish up. We'll get going." She looked him full on, her eyes deep brown. "If it helps," she said, "I didn't plan it. I'm not even sure why I did it. I mean, I'm not the sort to jump into bed with anyone who wears pants, okay?"

Vande Velde raised his index finger gently to her lips. "Shhh," he said.

Gloria poured two cups of coffee to go and led him outside.

The first thing Vande Velde saw when Gloria stopped the SUV at the property for sale was a bald eagle that swooped lazily from a stand of oak over the smooth water of Oxford Lake and like a dark arrow into the morning sun. He had already made his decision, but he let her walk him over the property.

"Everything to the north," she said, "is state land. To the south, federal. Someone owns a few acres alongside of the section we're looking at. I've never heard of him doing anything with the land."

Vande Velde nodded.

"Over there is what we call the Oxford Swamp. It's in the watershed of the Pere Marquette River. In fact, you can kayak the streams right into the Pere and find terrific fishing. There's only one structure on the land," she said, "and it ain't much."

They crossed scrub land tangled by brush. Backed against a deeper stand of pine and maple was a log cabin. Shutters hung askew. The front steps caved in. The front door was broken. They pushed the door aside and entered.

"Obviously you're not buying for the housing boom," Gloria observed.

The whole cabin was one fair-sized room, maybe fourteen by twenty feet. It had a fireplace, rough built from native stone. *Probably have to be torn down and redone*, Vande Velde thought. Cupboards and empty bookshelves lined one wall. A long bench lined another. A propane stove. A pump handle at the sink for water. It seemed primitive. Signs of animals were everywhere. The walls needed to be caulked or chinked or whatever you called it.

"How much did you say?"

"Forty-nine thousand."

"Is that a fair price?"

"It might be a little speculative. But remember, I listed it."

"Fine," Vande Velde said.

They rode back to Croton to sign off the paperwork. Vande Velde cut a check for the full amount. He gave her his fax numbers for the papers and they set a date to close.

On the way back to Chicago, he made another detour. Following Gloria's hand-drawn map, he found Highway 127 and followed it to 96, then down on 23 past Ann Arbor to Dundee. It would be an easy kick back to I-94 and Chicago, but he wanted to stop at the massive hunting and outdoor recreation goods store. It had never worked out to stop there before. Now he had a reason.

For that matter, he probably could have gotten materials from one of any big box sporting goods store in Chicago, some of them probably in malls he had helped develop. When he entered this store, though, he felt like he was in another world, a fantasyland of the outdoors, a dream-shaper.

He started with a waterproof parka and matching pants. He moved to the boots section and stood bewildered before endless racks. A clerk fitted him for a pair of sturdy boots and, after Vande Velde described the terrain, a set of knee length waders. Crossing to the optics department, he picked up a six watt LED waterproof flashlight. Again, at optics, he relied on a clerk to guide him. He found most of the binoculars too bulky and settled instead on a lightweight pair. On the way to the checkout counter he loaded on his shopping cart a self-inflating sleeping pad and a sleeping bag. Most everything else, he figured, he could get in a sporting goods shop in Chicago or a hardware store in Croton.

All his merchandise choices rang up to $3,455.60. *Not bad,* Vande Velde thought. *Not when I've just saved a million or two by not living in a beehive on the shoreline.*

It was his second year in Croton and Vande Velde felt that he had time to relax and enjoy it. The summer before he was usually out of Chicago by Friday morning, just hoping his son didn't screw up the family business too badly. It wasn't all about construction, although his son's engineering degree helped there; it was about sales. The art of the schmooze. That's where George worried about his son. But he forgot about it all once his SUV hit the Dan Ryan Expressway.

His first summer at his new house he had to go to White Cloud to find a firm that could deliver the lumber supplies, generator and power tools he ordered. They had to custom fabricate the metal, lockable shutters and sash windows he wanted. The framed steel door was easy to get. The work went smoothly. He was the craftsman again, not the developer. He worked the outside first, keeping the tools in the cabin. A stonemason worked alongside him, rebuilding the fireplace and chimney. By late August he had some furniture delivered. He locked the shutters and the steel door and called it a very good year.

It was Saturday, July 5, and only the third time Vande Velde had been up to his cabin in his second year of owning it. He missed it. Missed the smell, the emptiness, the song of the forest. The damp air felt pristine, like every particle of dirt and smog had been washed away by the ground fog. It was as quiet as a whisper. He had the binoculars trained on two blue herons shoreline wading. One of them had caught a small sunfish. In an acrobatic feat that gave Vande Velde shivers, the bird flung the fish into the air, gaped its beak and caught the fish head down. Through the lens he could see the fish bob down the gullet.

Suddenly the herons startled and climbed into a hopping, ungainly flight.

Vande Velde heard the racket before he spotted the source. There on the south shore was a man banging an aluminum boat out of a dilapidated truck. From 300 yards away Vande Velde could pick out every detail through the binoculars. Quickly he adjusted the lens. *There. What is he loading into that derelict? Nets or traps of some sort.*

Vande Velde hunkered down in a squat. This was interesting. He watched as the man slid the boat into the water, driving long stakes near shore, wiring the contraptions to them. Was that a chicken head? He watched the boat move out onto the lake.

Something was floating out there. It looked like a faded balloon or buoy of some kind.

The guy in the boat passed it and turned. He watched through the binoculars as the man screamed, vomited and paddled furiously toward shore. He couldn't follow everything after the man pulled his boat out of the water.

Vande Velde tweaked the focus of the binoculars, bringing what he thought was a buoy full into the lens. Through the binoculars it seemed like he was standing on top of it. Immediately he began digging in his pockets before realizing that his cellular phone was in the cabin. Then he was running, running hard, to call 911.

Part II

The Crime

"So cold, so icy that one burns one's fingers on him!"

Friedrich Nietzsche
Beyond Good and Evil, Epigram 91

Chapter 3

The Card Game

Rachel was happy. Happier, she thought, than she had ever been in her life.

She sat on the porch steps, admiring the antics of her three-month-old daughter, Shannon. Her pink, chubby fists flailed at the satin-edged blanket. Shannon's sky-blue eyes glittered in the sunlight, her silken hair tufted after her bath.

"She's so beautiful," Rachel's sister Sara said, holding out a finger to the tight little fist. The baby latched out, holding the finger to her mouth.

"She's hungry again," Sara laughed.

"She's always hungry. But you have to wait, beautiful baby," Rachel nuzzled her daughter's cheek. "Else you'll grow like a big old beach ball." She turned to Sara. "Can you believe she's in six-month diapers?"

"I know. I change enough of them."

Rachel's mouth spread in a grin as wide as the sun. It was a good day to be alive.

She had been smart, Rachel thought, to postpone marriage to the baby's father. Not that she had anything against him. He was a good person and Rachel loved his mother. But she wasn't sure she loved him. Not enough to marry, anyway. When she married she definitely wanted to be in love; she wanted it to last.

Who knows, she sometimes thought. *Maybe we will marry some-day. But not now; not yet.* After all, they had only been seeing each other a few months when she got pregnant. *Stupid*, she thought. She knew better. They started teaching birth control in, like, third grade now. But Shannon was her gift. Her special gift.

If only she had her own place—small, just for her and Shan-non—it would be perfect. Maybe it could work. She had some ideas to add to the small amount of child support and food stamps she received. She nibbled her daughter's ear.

Yes, she was happy. Even when Shannon woke her during the night, she thought, *This is my daughter calling.*

"She sure is the spitting image of you," Sara said.

"She is beautiful, my Shannon-go-Bannon."

The two sisters stretched out on the steps, letting the sun work slowly up their legs on this warm day.

"Do you have to work today?" she asked Sara.

"Yeah. Isaac's picking me up."

"Drop me off at Dad's, will you? I want to hang out there for a while. Maybe take a dip in the pool and mooch some goodies off Lyn."

"She is one of the world's best cooks. Okay. Figure on leaving by one-thirty, latest."

As Rachel relaxed by her father's pool later that day, Shannon on her lap delighting in the occasional sprinkle of water on her damp toes, she felt the past tug even more urgently at the edges of her mind.

She had been lucky, she knew, reflecting on the events of the past few months. Probation instead of five months in jail.

What would she have done without her baby for five months?

True, arrangements could have been made. The baby's father and his mother offered to take Shannon full time. Of course, her own dad and stepmom would have helped in any way possible. They always did.

Five months! She couldn't imagine what that would be like. At least she got probation.

She had a friend, Wayne Davis, who was a veteran living on disability. Often a few friends gathered at his house on the weekend to drink beer and play card games. Sometimes a couple of them brought along marijuana if they scored at a party store on what they called "Hunter's Highway." Rachel had given up beer and weed during her pregnancy but figured there was nothing wrong with enjoying the smell as the cards slid across the table.

"So," she said during a break from the card game one night in her seventh month of pregnancy, "how can I score some cash? You seen the price of diapers?"

"Ain't needed any of those lately," Wayne said.

"You gonna drink any more beer?" This from Angel, a tall, dark-haired guy. A contractor, Angel had been laid off this past winter. It seemed everyone in Michigan was laid off.

Instead, they played cards, drank beer and smoked weed.

"Here's the deal," Wayne said. "Take a weapon from my back room. Any old weapon. Hell, take that AK-47 I smuggled back. Ever tell you how I did that?"

"'Bout a million and six times," Angel said.

"Broke it down and put it in a speaker."

"Million and seven."

"Here's the thing. Hell, I'll go with you. Take ourselves a couple weapons and raid some of those hunters' cabins. Cool. They'll all be bouncing on some whore out of Baldwin anyway."

"Wayne, you're nuts," Rachel said.

"That's true," he said. "See, we'll wear hoods. Scare the shit outta them townies. A big canvas bag to dump the pro...pro...cedurals in."

"Yeah and they'll be looking for a little scrawny guy and a woman with a belly as big as Newaygo County. You're nuts."

"You already said that and I agreed. That's why I'm on disability."

Nobody was particularly surprised that Rachel was good friends with Wayne, even though he was about thirty years older than she was. He had little money, but enough heart to fill a treasure vault. People who didn't know him, especially when they saw him in the worn Army jacket that he never seemed to take off, usually called him a bit odd. Rachel didn't care. She figured most people were odd in one way or another. They had a right to it. And Wayne was one of the kindest guys she knew. He never wanted something for himself if he knew someone else who needed it more.

Wayne's wounds were in his head. Occasionally he tried to explain—post-traumatic stress syndrome—but people made rude comments. So Wayne quit talking about it and pointed at a small scar under his chin instead.

What nobody saw was the other scar, the one under the unkempt long hair near the rear of the skull. It was a star-shaped pattern with jagged edges and it bulged slightly from the metal plate the surgeons used to hold together the skin they harvested from his butt cheek.

He was certified as being on full disability and now wore his field coat with the 25th Infantry patch and corporal stripes in his house. "Could of made Sergeant," he told Rachel once, "but after slogging along the Mekong for eleven months I got foot rot so bad they shipped me out to a rear base. Feet are still half rotted. Purple and green. Wanna see them?"

While playing cards at Wayne's trailer that night, Angel had slipped three small bags of weed into Rachel's jacket pocket. "Just in case you need it," he said.

"I can't smoke when I'm pregnant."

"Hey, you inhale enough just sitting in on a game here. And you're complaining about how your back hurts and you're nervous about delivering. Here's what Doctor Angel ordered. Just hang on to it. My present."

She laughed. "No thanks, Angel. I've been good. Won't change now."

But she hadn't returned the baggies. *Maybe after I deliver*, she thought.

Rachel never got the chance. The sheriff picked her up on a tip some time later and confiscated the marijuana.

She had spent five days in the county jail before she even met her court appointed attorney, a young bearded guy with horn-rimmed glasses who seemed to Rachel not a day older than herself. She could see why he had grown the beard: To look older, sure, but he also had a river of acne scars coursing through the beard. His threadbare green suit and the worn and scuffed brown shoes didn't help much either. He was the kind of guy she'd turn down for a date in a heartbeat.

But he was all she had.

Thomas McHenry was his name. His voice was a deep, pleasant baritone, surprising out of his stalky frame. In his green suit he reminded Rachel of celery.

McHenry went over the prosecutor's charges. The thing that caught her attention was the guideline year of jail time on a misdemeanor.

"I can't go to jail," she protested to McHenry. "I mean, I can't stay in jail. I'd lose my baby. Can't you do something for me?"

"I already have," he said. "The prosecutor is giving you a plea deal. Five months in jail."

"I'm supposed to give birth in a jail cell?"

"I think I have that worked out, too. I'm going to have another run at the prosecution for straight probation on just that angle."

"Sounds wonderful," Rachel said. She almost jumped up to hug the man but thought better of it. She might crush him.

When Rachel watched his thin form slip out of the room, replaced by the female guard to lead her back to the cell, she felt weight slip off her shoulders.

Probation, she thought. *Thank you, Jesus.*

Funny, she thought, she hadn't said that since she was a little girl. There hadn't been a whole lot to be thankful for.

The red light on the prosecutor's phone blinked. It was Angie, the prosecutor's receptionist-secretary-paralegal out here in what the

prosecutor considered Wasteland, USA. The only thing held in common in Newaygo County is that everyone wished they weren't in
Newaygo County. She picked up the phone.

"Yes, Angie." The prosecutor answered.

"Your 4:50 appointment. Thomas McHenry."

"Send him in. Say, Angie, does he have that suit on?"

"Yes, ma'am."

"Take his jacket and hang it up. I don't want to puke."

Angie laughed and cut the line.

McHenry knocked shyly at the door a few moments later.
"Come in," the prosecutor roared.

McHenry stuck his head in. His body followed like a slinky toy.
"Shall I leave it open?" he asked.

"Sit down and say what you've got to say. I'm beat. Know what
the worst cases in the world are?"

"Domestic violence," McHenry replied.

"How'd you know that?"

"Fifty-two percent of the plaintiffs recant or fail to show."

"Right. Then how do you prosecute them?"

"It's a problem, ma'am."

"What's on your mind?" the prosecutor asked McHenry.

"I have a client, Rachel Timmerman."

"Court appointed, right?"

"Yes, ma'am. See, your assistant offered five months of child care
time, then five in jail."

The prosecutor nodded.

"What I'm thinking," McHenry began, "is that we let Rachel
loose on one-year probation under a strict gag order.

"See, here's what we have now," he continued. "She has five
months to deliver and wean her baby. Does it make sense to haul her
in then? Can you imagine the outcry? 'Mother separated from child
to do jail term!' And what happens to the kid? Put her in foster care?
Look at the expense.

"Besides," he added, "she had a clean sheet."

"Yes, she did."

McHenry spread his hands and looked pathetic.

"The hearing is when?"

"Next Tuesday," he said.

"Okay. Consider it done. I want you to get the papers on my desk first thing tomorrow. I want that probation to sound like a jail term. No known associates. No booze. No drugs. Unannounced visits. That sort of thing. Put the fear of evil in her."

"Will do, Ma'am. Ah, Ms..."

"Get out of here, McHenry."

The prosecutor was probably thinking that it was so much better this way. McHenry would owe her one. Judge Judy Bolton never would have gone for jail time anyway. Bleeding heart liberal and full-time feminist, Bolton would have kicked the case out.

Chapter 4

Bad Losers

"I just can't tonight, Rachel." Sara leaned against the kitchen counter on a warm August night, drinking from a large mug of coffee. Dark black, regular. She had her sister's blonde hair, almost white. The same blue eyes like chips of periwinkle. If someone they didn't know saw Rachel, Sara and baby Shannon in the trailer kitchen, he or she would think they were all sisters.

"I'm dead on my feet already. And Isaac wants to pick me up for a beer. I'd have to cancel on him."

"Please." Rachel's voice took on a pleading undertone. "All I've been doing for the last three months is sitting here. Besides, I'm just going to Wayne's to play some cards."

"Try standing on your feet for eight hours serving processed beef sandwiches. And the smell of those fries! Like a backed-up sewer. I swear that's what they fry them in. Sewer juice."

Sara downed her coffee. "The caffeine doesn't seem to be working," she noted. "Besides," she added, returning to the topic, "Wayne is seriously screwed up. It looks like he got run over and he never goes anywhere without that stupid Army jacket. I bet that thing could stand up and wave its arms all by itself."

"He's nice to me. I just don't want to take Shannon along." She looked at Shannon's soft pink baby cheeks puffing at her little fist shoved between her lips. "She's asleep already."

"So stay home and take care of her."

"Sara, that's all I *do*!"

"So is that my fault? Remember, you're on probation. Do I have to spell it? You could be sitting in county jail eating baloney sandwiches."

"I won't be home late. You could go to sleep. She sleeps the night, you know. Please. Pleasepleaseplease."

"Okay. Forget it. Go play a while. I'll stay here. I really don't want to go out with Isaac anyway."

"I love you too, Sara."

Sara had her cell phone open before Rachel could respond further.

"Isaac? Yeah, gotta take a rain check. Sicker than a dog over here. No, you don't want to come over and watch me vomit."

The card game was at a new guy's trailer that night. Brian Anderson was his name. Rachel walked the mile to the trailer through humidity thickening by the minute. Mosquitoes swarmed out of the brush. She slapped at her bare arms and legs. *Must be a million blood-blobs on me*, she thought. Nine o'clock and it was still light. Still hot. August hot when the humidity never let up, as though the daytime sun sucked at every ditch and gully of water then spat it out over people stupid enough to be walking through mosquito grounds at night.

Now and then a car slowed, beeped the horn and crept alongside a few paces. *Drunken old billy goats*, she thought. *I'd rather be prime rib for the bugs than crawl into one of those cars.*

Rachel hurried when she turned at the hill to the trailer. It stood in a copse of jack pine, the ground layered with needles. At the base of the hill, the grocery store was hopping. Kids in the parking lot had their car radios up. They were dancing or leaning against fenders of broken down pickups. She saw a convertible. *I wouldn't mind riding in that*, she thought. *Wind in my hair, breeze on my face. And these annoying mosquitoes splatting on the windshield.*

"Don't let the bugs in," Wayne shouted as Rachel stepped into the trailer.

"Hey. I'm inside. Get an air conditioner, why don't you?" She twirled with her hands over her head, her smile wide. "I lost twenty pounds to bugs chewing on me," she laughed.

An old fan sputtered in the kitchen window.

"You're wearing that jacket on a night like this?" Rachel asked.

"Man," said Wayne, "if I took this old Army jacket off half my skin would peel off with it."

"They'll bury you in it," Angel said. "Glad you're here, Rachel. Now we got a fourth."

"Where's the other guy?"

"Passed out in the TV room. Drunk as a skunk. Called some friend of his to fill in before he looped."

Rachel stepped through the kitchen to the narrow living room. A television set was on. In a cracked leather recliner of a burgundy color, Brian Anderson snored. His head was crooked to one side like a baby's. His hands were folded over the paunch of his belly. His T-shirt was ripped and soiled.

"I ain't picking him up," Wayne said. "I'd get about six hernias if I tried."

Angel kicked out a chair for Rachel. "Beer?" he asked. Angel was a strange one. When he was drunk he thought he was some kind of superman. He was very laid-back and spent his extra time selling deer hunters' bait to earn a few extra bucks.

"Sure. Why not?" She wasn't nursing anymore. The hot August night pressed at the screen door. A moth fluttered lazily around the outdoor light. The fan coughed at the window screen.

The beer tasted good. She was still sweaty from walking and her legs and arms were sprinkled with bites. Someone told her once that bugs loved blondes. *Could be true,* she considered.

The screen door crashed open. The big man at the doorway brushed the frame when he walked through. Black hair stabbed to a widow's peak on his forehead. He laid two twelve packs of beer on the counter, opened one, cracked the can and guzzled it down. His murky blue eyes drifted across the table, caught Rachel's eyes and held them along the barrel of the beer can.

"Only way to cool off," he said, lowering the can from his mouth. "Keep drinking beer."

"If you ain't too drunk," said Wayne, "pull up a chair. Racehorse pinochle tonight. Think you can handle that?"

The big man straddled a chair backwards. "Rachel can count," he said. "She's good at keeping track of things."

"How do you know my name?"

"Good looking woman like you? Everyone knows your name."

"Yeah. Sure." Rachel resisted rolling her eyes.

"I'm Marvin Gabrion."

For his size, his voice was surprisingly high-pitched. *Sort of nerve-wracking*, Rachel thought. It reminded her of a snake for some reason.

"Deal," she said to Angel. He began shuffling the double deck of cards like pieces of ice gliding smoothly between his fingers. When he cut, the cards snapped. He dealt by threes. Halfway through the deal, the door opened.

A red-cheeked boy, maybe fourteen or fifteen, stood uncertainly in the doorway. He had long arms that dangled at his sides as if he didn't know what to do with them.

"Oh, shit," Wayne said. "Don't just stand there with the door open, Charlie. You're letting the damn bugs in."
The boy moved forward and the screen door slammed.

"Charlie," Marvin said, "Go watch TV while we play cards." He turned to Rachel. "My neighbor's kid," he explained.

Charlie walked across the kitchen. Mud fell off his shoes.

"Dammit, Marv. He's getting the floor all dirty."

Marvin stared at Wayne. His eyes were flat pools. He said nothing. Wayne turned back to the table.

"Finish dealing," he said to Angel.

"Hey, little man," Marvin said to the boy as he stood up from the table. "Here. Have a beer and watch the TV." He popped a beer from a twelve-pack.

"But Marv," the boy said, "there's no noise."

"So turn the volume up," Marvin answered. He handed the beer to the boy.

When he got back to the table, Marvin Gabrion was angry.

"Deal," he barked at Angel. Everyone was silent, studying their cards while the deal slid around.

His mood got worse as the night wore on. They played two on two—Rachel and Angel against Marvin and Wayne. After three rounds Rachel and Angel were up by 130 points. Marvin cursed at his cards. Wayne made a half-assed bid on a round, forty points with nothing in his hand. Even so, in racehorse pinochle he should be able to cover forty. But Angel held five aces and Rachel two. Wayne and Marvin went down like a battleship.

Marvin hurled his half empty beer can against the wall. "That's the dumbest motherfucking bid I've ever seen. What did you have?"

"I sort of expected you'd give some help," Wayne said. "You played a dumb ass nine on my ace."

"I didn't take the bid."

"Just play the game," Wayne said. "Or go in the TV room and sleep it off."

"You telling me I'm drunk?" Gabrion stood. "Huh? You calling me drunk?" He grabbed Wayne by the throat, half lifting him from the chair. "You little motherfucker. I'll strangle you with that damn jacket."

"No, Marvin. I never said you were drunk."

Marvin was breathing hard, his eyes sweeping the others.

"Hey guys," Angel said. "Let's take a break already."

"Bunch of motherfuckers. Should kill you all. I've gotta take a leak," Marvin said. He banged open the screen door and went outside. Rachel went to use the bathroom. Wayne grabbed a newspaper flyer off the shelf and wiped up the spilled beer. A mound of empty cans overflowed the waste basket.

When Rachel returned to the kitchen, she started throwing the empty cans into a garbage bag for Wayne. Ten cents each deposit. Sometimes when Wayne's disability check ran short, he scoured the highways, walking along with a garbage bag for discarded cans. He went to the hunting and fishing camps. He knew all the necking spots and often pulled a couple of cases of empties from around cold camp-fires. He got by.

Wayne hated the process of recycling them though. He had to drive all the way over to the grocery store in Croton, put each stinking can through a machine and cash out the tally sheet. Usually, when he had a few garbage bags of cans behind the house, he turned them over to Kenny Mochenrose for a fifty-fifty split. Fair enough, in Wayne's opinion. Kenny had to pay for the gas.

"Not quitting already, are you?" Marvin said. The door had closed quietly behind him without anyone noticing. He had been doing more than taking a leak out there. The pupils in his murky blue eyes were slightly dilated, his smile easy. "Man, I'm just getting warmed up." He laughed loudly at some private joke.

"I should really get back," Rachel said. "My sister's babysitting for me."

"Yeah and I got a job doing some electrical work tomorrow," Angel said. "'Bout time I headed out. Got to be there at eight in the morning. The guy wants to put a 200 amp service in his barn."

Angel said good night and left the trailer.

"I'll walk Rachel along," Wayne said. "I just live about a mile past."

"Right. Let's get going." Rachel agreed.

"Wait just one minute," Marvin said. "Why you all walking? Let me give you a ride in my new car—a convertible. Better than having the bugs eat you up, sucking all your blood out."

"That convertible's yours?" Rachel asked.

"Sure is."

"What do you think, Wayne?"

"Better than walking."

"Wake up Charlie," Marvin instructed the others. "I'll drive it up the hill. Left it down by the store under the lights." He turned out the door.

Better than getting eaten alive by mosquitoes, Rachel thought as they turned out onto the road. The breeze felt cool on her face. Her hair lifted, snapped playfully in the wind. She sat in the passenger seat with Wayne and Charlie in the back. She dangled her arm out into the wind.

"My house is coming right up," Rachel said. "Up there on the left. Slow down."

He didn't. Marvin reached his arm along the seat, his hand kneading her shoulder. "Let's ride a little," he said.

"No. My sister's waiting for me."

She felt his big hand tighten at the back of her neck. She tried to pull away.

"Where are we going?"

"Just a little ride. Relax."

At least, Rachel thought, *Wayne and Charlie are along. He won't dare try anything, not with them along.*

Marvin slowed the car. "Hey," he said, "I sort of like this here road." He turned down a dirt road. The convertible bottomed going in. Marvin floored it, the back end of the car fishtailing back and forth.

"Whooee," shouted Charlie. "Ride her, Marv."

Marvin smiled. "I aim to," he said. "Yessir, I aim to do just that."

Chapter 5

"You Better Like It"

T he turnoff led into a rutted two-track. Under the sweating trees, swarms of bugs alighted on the convertible.

"Where we going, Marvin?" asked Charlie.

"Maybe going swimming at Rosie's Run," Rachel tried to keep it light. "Down by the river."

"Yeah," muttered Wayne. He was half asleep and pretty drunk. "Get away from these damn bugs. Afore they carry me away." He laughed.

"Yeah," said Charlie. "Go swimming."

The convertible groaned over some rocks and stopped. They were deep in the trees now, the night a sheet of impenetrable black. Marvin turned to Charlie and Wayne. "Get out," he said.

"Why, Marvin? It's dark," said Charlie.

"Get the fuck out."

"I ain't getting out," Charlie said. "I don't know my way out, man."

"Get the fuck out. Do you think I'm kidding you? I'll kill you in a minute without worrying about it."

Rachel tried to catch Wayne's eye. A silent plea. But it was too dark.

"I'll pick you up on the way back," Marvin said. His words were chips of ice.

Looking back over his shoulder, Wayne clumsily crawled out the backseat, over the side of the car. Charlie followed. They stood there, two pale ghosts against the forest.

The convertible edged forward.

"Where do you think you're going?" Rachel said.

Marvin slowed the car. His right hand squeezed Rachel's neck, twisting her toward him. He began kissing her, trying to pry her lips apart.

Rachel broke away. "Stop."

"You wanted to go to Rosie's Run, didn't you? Swim naked in the river?"

"I was kidding."

"Don't kid with Marvin." He put the car in Park, opened his door and got out. He waited a couple of seconds and then told Rachel to get out.

"Why?"

"Quit asking questions. Take a walk."

Rachel had a smart-ass response, but bit it off. *This guy's temper is all over the map*, she thought. *Maybe it's best to play along. Maybe I can make it back to Wayne and Charlie.*

You think I'm kidding? I'd kill you in a minute without worrying about it. Marvin's words echoed in Rachel's mind. *And probably dump the bodies in the river*, she thought. She slid out of the car.

They started walking down the two-track slowly, as if Marvin were looking for something nobody could see in the dark. They passed a slight berm, a sandy stretch. Rachel heard him stop, just a sudden disappearance of footsteps. She kept walking.

I could disappear, she thought. *Slip into the trees and hide. He wouldn't find me.*

But if he did?

He's testing me.

As if reading her mind, Marvin said, "That's far enough. I know what you're thinking." His voice wasn't loud, but all the worse for that. It cut inside her like pieces of ice.

"Now turn around and come back here."

He had undone the buttons on his shirt and didn't seem to mind the bugs at his bare skin.

"Sit down. No, not over there. We're not at a campfire, girl. Right here next to me. Just the two of us. Nice and cozy."

His hands were like vise grips. They pincered her shoulders and pulled her toward him. The pressure of his lips pried her neck backward. A crushing grip was on her breast.

"Ow," Rachel said. "They're sore. I just had a baby..."

"Nice and big for Daddy."

He bent her to the ground. He had her shirt off now, yanking her bra loose. One cold hand slid down her shorts, inside her panties, massaging her crotch.

"Just for Daddy," he said again.

"No. Stop it. Get the fuck off me."

Marvin laughed. He probed harder, his fingers rough and calloused as they entered her. "You can yell all you want," he said. "No one's going to hear you."

"I'm serious," she screamed. "I don't want it."

She squirmed, got one leg free from under him, kicked out wildly. She felt it connect. She kicked with both legs, slamming them into Marvin. He hovered over her, laughing, hot breath suffocating her. He grabbed one flailing fist and bent it back to the ground.

Rachel screamed. She hoped Wayne and Charlie would hear. "If you're going to do me, you'd better kill me, because I will press charges. You'll rot in jail."

Marvin grabbed her head and pounded it into the ground, over and over. Rachel felt stones embed in her scalp. She twisted and fought against the iron hands. She thought he was going to kiss her. But instead he twisted his head and sunk his teeth into her nose. He jerked his jaw. Rachel felt the snap of cartilage. Blood clogged her sinuses.

He reared back on his knees, breathing hoarsely. "Are you sure this is the way you want to die?" He began unfastening his pants. "Huh? Easy enough. I don't care."

Rachel was exhausted. She lay in the dirt trembling, pain ripping across her scalp. She thought of Shannon. What would it be like to grow up alone, without a mother? She held Shannon's face firmly in her mind. "Just do what you want," she mumbled.

"You better like it," he growled.

He pulled off her clothes. Bugs and mosquitoes were everywhere. He was on top of her. He banged at her until he found entrance. He kissed her, pushing with his tongue and his green teeth.

Rachel let him. She let her lips fall open. Let anything. Let him bite on her breasts. She thought of Shannon. Bites will heal.

Finally he came. She felt his repulsive body shudder and he fell on her.

He rolled off. Rachel dug in the pocket of her pants and pulled out a cigarette. The flame of her lighter kept missing the tip before she finally lit it. She started to dress and found herself too tired. She sat on the ground with her blouse wrapped around her shoulders. Her mind went blank. A darkness. She watched the glow of her cigarette as if it were a searchlight.

Marvin sat there naked, his legs stretched out, his cock puddled in his lap.

"Know why my mama called me Marvin?"

Rachel turned her head.

"When I came out I was already hanging a marvelous six inches long." He laughed.

He looked at Rachel with a sudden fury. "I'm going to kill you anyway, bitch. I'd rather kill you any day than go to jail." He flung rocks at trees he couldn't see.

"What does it matter anyway?" he said. "You've been begging me to fuck you all night. That's why you kicked those guys out of the car."

"I did not." Rachel realized then that Charlie and Wayne were probably long gone.

"Call me a liar!" Once again he was on her, once again he shuddered convulsively, once again he fell against her.

They got up slowly. Both dressed. They walked back toward the car. *It's finally over,* Rachel thought.

"Where's the fucking river?"

"Why?"

"Either you take a bath in it or die."

"I think it's down here. There's a gully though. I'd have to walk."

She entered the dark press of trees. Rachel pulled out her lighter to see the way. Like a streak of darkness, a big hand reached around her and seized it.

"Don't even think of running, cunt."

Rachel walked into the darkness. She couldn't find the river in the dark. Suddenly she had to pee. She lowered her pants and went in the path. She turned back.

Marvin was sitting on the ground not twenty feet from her. It felt as those wolfish eyes could see through the darkness. Rachel shuddered.

"Sit down," he ordered.

She did. Rachel was too exhausted to do anything. Marvin started pulling off her clothes. *No*, she thought. She couldn't even picture Shannon's face anymore. Again he was on her. Again the convulsive pounding, the shudder, the falling on her, his weight pinning her to the ground.

He didn't roll off. He made strange deep sounds. Like a groaning from his belly. He rolled Rachel on top of him. His large hands on her hips thrust her back and forth fiercely. He came again.

They got dressed, began walking back to the car. *And now he's done with me*, Rachel thought. *Used up. Now I die. Think of something. Think.*

Marvin put his arm around her, squeezed her breast.

No, she thought, *here it comes again. I can't…*

"Listen," she said. "Let's go back to my house. It's more comfortable than this sand and dirt."

"You liked it, though, didn't you?" He giggled. He sounded like Charlie. "We call it roughing it." He laughed.

"Still better in bed, though," Rachel said. She wondered why she said it. She just had to get out of here. Find some other people.

"Okay," he said.

They got in the car. Marvin backed up to a turnaround, straightened and drove slowly down the two-track.

"They're gone," Rachel said.

"Wayne and Charlie? 'Course they are. Asses are probably bitten off by bugs. They can walk. Sober them up. Me? I could use a few more beers."

When they got on the asphalt road, he slung his arm over Rachel's shoulder and began squeezing her breast again. A stab of pain hit her.

"Can't you wait until we get in bed?" she said.

"Maybe," he said. He removed his hand.

The convertible lurched slowly up the steep drive to Rachel's house. Halfway up, Rachel flung open the door and raced toward the trailer.

"Hey!" Marvin shouted at her. "Where you going?" He gunned the car. It spun futilely in the ruts.

"I have to pee," Rachel called over her shoulder.

The car slowed.

The door to the trailer was unlocked. *Good.* Rachel flung it open. Wayne and Charlie dozed in chairs in the kitchen. "Don't let him in," she screamed at them.

She raced to the bathroom, locked the door and leaned against it. An old hammer was on the floor under the sink. She reached out and squeezed the wooden handle in her fists.

If only I had this earlier, she thought.

She heard voices in the kitchen. *They let him in!* Heavy footsteps toward the bathroom door. The knob twisted. She braced her back against the pressure. "I'm sick," she shouted. "You broke my nose and I'm sucking blood."

Rachel heard Wayne say, "Just get out, Marvin. She wants you to leave."

There was muttering behind the door.

Then a voice: "What's going on here?"

"Sara. Stay out of it. Go back by my baby." Rachel called to her sister.

"Get out of here. All of you. Or I'll call the police. Now!"

Rachel heard footsteps and the slam of the door.

"You call the police," Marvin called. "But I'm calling them first. I work for the police, you know."

Rachel jumped up, furious. She flung the bathroom door open. "You go ahead and call the cops. We'll just see how much trouble you're in."

She locked the trailer door. From outside she heard Marvin shouting unintelligibly. Finally the sound of a car starting broke into the night. Gravel whipped against the trailer as he gunned the motor.

For the first time she looked at the digital clock on the microwave: 3:30 AM.

How could that be? The night seemed to have lasted forever. And ever. She collapsed on the couch, too exhausted to cry.

Rachel felt Sara's hand on her shoulder and thought at first, *he's back.* Her eyes were gritty, her body ached. Her nose felt swollen and swamped with blood.

"Shannon's awake."

"Unh."

"Get up. I have to get ready for work."

"Can you?"

"She's got dirty pants."

Rachel made it to the bathroom. Sore. Everything ached. She didn't know her own body. *Didn't own it,* she thought. She washed the blood off her face and went to change Shannon.

Rachel warmed a bottle and sat back heavily in the rocking chair. Shannon burbled at the bottle, spit the milk out a few times. *You want to play, little girl,* Rachel thought. She started crying. Finally Shannon began to feed.

Sara sat on the couch across from Rachel. "Tell me about it," she said.

"You can guess on your own," Rachel looked away.

Sara nodded. "I'm going to call your caseworker from the health department."

"I don't want to. I'm scared."

"Why?"

"He said he'd kill us all." Rachel looked at her sister with fear in her eyes.

"You believe that?"

"Yes."

"I'm calling her anyway."

The call went through and the caseworker, Nikki Wilson, made an appointment in the early afternoon to pick up Rachel and take her to the hospital. When she got there, Rachel was incoherent with fear—"petrified" was Wilson's word. The caseworker talked her into calling 911 to report the crime after the rape kit was administered.

Detective Sergeant Dave Babcock of the Newaygo County Sheriff Department had had run-ins with Marvin Gabrion before. He hadn't found much to like about the man. In fact, he had encouraged Marvin to move to adjoining Mecosta County for a time, saying to him, "Marvin, if you so much as sneeze in my county, I will arrest you for disturbing the peace."

After taking down the rape report, Babcock immediately began looking for Gabrion. Maybe this time he could make something stick to that slippery, frog-like hide. *The man,* he thought, *always smells like a swamp.*

It seemed like Marvin was gone. Long gone. Babcock couldn't find him.

Babcock tried another tactic, leaving word with anyone who knew Marvin that he was looking for him. *The man is an egomaniac,* he reasoned. *Thinks himself the cleverest manipulator around. Play on his instincts. Make him defend himself.*

It didn't take long. After a week Babcock got a fax from Marvin Gabrion, sent from a Grand Rapids grocery store. Gabrion claimed the whole thing was Rachel's idea. The woman was wild. Seduced him. She wanted to have sex with him, but he was afraid of getting her pregnant again. So all he let her do was perform oral sex on him. But she tricked him. Rachel got his semen on her fingers and rubbed it into her vagina.

Babcock obtained a warrant issued for his arrest on a rape charge.

But Marvin had disappeared again.

Newaygo County is a good place to get lost. Unless the state police are running the show, it's also a good place to let some crimes slide. The deputies were busy with domestic violence, deer hunter parties, out-of-control kids and the like.

In one of those oddities of justice, Rachel was arrested before Marvin Gabrion. In late autumn, someone called in a tip to her probation officer that Rachel was throwing wild parties and drinking. In fact, the tip suggested, her garbage can was usually overflowing with empty bottles of hard liquor. The probation officer sent to investigate that next morning found two empty bottles on top of the garbage.

No question. The prosecutor would move to revoke probation and put her in jail for five months.

On January 11, Rachel reported to the Newaygo County Jail.

Eventually, the sheriff's department put together a series of leads, located Gabrion and on January 20 put him in the county jail on the charge of rape. At the arraignment, Judge Bolton looked at him with that glare intended to make men wither. She meant it. Wife-beaters were scum of the earth. Fathers past due on child support were evil. If she had her way she would lock them in stocks in the public square and let the women heave rocks at them—from five feet away. But the very worst, in her judgment, were rapists, which she soundly and persuasively equated with murder. She would give them the same fate if she could. Unfortunately, bail guidelines made a distinction. She transgressed only slightly, setting Marvin's bond at $75,000.

It might have been higher, depending upon how one viewed his rap sheet they had available at the time. It wasn't pretty, but it wasn't deadly. A host of assaults that testified to his violence. A few robberies, none of them armed, burglary, an extensive list of DUIs. The man was a serial binge drinker. *Taken altogether*, the judge thought, *I can* *throw his ass in Jackson for ten to fifteen years. No one around here can cough up the $75,000 bail anyway.*

It didn't work quite that way either. Somehow Gabrion's lawyers got bail reduced to $40,000. This was more manageable. Gabrion's parents, not wanting him to face a long prison sentence, scrabbled together his $40,000 bond and bailed him out.

Marvin walked out of county jail on February 4 and never looked back. No way did he intend to spend ten to fifteen years in a prison cell.

He disappeared.

Chapter 6

Letters from Jail

Rachel stared at the gray walls of the cell—a tank really, holding seven other women. If only something would move besides her large cell mate, who lay in bunk above her most of the day. That woman acted like she was on vacation. The only work she did was to lift her industrial-sized ass and fart. Great, thunderous farts that shattered the cell like a thermite hand grenade. She had a variation she sometimes used—a long, staccato stream of farts like a burp gun. "Shut up," Rachel once yelled at her.

"Wha? Was I snoring again? My guy never did like my snoring."

It's enough to make a person weep, Rachel thought.

The shiny gray walls weren't particularly exciting. A washout. The hallway was some kind of lime green, like a lot of parrots had flown up and down crapping against the wall. Someone with a flourish for design had painted a dark green stripe right along the middle of the wall. A perfect stripe. Probably measured every inch. Rachel wondered if they measured from the ceiling or the floor. Which was more irregular?

At least the linoleum in the hallway was bright. Bright? The stuff glittered. You could see it staring back at the overhead lights, all nicely bound in their wire cages, the wires cabled to the plaster. Walk on that floor and you played hopscotch with light bulb reflections.

After two weeks of feeling sorry for herself, Rachel decided to do something about it. The change started when Rachel's bunkmate finished her time. It took a day for the air to clear. The next day Rachel and her cellmates scrubbed down the cell. She took a scrub brush and had at the toilet, even reaching her hand inside the rim and down the chute to work at the rust stains. Her new bunkmate came in the next night, a young-looking twenty-seven-year-old prostitute from Grand Rapids taking a bed leased out by Newaygo County. It was not an unusual arrangement. Kent County Jail could have had a whole floor for prostitutes. Once the woman came down from her crack high, Rachel became friends with her. It was easy. They talked about babies.

"I'd like to keep at least one of my kids," the woman said.

"Where are they?"

She shrugged. "Foster care. Adopted. I hope they got good families."

Rachel made friends with others—Charlotte, Ellen—talking about kids, families and whether the women had them or not. Most of the women seemed to be in on drug charges. Some had multiple DUIs. A few were in on burglary, obstruction of justice and such. Rachel found it easy to make friends.

But Rachel wanted to do something for herself, too. She enrolled in GED courses to earn her high school diploma, left behind with the discovery of her pregnancy. To strengthen her own resolve, Rachel wrote down her goals:

My vow to myself.

> While I'm incarcerated in Newaygo County Jail I would like to use the time to the best of my ability both mentally and physically. I would like to earn my GED. I would also love to lose some weight. I would above all like to get in touch with the Father, the Son and the Holy Spirit. I would like to do all these things for myself and my daughter. I am writing and fulfilling these dreams freely and completely of my own will! If I ever feel I cannot accomplish these things I will look over this paper and reread it. Thank you, Jesus.

Every inmate longs for two things: cards or letters from family or friends and visits—that one day a week of looking through the thick plastic window and talking on the telephone. It is the longing for the outside, for familiarity, for a life beyond bars. Shannon's paternal grandmother was caring for the baby and faithfully brought her for visits. So did Rachel's father Tim, who had to tangle the long legs of his six feet six inches frame into the tiny space, balancing on the wobbly stool.

Ecstatic to see her growing daughter, Rachel's heart nonetheless twisted like a pneumatic drill every time they left. *Will Shannon still remember me?* She wondered. *Remember what my arms are like?* Five months, now four, seemed more and more like an eternity marked by gray and green walls. However much she looked forward to the visits, a well of depression opened in her when the visitors left.

One day she found two surprises in her mail. The first was a brief letter from her beloved grandfather:

February 9

Dear Rachel,

I finally got your address, so now I can express both my concern and affection. Grandma and I enjoyed you so much as a child and saw so much promise in you that it is difficult for me to believe that you are where you are.

I don't know why you are there, but I pray and trust that it is a place where you can be helped to become again what you were.

I know grandpas don't usually send valentines to grandchildren, but since your dear grandma is gone I think you would like a valentine for her memory. I enclose a check for you and I hope you will have the patience and the pluck to leave this place, when your sentence has been served, to live a better life than you were living.

Love,

Grandpa

The second was a card from her Aunt Pat, who lived in Grand Rapids. Although they were close when Rachel was young, they hadn't seen each other for several years. What could she say? Rachel tore the envelope open.

Dear Rachel,

I heard from Grandpa that you are spending some time in jail. Honey, I don't know what the situation was that caused you to be sentenced to be there. But I want you to know for sure that God loves you and He is with you. He can help you with whatever situation or struggles you have had. I know that life hasn't been easy for you. And I feel very sad for you for that. Life can be very hard sometimes. We've had some hard times that we never planned on in our family, too.

I just wanted to let you know that I care and that I will be praying for you. If you want to write back, I would be happy to know how you are doing.

Love,

Aunt Pat

Rachel cried quietly in her cell.

The correspondence with her aunt developed into a relationship. Rachel found it easy to let down her guard with her non-judgmental aunt, sensing almost against her expectations that here was someone who really cared about her—just as she was. This came through in the tentative tone of her earliest return letter in February:

Dear Aunt Pat,

How are you and the family? I am doing fine. I'm not sitting in my dream location. But at least once in our life God has to put our faith to the test, right?

I'm sorry it took me so long to write back. I guess I just am not sure what to say.

I guess I can honestly say one good thing is coming from me being incarcerated: I'm getting my GED. I have taken three of the tests already and next Wednesday I'm taking the last two. I guess even in here I still have the family genes because I passed all three of the tests above 98 percent.

Did my dad ever send you pictures of my daughter? I know he said he'd get around to sending the pictures because I did not have any addresses. Well, if not I have a beautiful baby girl. She has curly hair and blue eyes and two teeth. She's twenty-nine inches long and weighs twenty-five pounds. She's a gorgeous baby, really. When her daddy's parents get pictures I'll send you one.

I'm not sure how much longer I'll be here. I'm hoping they'll give me early release after I get my GED and have an apartment ready at a program called Liz's House. So if you get an extra minute or two I'd appreciate it if you'd pray for me. I need all the help I can get.

Thank you for taking the time out of your busy life to write to me, even though I'm the black sheep so to say. Though Jesus loves all his sheep, right?

Well I'm surviving on three hours of sleep since 7 a.m. and it's 1 a.m. now so I think I should go to bed.

Love,

Rachel

P.S. Write back if you can. Mail's the highlight of everyone's life in here.

Rachel celebrated her nineteenth birthday in jail. Her aunt remembered with a card and a note:

April 5

Dear Rachel,

I'm sorry that this card is a little bit late for your birthday. I'm sure that this birthday is much different than any other birthday you've ever had. But I hope that you have had some special joy and blessing in it. I'm hoping that you have been able to visit with Shannon.

It's exciting to hear that some of your cellmates have been Christian ladies who want to study the Bible. Sometimes God speaks the most clearly to our hearts when our situations seem the most hopeless. When we realize that God is the only change-less One, the One we can *always* depend on, even in the hardest, saddest times then we can let Him work in our hearts. And His Spirit can change us and give us peace and power that we never thought would be possible.

Rachel, I remember you being such a precious little girl: I know that God has a very special plan for your life and that you have infinite value to Him. God loves you so much that He gave His own son Jesus to die for your sins and mine. That's pretty great love, isn't it!

Happy birthday!

Lots of love and prayers,

Aunt Pat

Rachel wrote back:

Dear Aunt Pat,

Hello, how are you? I'm fine I guess.

I'm sorry it took me so long to write back. I was hoping I'd be out and able to call.

Hopefully I'll be out of here soon. I just heard Wednesday that they've broken some rules to get me incarcerated.

Lyn called my probation officer and offered for me to go stay with her and my dad until there is a place at Liz's House for me. If that doesn't work a friend of mine has some good friends in high places who will talk to the judge. If that doesn't work I'm going to ask a friend of mine to get a lawyer.

My daughter is getting huge. She's growing up so fast and she's growing more and more beautiful each day.

Thank you for the birthday card. It was very beautiful.

Well I'm going to sign off now. Thank you for writing. I'm very grateful for mail.

Please pray for me.

Love,

Rachel

Almost by definition, jail is uncertainty. Someone else—some system—has power over you. Sometimes it takes the form of the corrections officers, who can easily make the time more harsh. Sometimes it's a cellmate. In her letters, Aunt Pat poured encouragement into Rachel.

Then, in late March, Aunt Pat broached a question:

Dear Rachel,

I was just rereading your letter. I'm glad that you wrote back to me.

You asked if I had seen a picture of your daughter. No, your dad didn't send any. But Grandpa did show me a picture he had. She looks like a beautiful baby. I'll bet that you miss her a great deal. Does she come with her daddy to see you? I'm happy to hear that her daddy and his family are able to take care of her while you are unable to.

It sounds like you did really well on your GED tests. I'll bet it makes you feel really good to have that accomplished.

Do you have a date yet for when you will be released? You mentioned you will be going to Liz's House. I've heard good things about the help that they are able to give to women while they get "back on their feet" after going through difficult situations.

Grandpa comes here every Sunday for dinner. He is doing better now than he was doing. He has had a very hard time adjusting to life without Grandma. He misses not being able to talk to Grandma about his grandchildren and the concerns he has about all of them.

My son, your cousin, is having a real great year at school. He has made the honor roll twice so far this year. He's very proud of that.

I keep busy with our family. For several years I have volunteered as a nurse at a clinic here in Grand Rapids for homeless people. I'm going to work there two days this week as a patient coordinator. I work on call as an employee when they are short-staffed. It's a very rewarding though at times a very sad place to work. There are so many homeless people who have so little in life. The clinic is a clinic of St. Mary's Hospital.

Rachel, you are right that God loves all His sheep. God does love you very much. He is right there beside you all the time. Even when bad things happen to us. He can turn it into something good. But we have to cooperate with Him. We have to trust in

Him and obey Him—go by His rules. Because He knows what's really best for us. I hope that you have a Bible with you. If you don't, let me know and I'll be sure to get you one if you would like.

Take good care of yourself.

Love,

Aunt Pat

Rachel wrote back:

Dear Aunt Pat,

Hello, how are you and the family? I hope you are all well.

I'm glad Grandpa goes there every Sunday for dinner, he needs a good old fashioned Sunday dinner.

Shannon's daddy brings Shannon and her grandma up here every week to see me. Shannon's dad probably wouldn't come at all, except his stepmom won't drive. She hasn't for years.

I'm going to put a couple of pictures of Shannon in with this letter. They were taken on Christmas day at my dad's house.

Shannon's grandparents are videotaping her so I don't miss too much. Yeah, right, I miss her more than anything in this world!

No, I don't have a Bible in here. I asked my dad for one in a letter, but apparently he never got the letter. I would appreciate it a great deal if you got one for me. I don't even have one at home; otherwise I would have had it brought in.

I'm glad my cousin is shaping up to be very smart. I still remember when you were pregnant with him. You were very big!

I have no specific release date yet but my probation officer came last Wednesday and told me she was going to put my name on the waiting list for Liz's House.

I don't think I could be a nurse, too much death and other problems for me. I guess I just don't have an iron belly.

I'm not sure what I will do when I get out of here. Liz's House puts you into college. I'm just not sure what to major in.

I'm thinking computers, but since the opportunity has become real there are lots of things I'd like to do.

Well I should go now. Thank you for writing me. Mail is gold in here.

Love,

Rachel

P.S. Give my other cousin my best wishes seeing as how I didn't make it to her wedding and haven't had any chance to come into contact with her.

Shortly thereafter, a package arrived for Rachel, sent by a publisher since books couldn't be mailed to prisoners individually. Too easy to conceal contraband. Inside was a new leather-bound Bible from her Aunt Pat. Several weeks later, Rachel wrote her aunt announcing that she had become a Christian.

In one of her final letters, with discharge approaching, Rachel wrote:

Dear Aunt Pat,

Hello, how are you? I suppose I'm fine.

There is a woman in our cell who thinks she is perfect and gets to rule everything, but this is jail and I have to live with it.

Thank you very much for the Bible. I've already almost read the study patterns for the first two weeks.

Yes Shannon is a beautiful, happy baby. Her grandma says she's getting quite the temper, but other than that. She only speaks three words: Mamma, Daddy and hot dogs. She hasn't even eaten hot dogs yet!

Does your church frown upon single parents, because when I get out I will need a church to go to. Believe it or not I've only attended four churches in my life. The one my brother and I went to Sunday school at in Howard City, Grandpa and Grandma's church, your church and Community church where Dad and Lyn got married. I haven't been to a real service since Grandma passed away.

Your passage Jeremiah 29:11 is right. God put me here to prosper me and to teach me patience and his path.

I realize now that I want my daughter to grow up knowing her heavenly father just as she will her flesh father.

One can always hope though that God's will has been done and that I can soon return to Shannon.

There is a wonderful woman named Ellen in my cell. I was here for four weeks or so when she came in. One day Ellen asked me if I believe in God; I said yes. She invited me to pray with her and I did. She had a friend she called on the telephone who had a gift to talk with God. This woman told Ellen to tell Charlotte to pray for a Wednesday. Wednesday this week Charlotte got out without any warning whatsoever. I wish Ellen could still call the woman, but Ellen is a federal detainee and they've blocked her calls. Without Ellen coming in here and having a friend over the phone I probably wouldn't be studying God. When Ellen came the whole cell prayed and read the Bible for a while. Charlotte prayed and read the Bible up until the day she left.

Ellen and I are the only ones who pray and talk to God in here. I don't know why I've told you all of this except maybe because I wanted to share with someone God's work.

I have a question. I read somewhere that only the people who believe in God the most are the ones who question him when bad things happen. Because they believe in God so much that they know it is his doing. Is that true? I know it's supposed to be something like that.

Well I have to go. Thank you for the Bible and for writing me.

Love,

Rachel

During Rachel's time in jail she passed the testing for a GED, a high school equivalency exam. Every Wednesday Rachel called Shannon's grandmother, Kim VerHage, and talked to her baby. Visiting hours were forty-five minutes on Sunday. It was so very hard for Rachel to see Shannon behind the thick glass and not be allowed to hold her in her arms. Her visitors didn't really like trying to balance the growing Shannon and the telephone on a wobbly little stool.

There is one more piece of correspondence from Rachel during her incarceration. Since her earliest years, Rachel had a lively creative impulse. Often she bent over a pad of lined writing paper, her smile wide as ever, her blonde hair falling forward and tenting her face. Near the end of her incarceration she sent Aunt Pat a poem:

About the End.
When will the end come?
Has God's will been done?
When will judgment take place?
Will there be enough space?
Will God let me in?
Despite all my sin?

Do not doubt the will of God!
For he has never been a fraud!
He will not lie,
about when we will die!
For it has been said,
Heaven will take our dead!
So despite all your fears,
open your ears!
Hear the sound
of those who've been found!
Trust in him,
and let him dwell within!
Then you will know,
where you will go.
The End

The words rattle in the mind as premonitory when one looks back upon them. Rachel had taken a fork in the road. It appeared to open on new and promising directions. Yet, any new path is fraught with blind spots, even traps and dangers. If only one could know about them in advance.

Not knowing—this is a parent's primal fear. Why? Because the child is the parent's responsibility? Surely that. When the toddler wanders off, panic rides a surge of adrenaline. When a child gets hurt, the parent comforts. These things beat in our souls like some primal drum. There is no need to romanticize it. A parent is the protector of innocence. When there are traps and dangers on that child's path, the parent needs to be there.

Perhaps the fear enters also because this child is part of the parent. No, a person doesn't remake herself through the child. But without the parent, the uniqueness, the person, of this child would not exist. If the parent doesn't care for her child, the parent probably doesn't really care for herself.

That's why we toss in bed at night while the minutes tick past. We wonder whom she is with, what she is doing. We wonder if that beat-up car he drives broke down on some empty stretch, whether he is freezing in the icy knife blades of the blizzard.

Missing. The awful unknown that opens a canyon inside us. To some degree, all have felt loss. We can't escape suffering on this earth, no matter what walls of power, pleasure or wealth we erect against it. Yet, we agree that the loss of a child, when the late night stretches into a day, another night, another day, is the cruelest trick the world can play on us.

What has happened to them? Where are they? Who has them? Are they suffering? The great unknown. We awaken to the morning light and want to howl at the sun.

What happened next is best related in a journal kept by Rachel's father, "Tim" Timmerman:

It was a warm day when Lyn brought Rachel home from the Newaygo County Jail. Rachel had a couple of changes of underwear and was wearing a worn, brown, one-piece snowmobile suit.

I was at work when Rachel came to our home on May 5. By the time I came home Lyn had bought Rachel some new clothes. Rachel gave me the biggest hug of her life, she was just so happy to be free. The next day she would be with Shannon again.

This was an unbelievably busy time at the Timmerman household on the northern fringe of Cedar Springs. Tim's youngest son, John, had been born with feet anomalies and had great difficulty walking at all. Very quickly Rachel established a close connection with her little brother. Gifted with a patience few had seen before, she held both of her brother's hands and helped him walk around the yard on his wobbly feet. Even while tending Shannon, she played hand puppets with him, satisfying his love to hold something soft and cuddly.

Tim and Lyn had scheduled a surgery on John's tendons to correct the curvature of his feet and ankles many months earlier. It didn't sound like a threatening surgery and it gave the hope that John could walk with greater ease. It was not successful. John never walked without assistance for the duration of his brief life.

Lyn brought two children of her own into the marriage. At about the same time Rachel was being discharged, her daughter had bought her own house and Lyn and her son were busy helping Lyn's daughter move while also preparing a room for Rachel and Shannon. Although still a boy of nine, Lyn's son was gifted with a burly strength beyond his years and helped with both moves. He and Rachel struck it off long before and had become close buddies. Now Rachel often preached to him on how bad jail was. Lyn's son didn't mind; they were together again.

About this time, Rachel began getting a lot of phone calls from boys. Lyn had mothered her about some of the topics of conversation, so Rachel began taking them outside. Lyn's son was often in the vicinity and in particular remembered many calls from one specific guy named Ian.

In spite of the circumstantial stress in the house, there was joy, the surging hope of new beginnings. Tim felt that his greatest challenge was teaching Rachel to drive. She needed the mobility to find work. The notebook continues.

Teaching Rachel to drive wasn't an easy experience. First there were some bureaucratic problems with the Secretary of State office and an unpaid traffic fine. Rachel told me that she had worked for a wood cutter, helping him load the wood to pay off the fine. We live in the country and were able to get in several practice drives on the unpaved back roads of Cedar Springs. She was under-confident, but getting better every time.

I was working underneath Lyn's daughter's new house on June 3. I was removing some old wiring when I hit my hand on a water pipe, fracturing a finger. I'm not sure what Rachel was doing at the time but that next morning, June 4, we were drinking coffee at the kitchen table. Rachel was playing with Shannon on the living room floor. "Grandpa, hold out your arms," Rachel said. It's almost like a videotape in my mind. Shannon toddled toward me. She was wearing a blue night dress. Her blonde hair was getting longer, her brilliant blue eyes, a proud smile on her face. These were Shannon's first steps for Grandpa.

That afternoon I was sitting outside, feeling sorry for myself because of my broken finger. Rachel came out to the patio. She was wearing new blue jeans, her long blonde hair pulled back into a pony tail. The thought crossed my mind for a moment that she might have too much makeup on. I decided to say nothing. Rachel told me that a boy named Ian had asked her out on a dinner date and she'd be back in a few hours.

Lyn had been helping out a lot with Shannon's care, so I asked, "What about Shannon?"

Rachel told me, "He asked me to bring Shannon, too."

She gave me a hug and a kiss. Rachel said, "Bye, Dad. I love you."

I sat back down and told her, "Bye. I love you, too, honey."

Later that night, we got a message on the telephone answering machine from her manager at the restaurant where she was working asking for Rachel to return his call when she got in. She never returned.

The next day, June 5, there was a pre-stamped space station hologram envelope in our mail with a letter from Rachel. The letter was postmarked Cedar Springs, Michigan, but the return address was "on vacation."

Dad,

I'm sorry I left without saying goodbye. That guy who picked me up is like the man of my dreams. Shannon bonded with him so well and so did I.

Right now we're on vacation. Maybe we might get eloped. He already asked me to marry him.

I'll be gone for a couple of weeks. I would call you on the phone, but I think you'd try to talk me out of it—marriage.

I'll write more letters and send you my address when I get one.

Love,

Rachel

Lyn and I thought it was quite goofy. Rachel didn't need a vacation from us—we were getting along well—or from her job—she'd only worked one week. Also she had said goodbye before her date. We just didn't understand. It just didn't seem to be her letter.

Sunday, June 15, was Father's Day and Shannon's first birthday. The weather was beautiful, yet I walked aimlessly around the yard all day. I felt that something was wrong. Rachel had always been very good about Father's Day, giving me a plaque or a card. She would have at the very least called collect from wherever she was. I was getting worried and anxious. There was no way Rachel would have Shannon miss getting her birthday presents.

On Monday, June 16, Dave Babcock came to inquire about Rachel. The Newaygo County Prosecutor had received a letter from Rachel, postmarked from Little Rock, Arkansas. Dave didn't know what kind of envelope it was in; he assumed the secretary threw it away. He did know that the return address was our house and he wanted to talk with Rachel.

He showed us the letter:

Dear Chrystal Roach,

I am writing you in hopes that you won't press charges on me for falsifying a police report. Marvin Gabrion did not rape me. I was mad at him, because he called my mother and sister prostitutes at a card party.

A short time later we made up. Then we went down by the river where I performed oral sex on him. When he wouldn't have intercourse with me I decided to teach him a lesson. The final straw was when his puppy bit me on the nose. I pushed the come up on my vagina. Then I pinched myself so I'd be bruised.

I am madly in love with an honest Christian man. And I can't bear the thought of trying to lock up an innocent man.

Thank you,

Rachel Timmerman

Reading the letter we were shocked. Was it really from Rachel? If so, what made her write these words? That same day we received a second letter from Rachel. This was another pre-stamped space station hologram envelope, bearing a postmark from Little Rock, Arkansas.

Dear Dad,

Hello, how are you? I am fine.

Delbert just got a job in Little Rock, Arkansas. All the people here are so nice. I am considering living out here forever. Shannon is doing great. She misses you guys but she's adjusting to life out here really well. I don't know for sure yet when I'll be home. But we will at least come for a visit in the near future.

I'm pretty sure you and Delbert will get along. He's a really good guy. When I decide what I'm doing for the future I will write you back and let you know. Pass on my love to the others and tell them I'll miss 'em 'til I see them again.

Love ya loads.

Love,

Rachel

This letter was also confusing. Rachel had told me she was going on a dinner date with a man named Ian. Now in the letter postmarked from Little Rock, she wrote that she had fallen in love with a man named "Delbert." What was the real story? What was really going on? Where was Rachel?

It was on that Saturday, July 5, George Vande Velde went to his place on Oxford Lake. He owned some vacation property there. That was when he thought he saw something in the lake and called the Newaygo County Sheriff Department.

On Tuesday there was a news conference in Newaygo County. The police weren't saying much, just that they had found an unidentified body in a very remote lake. Ken Kolker, a reporter from the *Grand Rapids Press*, asked for more information, something he could tell the readers and maybe help to identify the body. The police then released the fact that the body had a cross tattooed on the web of the hand.

On Thursday, July 10, I went to work as usual. I received a note from Lyn. Sergeant Miller from the Michigan State Police had called. He wanted to talk to me. I told my boss that I was afraid my daughter was in trouble for not testifying at her rapist's trial.

Sergeant Babcock, whom we'd already met, and Sergeant Miller arrived at our home soon after I did. They weren't saying much, but they were investigating missing persons reports. They felt it wasn't likely that it was Rachel's body found in Oxford Lake; the woman appeared to be much older. They were just checking every possibility. Could I give them a further description of Rachel? Did she have any scars or tattoos?

I told them Rachel did have a large scar on her thigh, where she had hip surgery. As I described Rachel I saw some furtive, knowing looks pass back and forth between the two detectives. They didn't say much more, but asked for her dental records and didn't stay long. Lyn and I talked a little after they left, assuring each other that it couldn't be Rachel.

I went back to work. At lunchtime I went outside on the front lawn of the factory to eat and read yesterday's newspaper. I read Ken Kolker's description of the body in Oxford Lake: "She apparently died after her killer bound and gagged her, secured her with weights and dumped her in a remote lake. Detectives haven't identified the victim." When the article described a white woman five feet ten inches with shoulder length blondish-brown hair, I got a dreadful sinking feeling that grew as I continued reading. "They say she has tattoos, including a cross on her left hand where the thumb and forefinger meet."

The article continued: "Investigators said they've checked missing persons reports from adjacent counties, including Kent, but found nobody matching the description of the body. A preliminary autopsy by Dr. Stephen Cohle at Blodgett Memorial Medical Center shows the woman likely drowned within the last thirty days."

State Police Detective Sergeant Richard Miller was quoted as saying he hoped to identify the victim from fingerprints and dental records: "The victim had good dental hygiene; there should be dental records somewhere."

Sergeant Miller had asked the name of our dentist. My anxiety intensified. The only thing to do was walk. Walk and think.

The next morning I called the phone numbers on the business cards the officers had given us. Sergeants Miller and Babcock weren't available, but someone did return our calls. He advised me not to go to work, that the detectives would be coming to our home later.

It turned out to be an emotionally devastating afternoon, one that even Sergeant Miller's kindness couldn't assuage. He looked me in the eye, grasped my hand tightly and said, "I'm sorry, Mr. Timmerman. We are about 99 percent sure that it is Rachel's body we recovered from Oxford Lake." He had been at the lake since day one. He cut the chains off Rachel's dead body. He had a personal investment in the case from the start. He also had a job to do and nobody wanted to do it more.

The very first question I had, almost a shout, was "Where is Shannon?"

There was no answer.

We answered their questions for about an hour, but I was in too much of a state of shock to really be aware. It wasn't until after the police left that Lyn pointed out that they had asked us all of those questions because they thought that we were suspects.

I really hadn't known the extent of Marvin Gabrion's threats toward Rachel. When I talked to her older brother, there was no doubt in his mind. "Dad, it was Marvin Gabrion who killed her."

By Saturday we were incredibly numb. I went out to the barn and sorted through a box of Rachel's papers.

In the box of Rachel's papers, Tim found Rachel's diary from her time in county jail. Tentatively he flipped through a few pages. Needing to feel a connection to Rachel, he stopped on a page and began reading:

Rachel's Diary
Ever since I was fourteen years old, everyone has told me I should write a book on my life.

Well here it is. I am eighteen years old, the date is February 19 and I'm sitting in the Newaygo County Jail for the next few months plus I've been here since January 8.

My crime was I loved being high on marijuana or anything else. My charge is selling dope. I guess my thoughts were anything to get a buzz. As if this isn't enough I have an eight-month-old baby. She lives with her father and his parents while I do my time.

My Crazy Life
My story really starts when I was thirteen or so, but in order for you to understand just why things happened the way they did, I will have to tell you an outline of my childhood.

I guess I had an ordinary life for children growing up in the late 1970s, early 1980s. My parents didn't have a lot of money and there were three children. My brother was born in 1976. I was born in 1978 and my sister Sara was born in 1981. Our parents always provided for us. We wore homemade or used clothes. We got most of our toys from garage sales or thrift shops. My father grew most of our vegetables and my mother made homemade jams and ketchups. She canned vegetables and fruits.

Basically, all in all my life was pure sunshine in the early years. I don't ever remember being alone, cold or hungry. I had siblings to play with, parents who loved us and a good warm wood stove to cuddle up next to.

Then, in 1983, everything changed. There were four of us then. We had a baby sister named Rebecca Kay. I only have a few precious memories of Becca. I had my own problems.

My lifelong babysitters were all a big family that lived down the road. There was Nancy, the mother, then Walter, her oldest child, then Christine in the middle and last but not least, Matt. Nancy was a strict short lady. Their house never had running water and it always smelled strange. I don't remember Walter much, except once or twice when he stopped Matt from doing it to me. Walter went away to one of the armed services or somewhere, was injured and became confined to a wheelchair. Not only was Walter a hero of the United States, but also he was my hero for stopping Matt. Then there was Matt. He was a child-molester who thought a five-year-old looked good. I have more memories of him in my childhood than anything else.

I told my parents that he was touching me and they called the police and pressed charges, but nothing ever happened to him because I was a child and my testimony wouldn't stand up in a court of law. I have heard that he has a wife and children of his own now. In the end, my parents decided that he couldn't babysit us anymore. Nancy and Christine still did, but only in our own home.

On December 25, 1983, my two-month-old sister died from SIDS at about 10:00 at night. I woke up by being pulled out of bed by my hair. It was Nancy. She said, "Rebecca's dead. You're coming with me. If you don't believe me the ambulance is still outside."

Changes

Our parents split us children up between my father's siblings. I don't remember where my brother went, but I went to my one aunt's and Sara went to Aunt Pat's.

We all attended the funeral where I was told by my ten-year-old cousin that I was a baby because I was crying. I told her to shut up, because she'd cry too if it was her sister who died.

Then we all went to the graveyard to bury Becca. The snow was so deep that my Aunt Pat picked me up and carried me to the grave.

Then we all stood holding hands in a circle and recited the Lord's Prayer.

After the funeral, we all went back to our designated relatives and there we sat for a while, I'm not sure how long. It must have been close to a month. While my parents went through a breakdown. I never even understood until I was much older.

When we finally went home and went back to school, things were really out of whack. There was no more everlasting sunshine. My mom was always crying; then she went into a rehabilitation center for a while.

Things between my mom and dad weren't good either. Truthfully, they never recovered, especially after future events took place. In June of 1984, we moved from our home in the country to a nice home in a nice upper-middle class neighborhood in the southeast suburbs of Grand Rapids. I hated the city at first. We couldn't run around half-naked anymore and we broke our sibling bond, because there were at least ten kids on our street alone to play with. As time traveled on, I grew to love city life. Crime didn't hit us and my mother seemed to be getting better.

In June of 1986 my parents had another child, a boy. And disaster struck again. The baby was born with numerous physical and mental disabilities.

The handicapped child put more stress on my parents. They each accused the other of being the one who had caused the defect. The fighting was getting bad and they seemed to have forgotten that they had three healthy children who desperately needed them. The only plus was that we got to spend a lot of time with our wonderful grandparents.

Disaster

Toward the end of the summer of 1988, my parents split for good. My mother left with us children for a while. First we stayed at my mother's friend's house. Then I went to stay with another one of my mother's friend's because she had daughters my age. It was fun for a while, but all we did was watch television and swim in the swimming pool.

Finally, in the end we wound up camping at Gun Lake. We were going to stay there the whole summer. Then one day while I was down at the lake swimming, my dad came to the campsite. He forced my mother to leave. Then he took over the campsite. The next day he packed our stuff, collected the money from the days she didn't use and we went home.

I'll never forget coming home. There were four wilting roses on the porch step and a card that said she loved us. Inside, my mother had cleaned the house and did the dishes one last time. The most vivid detail in my mind was that she left the dishwater in the sink. My mother never did that.

We pretty much stayed with our Aunt Pat and her husband for the rest of the summer. We went to Bible school every day and had our cousins to play with. But I still missed my mother. How was I supposed to start fourth grade without my mother? I didn't see my mother for many months.

She went off to be with her family out West and got sick in California. She was forced to stay there for a couple of more months than she wanted because she was sick and quarantined.

When my mother finally returned, my parents had a custody trial. My mother lost and my father ended up with custody of all of us, except my little brother, who lived with his foster family.

New Beginnings
My father didn't date much until a year and a half to two years after my parents split. My mother, on the other hand, was always dating. This man, that man. A select few I liked, but most I couldn't stand. There was one man in particular whom I adored. He was excellent to us children, especially me. He was always buying me expensive gifts and clothes. The bad thing about him was that he was always in and out of prison. Three quarters of the times I saw him was at county jails or Michigan State Prison in Jackson.

Although he and my mom were together on and off until he died in 1995, they were mostly together in the late 1980s when my mother had a little apartment on Plainfield Avenue.

I will always love that beautiful apartment. There were a lot of good times in that little one-room apartment, but there were a few bad times too.

When I was ten years old, maybe eleven, this was the first time all of us children went to stay at Mommy's house. My mom was still unpacking her stuff and she was in her bedroom putting a box on the shelf in her closet when a garment bag fell right into her eyes.

My mother came running out of the bedroom screaming. She had blood running down her face. She had her hand cupped over her eye. I thought her eye fell out. My brother was screaming, "Mom, Mom, what do I do?" She was yelling, "Call your father. Call your father." My sister and I were standing on the side, scared. My brother got my father on the phone, then handed the phone to my mother. She was screaming over the phone, "Mr. Timmerman, I've lost my eyes." I ran outside screaming. "My parents got divorced, now my mother poked her eye out." I remember a lady stopped and asked me what was wrong. "My mother poked her eye out." I went on crying. I cried so hard I barely noticed when my dad and the ambulance showed up.

My father drove us all right behind the ambulance to the hospital. It seemed like it took forever for the doctor to come and tell us she didn't lose her eye. She just scratched the lens of her eye and she tore apart her eyelid. My mother was then rushed into emergency eye surgery and plastic surgery where they had to piece her eyelid back together like a jigsaw puzzle. So we went home with a promise to come back the next day.

My mother got out of the hospital a few days later. My father, my brother, my sister and I all went to pick her up. We all had dinner together for the first and last time since their separation.

My dad brought a huge dish of my grandma's Abominable Spaghetti. No matter how much you ate out of the pan, there was always more. We sat around on my mother's floor (she didn't have any furniture yet) and ate spaghetti and talked and laughed like a real family.

My brother and sister and I all hoped our parents would get back together. My dad said if my mom got a job, he'd give her another chance. My mom got a job, but they still never got back together.

Then when I was eleven years old my dad met Lyn. Lyn was just starting a divorce with her husband when my dad asked her out. Lyn had two kids, a ten-year-old and an eighteen-month-old or so. The ten-year-old and I got along real well.

Lyn was all right at first, but it was obvious that her daughter was the brightest star in her sky. We all got along perfectly for a while. We went on long car trips to Florida, all seven of us in one car. We went camping and to the movies, just like most families. The worst was yet to come.

When I was twelve years old I broke my hip. It had been gradually falling out of place for months. My dad said it was because I was getting heavy. I tried explaining to him that I was getting fat because I could barely walk. On December 6, 1990, I had a dream that I was jumping over mud puddles. My leg kicked up in my sleep and made my hip fall the rest of the way out of its socket. I awoke in screams. My dad came running into my room. When I told him what was wrong, he didn't believe me. I told him I couldn't move. I told him if I so much as twitched a finger or took a breath, it knocked me into severe pain. He didn't believe me so he stood me up and I fell like a limp dishrag to the floor. Then he knew something was wrong.

My father called the doctor, then he carried me out to the car and we were off. Every bump we hit, I wanted to die. I was glad when we finally made it to the doctor's office. It took a while for the doctor to see me, but when he did it took not even two minutes for his diagnosis. "Get this girl to the hospital!" He told my dad that I should go in an ambulance, but since I had made it so far by car, he could drive me.

When we got to the hospital, it took a few hours to be admitted. Then they drew lots of blood and took tons of X-rays. Their diagnosis was that I had a slipped hip and they needed to do an emergency surgery to pin it back into place, because the misplaced bone was cutting off the blood supply to my leg.

I barely had time to call my mother from my hospital room before they prepared me for surgery. I was so scared I brought my teddy, named Mr. Bear, into the operating room with me. Then there was blackness. When I woke up, I was back in my hospital room. There were flowers and balloons all scattered through the room, but no mother. I asked my dad where my mom was and he said she had been there, but had to leave. I was in the hospital a little over a week before I could go home.

A lot of things were different after my surgery. I was no longer like a normal child. I walked on crutches for three months. I couldn't go outside and play.

As Tim continued to read Rachel's writings, he was overwhelmed to see a letter from Marvin's mother. This woman told Rachel to do exactly what had happened.

First, Elaine stated that they couldn't afford to have Marvin convicted on the rape charge. She said that this was their life savings and if they put up his $4,000 bond and he was convicted they wouldn't get it back. The words resonated in Tim's mind. Marvin's mother went on to tell Rachel that she must write a letter to the county prosecutor: "Tell her that you were mad at Marvin, you wanted to hurt him and the rape never really happened."

Tim's notebook entry continues:

Our disbelief escalated when we found an earlier letter written to the Newaygo County jail. In the earlier letter Marvin's mother inquires about Shannon's schedule, how much was she eating and sleeping. How would Rachel know? She was in jail and Shannon was staying with her paternal grandmother. More importantly, why would Marvin's mother want to know the details of Shannon's schedule? Perhaps she thought she was going to be taking over her care.

Questions and theories about the man Rachel was supposed to have been with and the man who had raped her filled our waking hours and our dreams.

I was paranoid and nervous. I called Sergeant Miller, but he wasn't available. I told the officer who answered the phone at the Newaygo State Police Post, "I have some information about the murder at Oxford Lake. Is this phone secure for me to talk about it?"

Chapter 7

"I'm Going Fishing Today"

Rachel's funeral was held in Cedar Springs on July 17. The small chapel was packed with Rachel's friends, sporting a creative array of tattoos, piercings and outfits. The officiating pastor was Reverend Walker. He stood before the casket, upon which rested the Bible from Aunt Pat, and said in a deep, gravelly voice: "I'm going fishing today." He had the young people with him at every word.

Reverend Walker selected two passages for his sermon: Psalm 27 and Mark 4:35-41. David's Psalm registers a note of confidence in God even when pursued by enemies. Reverend Walker pointed out:

> The Lord is my light and my salvation;
> Whom shall I fear?
> The Lord is the stronghold of my life;
> Of whom shall I be afraid?

Rachel lived her final hours in desperate fear. She couldn't deliver herself under her own strength. Yet, Reverend Walker insisted, God provided a way of escape for Rachel when her enemy thought he had destroyed her. Her last breath on earth was her first breath in heaven. God sent his angels to rescue her, to meet her and to take her into heaven.

But, we in our human condition wonder, why did she have to die at all? There's the great mystery. We hate suffering; yet, none of us escapes its carnage. And it seems worse yet when it happens to those with their whole lives spread before them: our children.

Every person in the chapel that day knew this. All had learned grief. Reverend Walker turned their attention to Mark 4.

In the story, Jesus had been teaching at the shore of the Sea of Galilee and, because of the crowds, had to retreat to a boat offshore. As night drew near, Jesus directed his disciples to set sail for the far side of the sea. Exhausted from the long hours of teaching, Jesus fell asleep in the stern, apparently oblivious to a sudden storm that lashed the sea, filling the boat to the point of capsizing. The disciples jostled Jesus awake, "Teacher, do you not care if we perish?"

Two things followed. First, Jesus commanded the sea, "Peace! Be still!" Secondly, after the eerie calm settled, he turned to his disciples and asked, "Why are you afraid? Have you no faith?"

Reverend Walker knew full well that life could be hard in Newaygo County. He didn't sugarcoat grief and loss. He spoke from his heart to the broken-hearted, assuring them that even at the moment of Rachel's greatest need, Jesus did not forsake her.

Tim's elderly father said softly, "That was one of the two or three best sermons I've ever heard." *Out of how many thousands?* Tim wondered.

For the service, Rachel's sister Sara had written her own poem.
SECURE?
He is a rock,
He the God who does no wrong,
gives and He taketh away.
Even in pain and joy, I look to Him.
From the pit—
the eternal pit—
I saw a great redeeming light.
There went all of my fright.
Death in the pit
was emotionless.
Joy was lost,
and seemed meaningless.
When I woke up
with heartache and yearning

It was then in my life
I opened my covered eyes
and then I lifted my eyes to the skies.
Pain, sorrow and remorse
flooded my body.
I fell to my knees
and I cried.
My provider gave me an escape.
A thin rope—
for me to pull myself out with.
Many times
the light, the goal
seemed to fade,
and I would fall.
Satan would not give up,
he wanted me.
God's love was stronger.
He would always pick me up.
He always will.
The depths of life
are far behind me,
The shining light,
is far before me.
In our hearts
There are weaknesses and strengths.
The Lord never leaves us,
He holds us and carries us.
When my time comes,
I'll stand my ground.
Next to God, my precious Father,
I will be found.

Rachel's loved ones were left with one great unknown. The detectives
had recovered only one body. What had happened to baby Shannon?

Shortly after the funeral, Tim and Lyn received a number of

condolence cards from Rachel's cellmates. Through them, it almost seemed Tim was seeing Rachel again, connecting with her. The cards were laboriously crafted with intricate, hand-drawn designs and each testified to their love for Rachel.

Rachel and her cellmates had grown close through playing chess and praying together. Many of the letters spoke to Rachel's caring nature, saying she offered the other cellmates a shoulder to cry on and an ear to listen to their problems.

Other letters told of the love Rachel had expressed for Shannon to her cellmates. They knew that Rachel wanted the best for her daughter and had dreams of giving Shannon the opportunity to live a full life. Rachel's cellmate hoped and prayed for Shannon's safe return.

At times, the letters also expressed outrage and anger at the murderer.

The letters had a moving and comforting effect for Tim and Lyn. These were the women Rachel lived with for the last five months of her life. With them she was intimate. Together they storied their pasts and made plans for the future. Tim wrote and sent letters of gratitude to each one. With only one exception, he never heard anything back. The likeliest event, he figured, was that the letters were confiscated at the jail. Some months later he was able to confirm that almost none of the letters had been received.

That one exception, however, was a lifeline to his lost daughter. Sharlene Madden continued her correspondence. In a Christmas letter dated December 23, she offered whatever help she could. Moreover, her memory of Rachel's fears seemed far more detailed than earlier letters Tim had received. On January 16, Tim wrote back.

Dear Ms. Madden,

Thank you very much for your recent letter. Losing my Rachel was a tragic loss, but every day we are haunted by thoughts of our "missing" granddaughter. I have tried very hard to get nationwide publicity for Shannon, but it hasn't been easy.

You can't imagine how much I would like to hear about what Rachel told you about Marvin. She lived with me for a month after she got out of jail. She got a job at a restaurant and seemed to like working with the kids there. My wife, Lyn, took care of Shannon while Rachel was at work. I was teaching Rachel how to drive my car. Rachel never mentioned Marvin. She did get subpoenaed to testify in his rape case. I told her I'd go with her and I believed she would testify against him. Rachel left my home supposedly for a couple of hours with a boy she didn't introduce and never came back.

I have to ask . . . would you please take the time to share your memories of what Rachel shared with you. It won't hurt me. I believe Rachel is in a better place. The cops don't tell me the time of day. I've been very frustrated trying to learn more about the chain of events. Thank you very much.

Wishing you the best in your future, I appreciate your letter and pray that you will help me in my attempts to understand.

Sharlene Madden responded quickly, on January 27, with a long, detailed letter. In it she told Tim that she and Rachel played cards and had long talks while in jail together. She then went on to describe Rachel's version of the rape, which Rachel had told her during one of their many conversations. Sharlene's details of the events, as told to her by Rachel, were violent and concluded that Gabrion forced Rachel to have sex with him several times, pounded her head on the ground, bit her nose, twisted her nipples and burned her skin with cigarettes. Sharlene wrote that she could still see the scars on Rachel's nose and arms. Rachel described Gabrion as having spooky eyes and green teeth.

During the rape and shortly thereafter, Gabrion threatened many times to kill Rachel. Rachel told Sharlene that after she pressed charges Gabrion stalked her and continued to threaten her life. Sharlene explained in her letter that Rachel confided that she was terrified of Marvin Gabrion. On one occasion Gabrion told Rachel details about her family members—where they lived, what kinds of cars they drove and where they worked—and Rachel was scared he would hurt her family and her if he was released from the charges. Sharlene wrote that Rachel often asked the correction officers for information and updates about Gabrion, wanting to make sure he stayed locked up. Sharlene was positive Rachel would have never dropped the rape charges against Gabrion or written a letter saying the rape charges were false unless someone forced her.

Tim was happy to read that Sharlene had viewed Rachel as a daughter and guided her to finish her GED and to attend church. Rachel's love for Shannon was also prominent in Sharlene's letter.

Chapter 8

Land of Lost People

S outh Division Avenue in Grand Rapids is today graciously called the Heartside District. Once a booming industrial area, it still bears the red and gray hues of urban desolation. Sometime around the Korean War, it slid into decay. A factory closed down, perhaps; a building burned. Some windows now wear plywood; others stare vacantly upon the streets from out of dark recesses.

The post-Korean War era was a time of cheap construction and spacious suburbs. Like a vacuum, the suburban "industrial malls" sucked out the companies, the workers and the life of the district.

Then, like animals ferreting out a new burrow, others began to creep into the abandoned streets and buildings. They soon housed prostitutes and pimps, drug dealers and alcoholics, potholes, garbage, urine, sickness and death. The former inhabitants no longer dared drive down the streets lined with broken-down autos.

During the 1990s, as with inner cities nearly everywhere, dirt cheap property drew developers. In those years a very odd term came to life: *gentrification*. In reality, some areas never are truly gentrified. The hustlers still fight and kill for their turf. The mentally ill, armed with a couple bottles of pills in their pockets, are kicked out of economically nonviable mental hospitals and are told to be well and see their doctors if they think of it. South Division is home to missions, soup kitchens, free clothing stores and places for the homeless to hang out, drink coffee, work on puzzles or sleep. Gentrification has squeezed the homeless closer together, maybe a square mile. During winter, mattresses line the floors of shelters. When the temperature hits single digits, plus or minus, volunteers go out in the night and try to talk people who sleep on tarps and cardboard under the expressway bridges to come inside. Some come; some don't. Some die.

Others die for different reasons, but mainly from a coldness of soul. A knifed prostitute in an empty lot. Two or three men in a shootout at a bar, fast-food restaurant or pool hall. Sometimes others on the street know the deceased, sometimes not. The sixteen-year-old prostitute just in from Chicago? The one found in the gravel lot with her neck broken? No. Nobody knew her but her pimp. And he's not telling. "Never seen her before, man."

But sometimes, the law of the street, which is also the fear of the street, forces small bands of three or four despondent souls together. It reminds them of something they only dimly remember— security against the unknown. Or it gives it to them for the first time.

One was Robert Allen.

Mentally disabled and alcoholic, subsisting on a social security check and the missions, Robert Allen survived life on South Division.

It was not unusual for one of the street people to suddenly disappear. In spite of the increased security patrols of the rail yards just five blocks away, a ride on a freight was available anytime. Very rarely, a concerned family member might come looking. But not for Robert Allen. He had no one except three friends and the social security check that enabled him to live in a tiny one-room, subsidized apartment converted out of a nineteenth century hotel on Division Avenue. However tiny, he did have some guy living with him for a few weeks one winter. Every room in the six floors of the unit was subsidized. That left Allen enough money for wine. He ate at the missions, got clothes from the Big House Clothing Shop and hung out with his friends in the shade, out of the way, when the weather was warm. They walked a couple of blocks to the Grand River where they had a patch of grass staked out.

If anyone on South Division needed something special—say, a tooth pulled by a volunteer dentist, a new winter coat, some extra food to tide you over—he or she went to see Big Duane at the Big House. About a dozen or so churches had worked together, bought a two-story warehouse long before the prices rose and put in a row of self-contained showers and high capacity water heaters. They put in two fifty-cup coffee makers, both regular coffee only. The coffee came in dented and broken cans donated by wholesalers. The board of Big House was looking for a director when the pastor at the mission sent Big Duane their way. That was twenty years ago.

Big Duane was six feet six inches, 300 pounds and black as rubber tires steel-belted with a scar through his upper lip into his cheek. Big Duane was a three-time felon and a recovering addict. He named the place the Big House and was the closest thing to a constant presence of law that one could find on South Division. When there was a problem, you talked to Big Duane.

Robert and his friends didn't go to the Big House much. They looked out for one another, not that any of them could do much by way of defense. It was being together that counted. Three or four always seemed stronger than one or two. It was one of the illusions by which the people of South Division lived. There was no such thing as safety.

When Robert Allen first went missing one summer, his buddies thought maybe he just needed a change of scenery. When they walked down to the Grand River the next day, they half expected to find Allen sprawled in the grass. Social security payments had come in two days previously. Maybe he really tied one on. Fallen asleep in a bar, perhaps. Got kicked out and found his way down to the river to sleep it off.

Although, his friends rationalized, Robert Allen would no more go near a bar than any one of them would. Pay those prices? No way. And they didn't like bars. It was too easy to get hurt. Allen's friends stood by the railing of the river and thought it over. A tumble of concrete blocks sprawled down the bank. It had been dry this summer, but the black flow of water looked deep and cold. They began to worry; not one of them wanted to say what they were worried about.

On the fifth day, they began to feel they had to do something. Nobody said anything at first. They sat in the shade passing a gallon box of something red and wet and 13 percent alcohol.

"Think we ought to do something," one said. It was not a question; it was a decision. The others nodded and passed around the gallon. No one said anything for a long time. Then, "Port City," said one.

"What's that?" another asked.

"Port City wine," the first replied.

"It is." Someone stared at the label.

"This ain't a port city. Them's over by the lake," the third friend argued.

"True. So what?"

Silence. They drained the wine.

"Got a kick, though."

They fell asleep.

They awakened in the mid-afternoon and realized they had missed dinner at the mission. They stood up.

"What now?"

"Get in line for supper. Gotta eat an' keep my strength up."

"Stop an' see Big Duane on the way."

"Should tell him about Bob. I got a funny feeling," the first friend said.

The second man agreed. "He wouldn't just leave this long."

"No. What about his sisters?"

A long pause.

"I don't know. I think he likes his apartment too much."

"Got a funny feeling. Like I did with that guy," reiterated the first.

"Who?"

"Guy that stayed there. Few weeks. Last winter. Bert, I think his name was."

"Bart," the third man suggested.

"Nah. That's not right. Mart or Marv or something," the second friend supplied.

"Better go see Duane afore I fall back asleep."

"Yessir. All this thinking tires a body out."

"Duane'll know what to do." They nodded.

Big Duane had a second-story apartment at the Big House. The main floor was nearly empty with everyone out enjoying the sunshine. To the left were the shower rooms. To the rear of the building were rows of circular bins holding used clothing, enough winter coats to outfit a battalion. Never too many of those for the street in winter.

Big Duane had been sleeping. When the friends knocked, his voice hit the door like a tidal wave. At first he looked angry—300 pounds in a T-strap undershirt and khaki shorts as big as a circus tent. Then he listened. He nodded in dismissal and said, "I know Robert. I'll put the word out."

When no word came back after two days, Big Duane contacted the police and filed a formal report. It didn't matter, really. Street people disappeared left and right. Didn't matter. But it was his final, self-imposed obligation to his people. File the report.

The fact that Robert Allen disappeared didn't strike anyone as a particularly ominous event. Street people were, by definition, transients. Yet, Robert was a fixture. He had an apartment. He had a social security check coming in. He had buddies. He had good sisters who looked after him. He probably had something of a past, although longtime street people seldom talked about it.

When Big Duane filed a report, a rookie female cop, red hair tucked up under her blue cap and her bulletproof vest about doubling her size and weight, came down to the Big House to talk with him. People came to Big Duane, not the other way around. He didn't go the five blocks to the police department.

He was in his weightlifting room when she arrived—pushing out grunts and heaves and stink. Only free weights, no gadgets.

Rookie Officer O'Rourke followed him around a circuit, trying to keep her eyes off those biceps like tree limbs. She scratched down words in her pad when she could catch enough of them between grunts. She turned to leave when she thought she had enough.

"Officer," Big Duane barked as she neared the door.

She froze then turned slowly. "Yes?"

"Next time you come in the Big House, remember to take your hat off."

Nervously she touched the brim of her cap. "Yes," she said. "Thanks for the reminder."

Big Duane had done all he could.

Officer O'Rourke had done what she should. She filed the report.

Nobody seemed to notice in the weeks following that Robert Allen's social security check still was being cashed. Or that it was sent to a different address.

And nobody seemed to take note of the fact that a driver's license was issued to a Robert Allen in the state of Indiana.

No one on South Division, no one at the police department and surely no one in Newaygo County made any connection between the disappearances of Rachel and Shannon one year later with that of Robert Allen. Even though late that summer someone rented a room at a South Division house using Robert Allen's identification and social security check, such a connection had been rendered oblivious to most.

Besides, if Robert Allen's file was set aside at the police department—understandably so for a city steamrolled by crime—it never came to the attention of the newspaper. Why should it?

Then another unusual thing happened. Wayne Davis had an unusually wide circle of friends. Truly he could care less about winning friends and influencing people. It came naturally to him. Wayne Davis was a man without guile. He helped others when they needed it and as often as he could. On more than one occasion, he posted bond for someone. And a good portion of every disability check went to maintain his stock of beer, which he distributed freely.

Wayne Davis was thin, walked with a bad limp, had a metal plate in his head from a Vietnam injury, wore physical health like a shredded garment and was an alcoholic, but nearly everyone loved him. That included his estranged wife who was in a new relationship but wouldn't divorce Wayne. It included his children, scattered all over the United States. It surely included his many friends in his little corner of Newaygo County. Moreover, he had one claim to fame. It was said that Wayne Davis made the best pickles in all of Michigan.

So when people went checking on Wayne Davis, just days after Rachel's disappearance, they were surprised not to find him. He was, although a good deal older, a very good friend of Rachel's. Wouldn't he be out looking and concerned?

Then, inside his house, they found his old camouflage army jacket draped over a chair. Wayne never went anywhere without that jacket.

Detectives began studying the scene, now set off with yellow crime tape. No, they didn't find any blood or traces of violence inside. They did find a single set of footprints, leading from the back of the trailer to the woods.

Now the questions began to collide. Marvin Gabrion, Rachel, Shannon and Wayne Davis all seemed to have disappeared around the same time. What was the connection? Wayne Davis couldn't have been a perpetrator in any crime—at least he was highly unlikely to be one. For one thing, he didn't have the strength to do any violence. He wasn't physically capable. For another thing, Rachel was his friend and Wayne, the ex-infantryman, was fiercely loyal.

But, right there in the initial sheriff's report for Rachel's rape was the evidentiary witness statement of Wayne Davis, on August 7:

> He advised Ms. Timmerman and Marvin Gabrion had met for the first time. Davis stated they were in Marvin Gabrion's vehicle... Mr. Davis advised he, Ms. Timmerman, young Charlie and Marvin Gabrion went to Brian Anderson's house in the trailer park near 36th and Chestnut to a party. He advised at the party were the aforementioned subjects, Mr. Anderson and his young son were playing cards and the both of them continued to drink. He advised that Mr. Gabrion was intoxicated at the house while they were playing cards and that both of them continued to drink. He advised that Mr. Gabrion was very moody and attempted to pick a fight with him at one point, however,

Davis would not fight him telling him he was intoxicated and to relax. Davis also advised he did not notice any touching, kissing or feeling between Mr. Gabrion and Ms. Timmerman while at the residence.

Mr. Davis stated later that evening he, both the Gabrions and Ms. Timmerman left in Mr. Gabrion's convertible with the top down. Seating arrangements were Mr. Marvin Gabrion driving, Ms. Timmerman in the passenger seat, and Mr. Davis and young Gabrion in the back seat. He stated he drove east on 36th, then turned north on Newcosta where Marvin Gabrion stopped the vehicle and told young Charlie and Mr. Davis to "get the fuck out," which they obliged leaving Ms. Timmerman and Marvin Gabrion in the vehicle. R/O asked Mr. Davis if he had heard Mr. Gabrion ask Ms. Timmerman at any time while driving down the road if she liked to fuck women, to which Mr. Davis replied he couldn't hear anything due to the fact the top was down on the vehicle. Davis stated that he and young Gabrion walked to Ms. Timmerman's house where they stayed. Davis said awhile later, Ms. Timmerman came home, appearing to be very upset, was crying and noticed that her nose was bleeding. Mr. Davis stated that Ms. Timmerman went to the area near the bathroom in the trailer and Marvin Gabrion also came into the house. Davis stated at that point Ms. Timmerman told Mr. Davis to tell Marvin Gabrion to leave, which he did. At that point, Davis said Marvin Gabrion began pushing him around and Mr. Davis was able to get him out of the trailer and he locked the door. R/O asked Mr. Davis if Ms. Timmerman was in the bathroom, which he was unsure, however, he did state she did produce a hammer at one point. Davis advised that once Gabrion was out of the house, there was yelling by Mr. Gabrion and Ms. Timmerman. He said Mr. Gabrion, at one point, threatened to call the police, at which time Ms. Timmerman told him to go ahead and call the police, he would be the one that got in trouble and she was not going to call the police. R/O asked Mr. Davis if Marvin Gabrion and he were intoxicated, to which he advised definitely they were.

More pieces of the puzzle were coming together.

As the days grew long and empty of answers, thoughts of that June evening haunted Tim's mind. Over and over he saw his daughter's bright blue eyes sparkling when she had held Shannon who had just learned to take her first steps to her grandpa. The evening sun lit their light blonde hair. Two heads, side by side, lit like candles in the wind.

I love you, Dad.

Bye. I love you too, honey.

And she had turned and walked down the long driveway, past the stand of trees by the pole barn, entered a car and disappeared.

But with whom? It had to be someone she trusted. She was still afraid from the ordeal of the past year. Rachel simply would not have entered a car with someone she didn't know. But with whom?

Nobody seriously believed for a moment that she had taken off to Arkansas. But that simply left more mysteries, more questions. If the detectives could only find the man with whom she had left they would have a place to start.

Then another disappearance came to light through Lyn's sister. She had made a stop at the a store near where Rachel and Sara had lived together. While there, she overheard talk that a man named Ian Decker was missing. Curiously, the man's name had earlier been associated with Rachel.

Tim started by asking his other children if they had ever heard of him. Rachel's older brother knew of him, but hadn't met him. He did know the guy's name was Decker. Sara didn't know Ian's last name, but knew that he had called Rachel a few times. Could this have been the same Ian whom Lyn's son had overheard before Rachel disappeared?

Nowhere to go. Another disappearance. Another loose end leading anywhere and nowhere.

In the early days of Rachel and Shannon's disappearance, no clear link existed among any of these people. Only in their nightmares did Tim and Lyn have flickers of fear linking Rachel, Shannon and

Marvin Gabrion. Rachel, after all, had been scheduled to testify against him at the rape trial.

The empty days dragged by.

Not until Rachel's body surfaced, clad in her favorite red and black flannel shirt and the new jeans in which she had left the house on June 4, did the law have to work urgently for connections. Coincidence no longer was an issue.

The law agencies and investigating detectives multiplied quickly. Although many secondary investigators were involved, three people worked lead on the case.

Dick Miller, detective sergeant with the Michigan State Police, was the consummate professional, always honest and with something encouraging to say. Six feet tall, solidly built and wearing high quality suits, Miller sported two distinctive habits. First, he wore his hair "high and tight"—military style—with flecks of gray creeping in. If you want to know what's going on in Newaygo County, get a haircut at a local barbershop every week. Second was the fastidious neatness of his office. Above his desk was a corkboard, to which were pinned two photographs: one of Rachel with Shannon and one of Marvin Gabrion. Dick Miller had passions other than nailing criminals. Few things made him happier than trekking through the wilds of Michigan's Upper Peninsula hunting bear with a bow and arrow.

The second major lead was Detective Sergeant David Babcock of the Newaygo County Sheriff Office. Babcock knew people. He knew their backgrounds, their families, their criminal records.

The third lead came as a surprising twist. In the national forest-land of Newaygo County, boundary lines skirmish among federal, state, county and private ownership. It just so happens that a line bisects Oxford Lake, dividing state to the north and federal to the south. With the weight of the chains and blocks, Rachel's recovered body would have been sighted within inches of where she drowned. That spot was precisely 227 feet south of the line, well within federal territory.

Enter Special Agent Roberta Gilligan of the Federal Bureau of Investigation. Lyn's daughter referred to her as "the super cool FBI chick." It wasn't just because of her petite size or good looks, though that might be sufficient. From the outset and, in spite of her training that everyone is a suspect, she impressed Tim and Lyn with her determined, direct approach. Intelligent and insightful, Agent Gilligan initiated a series of interviews, comparing and contrasting recollections to get an accurate picture. She dressed like a professional agent: dark pantsuit, feminine blouse and a large gun in her purse.

Despite all the caricatures of FBI special agents in popular crime novels, Gilligan genuinely entered into the emotional distress of the family. Moreover, while she couldn't or wouldn't disclose many details of the case to Tim and Lyn, she did always respond to their calls and found something encouraging to say each time.

The investigation widened. Tip after tip pursued. Yet, there was no arrest. Tim and Lyn's dismay grew, as Tim's notebook entries reflected:

Three months, three weeks and two days have passed since Rachel and Shannon left us. We are encouraged by the involvement of a task force of state and federal agencies. We very much want some answers. We just don't know what the police are doing.

Part III

The Investigation

But behind the bewilderment
The truth was already gleaming.
The loathsome truth!

Fyodor Dostoevsky
Notes from Underground

Chapter 9

Parents of the Disappeared

E ven the best parents make mistakes. They do wrong. If they have any sense of moral ought-ness, they discipline their children. Sometimes they wonder if the punishment is too easy or too harsh. If they have any sense of the furious dangers that swirl about this world, they try to protect their children. Sometimes they wonder if they are merely shielding their children from a reality that can't be denied, sidestepped or avoided. Perhaps, too, parents make the awful mistake of trying to recreate themselves in their children. They give too much or too little, depending upon their own pasts. They reshape the contours of their own lives in the clay models of their offspring.

Human nature forces us to stumble along on the tightrope relationships with our children, often toppling headlong. The very worst paradigm, however, is simply to give up, not to care, to let the child wander his or her own way with our benign neglect. Complete freedom can be the most unpardonable sin visited upon a child, for at that point one ceases to be a parent in the truest sense. Rather, one has become a biological mercenary, sending the child alone to do battle in a fragmented universe.

Moreover, even the best children make mistakes. They, too, do wrong, sometimes grievous harm that rives the soul of the parent. It is the nature of most children to kick against the fencing of their parents' moral boundaries. It is the nature of children to explore the world beyond their traditional experiences, to wonder what if and test what might be. It is the nature of children to dissociate themselves from their parents. In the children's efforts to find their own identities, parents are often little more than an embarrassment, a relic of a way they choose not to go.

Such rebellion is also a part of human nature. We have all experienced it. Our children will also. Our children make mistakes. They do wrong.

Regardless of this delicate dance on the tightrope between parent and child, one thing is indissoluble: we are a part of each other. This is more than a matter of biology—the sequenced mystery of sperm and egg. Rather, it is a fusion of spirit. This is my child; this is my parent. For better or worse, despite all the mistakes in the world, this primal truth echoes since the world began.

For this reason, separation hurts so terribly. It may happen when the door shuts on the prisoner sentenced to jail. It may happen when the soldier leaves for a war zone or some distant assignment. Surely it happens when parent or child submits to surgical intervention that may alter a life for better or for worse. But in each of these instances there is a reasonable expectation, a hope that the person might return, that even though distance, danger or helplessness arise, nonetheless restoration may occur. This we can all understand.

What is incomprehensible, what begs understanding, is when a child disappears. The not knowing lacerates the soul. This is the state of parents of the disappeared: the not knowing.

Hope collides with uncertainty like thunderclaps. *What if* are the words hardly dared to be spoken. They are the words on the lips of many parents who have endured such anguish.

Then, perhaps, a day like this arrives—the very worst fears founded. In this case, the body of Rachel Timmerman was secured from the dark waters of Oxford Lake on July 6. Her body was virtually unidentifiable pending the medical examiner's report. The many days of submersion in the algae-ridden waters had bloated and disfigured the body. Initial impressions reported brown hair instead of blonde. The only readily identifiable marking was a tattoo of a cross on the webbing between the thumb and the forefinger. It was enough for her family. They knew.

Still, four days later the official press report was: "Police seek
I.D. of body in lake." The next day Detectives Miller and Babcock
called Tim out of work for an interview. They told him they were routinely investigating the missing persons reports and the possibility of
this being Rachel's body. Finally, on July 11, Sergeant Miller said,
"I'm sorry, Mr. Timmerman. We're about 99 percent sure that it was
Rachel's body in Oxford Lake."

There is something oddly comforting in at least knowing the
truth. But in this case the truth was only partial. In a sense, Rachel's
story had ended, but in another sense the full horror and trauma of
that story had only begun. The story of Rachel's infant daughter,
Shannon, was still open. It was a blank book and no one had found
words to enter on the mocking, empty pages.

Counselors and psychologists cautiously lay out the emotional
stages of grieving. They are classic; any elementary psychology student
knows them. Yet they seem oddly skewed for parents of murdered
children.

For one thing, of necessity the act happens apart from us. We
are robbed of that basic instinct of humanity—to protect and comfort
our children. A merciful numbness, like a gray vapor of fog, surrounds
us. Every synapse in the brain battles against the reality. *This can't
have happened. The worst nightmare is true. The nightmare! Never to
be awakened from, but true!*

The synapses overload and short out. The gray fog leaks across
the ruined landscape of the brain. Numb.

Late in the week, Tim drove to the hospital morgue where the
autopsy would be performed:

> Thursday morning I went to Blodgett Hospital and asked for
> directions to the morgue. A friendly technician of some sort
> guided me to the right elevator. He said that he saw me on TV:
> "Man, it must be tough." I finally found Dr. Stephen Cohle,
> our Kent County medical examiner. Dr. Cohle is a very under-
> standing, caring person. He seems to understand my need to

know something. There had been a 747 airplane that crashed into Guam days before. Dr. Cohle's wife, also a medical examiner, and a secretary are still in Guam. Dr. Cohle told me that he can hardly do his job without his secretary. They are scheduled to return this weekend. Dr. Cohle's wife will have a mountain of work ahead of her, but if I call next Wednesday I should be able to get a copy of the death certificate. Her cause of death will be broadly described as "homicidal means." Dr. Cohle was willing to tell me what happened. "Rachel's body came into the hospital in a black hazard bag. It was complete from the scene, with the cement blocks and a heavy, shiny, silver chain." He wasn't sure about the type of locks, but he did assure me that they removed all of the evidence. He stated that the handcuffs had to be cut off.

Some time later Tim was able to read the entire autopsy report. Is there anything more real, more final, than an autopsy report? The cover page was so bland in its black and white objectivity. The report number: A- 97-321. Meaningless.

Below, the reality:

    Name: Timmerman, Rachel   Birth date: 04/06/78

Below those presiding over the autopsy:

    Date & Hour of Death   06/03/97, unknown
    of Autopsy   07/07/97, 1300

That affirmed the necessities. And above the forensic pathologist's signature:

    Manner of Death: Homicide.

There was something about the finality of that period after *Homicide*. No doubt. The end of the matter. This was what happened to Rachel.

But it flung the door open to hundreds of questions: Who? When? How? Endless questions.

On the second page, more information appeared, again in the crisp, formal language of forensic evidence:

FINAL DIAGNOSES:

1. Homicidal means
   a. Body recovered from lake.
   b. Body wrapped in chains attached to cement blocks, wrists handcuffed behind back, and duct tape wrapped around eyes and mouth.
   c. Not found: evidence of injury, natural disease or intoxication.

CAUSE OF DEATH: Homicidal means.

With clinical dispassion, the report cut inward, first stripping away anything not biological. The inventory was carefully reported, mapping the initial investigation point:

PERSONAL INVENTORY:

The body is secured with a heavy link chain wrapped around the waist and secured in the back to a cement block. This chain is attached to another chain which is looped within one of the holes of a cement block. The second chain and block are wrapped around the legs. These are secured with two padlocks and three separate metal clips. The hands are handcuffed behind the back with white metal handcuffs. Duct tape is wrapped around the face over the eyes and mouth. The nose is exposed. The body is clad in a long sleeve red plaid shirt. There are designer jeans. There are no shoes or socks. The body is clad in a V-neck undershirt, white brassiere and black panties. In the right front pocket of the jeans there are two one-dollar bills, four dimes, seven nickels and a penny. There are two cloth bracelets around the left ankle. There is a discolored metal ring with one lavender stone on the fourth finger of the left hand.

The probing of the pathologist then moved inward, his eyes, his tools, his report examined the body in microscopic detail. "One healed piercing on the right ear. Two healed piercings on the left ear. Hair: approximately seven inches long."

This is my daughter, Tim thought.

The report continues. There were striae; there were symmetrically developed extremities. There was this intact and that intact. There was the weighing and examination of organs. Unremarkable. Unremarkable. The final words: "The remainder of the autopsy is without particular note." It stands there: black and white. Final.

This is my daughter.

Numbness settled down into the brain like a salve. Limbs were heavy, the body lethargic. It had received a traumatic psychological blow. Numb.

The feeling came down like a fogbank, obscuring everything. The fog was heavy, paralyzing.

Moreover, as the fog pressed inward it isolated and violated. It bared spaces that filled with a sense of failure—*this happened on my watch*. Depression moved in and took up residence. Its scaly hide and clacking feet scared away the shadow of happiness, if only a remembered happiness.

In his notebook, Tim quoted Samuel Taylor Coleridge: "A sadder and a wiser man, he rose the morrow morn."

For Rachel's father the investigation seemed to continue at a sputtering gait.

In midsummer the name Ian Decker began to factor more prominently in the investigation. From one of Lyn's relatives they learned that Ian Decker had gone missing about the time of Rachel's disappearance. In the family's own investigation they found a source who "had known Ian Decker forever." Moreover, this person had seen Rachel and Ian together and Ian had introduced Rachel to the source. She confirmed it was Rachel by reference to the cross tattoo. Lyn asked the source to describe Rachel's companion. "Ian is scruffy looking, shoulder length, dark colored hair. He's about five feet, ten inches tall. He's built kind of husky in the upper body, but has real thin legs." Could Ian Decker have been the same Ian who picked Rachel up that night for her date?

Then too it sometimes seemed to her father and stepmother that the only people being questioned were family members. In the process, Tim and Lyn wondered if the police were learning anything at all or if the investigators couldn't find anyone else to question.

It still surprised them a bit when detectives Dave Babcock and Roberta Gilligan requested a personal interview with Sara. She had given two interviews on the rape charge and had been informally questioned since Rachel's disappearance.

It was a warm summer day when Tim saw Babcock through the kitchen window, headed toward the back door. When he and Gilligan entered, they asked if they could speak with Sara in private. Tim, Lyn and Lyn's son Mitchell went outside where they could keep an eye on to the proceedings. Mitchell wrote in his own notebook, "Nobody ever asks me any questions about my sister, and I knew her better than anyone. I'm just a reflection in the glass." One of the things he did know and was not questioned about was that the man who had been calling Rachel was named Ian.

After Sara's interview, Tim left for work and Lyn began straightening up the house—busywork to distract herself. Or maybe it was fortuitous, for there on the carpet lay a small black microcassette recorder, no doubt left by one of the investigators. Crime victims just didn't get that lucky. Had it been an accident by Dave Babcock or on purpose? FBI trained Roberta Gilligan played everything top-secret and no comment. Tim joked that she would say "no comment" if you asked her the time of day and she was wearing a wristwatch.

Tim got home from work too late to reach one of the investigators. What would anyone do anyway? There was no sign on the recorder that read: *Don't Listen To Me*. Instead, he hurriedly transcribed the contents. Not all of it made sense at the time—apparently random notes and details. But two things did spring out. This was the first time they heard the name Robert Allen linked in any way with Marvin Gabrion. And it was the first time they heard Gabrion's current address—in Altona, Michigan.

With the questions that multiply insistently like moss in the dark, a double-edged axe slices into numbness of the frozen self.

The first edge is surely grief; for, while numbness is paralysis, grief is active. And because the violation is great, the grief is great.

The parents of the disappeared are still victims at this stage. Grief may be expressed communally, but finally it is an individual position. The response of others is consolation. Grief is a state of your soul when it is riven by the double-headed axe and laid mercilessly bare.

Comfort may come from many quarters: family, co-workers, friends. But Tim and Lyn needed to hear from others who had endured similar situations. It started with a friend's recommendation to read *How to Survive the Loss of a Child* by Catherine Sanders.

One day someone left a fat manila envelope at Tim's workstation. It was filled with materials from the National Organization of Parents of Murdered Children (POMC). A local chapter met in nearby Grand Rapids. The featured guest speakers often included police officers who explained the legal answers parents sought. Additionally, the POMC Web site (www.pomc.org) made available many resources.

It also gave Tim and Lyn a chance to share their story. They could put a face on grief.

As the days slipped into the New Year, the questions voiced by Tim grew:

February 12

We haven't heard from anybody lately about the search for Shannon. She is always in my thoughts. I walk from my barn to the house, in the sky is the full moon, showing me a happy face. I have hope, I have love, I try to give my love and show it to those I know who love me back.

The disappearance of Shannon. The murder of Rachel. The disappearance and possible murder of Wayne Davis. The disappearance of Ian Decker. What about the disappearance of Robert Allen?

As the case became more complicated, it seemed that Tim's desire for answers began to beat through the grief. Like the second head of that double-bladed axe, the rational need to know began to work alongside the emotional loss.

This driving urge to get answers is clearly evidenced in Tim's February 19 notebook entry:

> On my turn to talk at the POMC meeting I gave a very brief synopsis of my story. I mentioned that we'd talked to a lot of reporters, most were in a hurry, but the reporter who sought us out took her time, felt our pain, gave me a chance to correct mistakes or do better.
>
> I supported the concept of POMC because…from July through the long months I could really relate to the written materials, the stages I went through. I had experienced the pain and anger of having a child die of crib death (a daughter, Rebecca, who died of SIDS). I compared that pain to a grain of sand on the vast beach of rage I felt toward the individual who murdered my daughter.

Grief transforms to anger. And with anger comes more questions. The need to know every detail beats like frantic CPR into the numb heart. Like shifting pieces of a puzzle, these old questions frame the anger. Who did this to my child? Where? And when? How did the monster set it up? And maybe the best clues emerge from the question why. A notebook entry dated August 2 captures the transformation:

> Some weeks after the funeral, the psychological trauma begins to ebb. Our minds became less overwhelmed by the pain. We began to wonder, what happened? I started out by compiling simple timelines, recording when events occurred. We knew we had a missing granddaughter, but we didn't know what to do about it. We began to ask more and more questions. Frustrated by law enforcement's lack of answers, we started writing down questions and trying to find answers.

Worse, as more time passed, the parents seemed to be kept at the far periphery of any police investigation. They understood that to a certain degree this was necessary. Detectives have to protect the train of evidence. They think of "the case" and what they'll give the prosecutor to take to court.

But as parents they are ransacked by those questions: who, what, when, where, why, how. Like tiny planets, they wobble at the edge of dark space.

As the questions spin crazily, anger grows. Parents being to look for answers themselves.

Chapter 10

Searching

Cedar Springs lies equidistant between a state expressway to the west and a heavily travelled business route to the east. The intersection with the expressway has the typical highway megamall—several gas stations, fast food restaurants, a grocery store. At night the bright arc lights can be seen two miles away.

The megamall provides employment for some of the residents, especially teenagers who can stand on their feet inhaling grease fumes and flipping burgers at warp speed. Thirty-two hours a week at minimum wage. Many adults take one of the two thoroughfares south to Grand Rapids for work.

Cedar Springs itself is a pleasant little town, one that could be transplanted with any of a thousand Midwestern towns and not lose its identity. A main street runs north and south with a traffic light at the intersection of the county road. A block or two north is the second traffic light, there for no compelling reason. Auto parts stores, a couple of restaurants and a few businesses marked more by hope than success dead-end into a car dealership. There the road forks and the north country begins.

Just a few signs first appear of what lies ahead. A Christmas tree farm. A small swampy area. Forest and farms playing tug of war. Here a gated mansion with a driveway as smooth and glistening as a new freeway. Around the bend a few trailers jacked haphazardly among the trees.

Tim walked along the old railroad path—one he had walked a thousand times. The dew was heavy. He could see it collect on the pine trees, hanging in tiny transparent globes from the needles. The ground fog was caught in the brush and trees at the south end of his property. It seemed to crawl up out of the brush and wrap around the two-story farmhouse that he and Lyn had restored. He loved that house, as if the muscle and planning had somehow fused a part of his own spirit into wood and concrete, glass and aluminum.

Then he thought of the last times he had seen Rachel here. Playing by the pool with Shannon in the glow of a golden sun. Or walking away with Shannon on a June evening.

Bye, Dad. I love you.

Bye. I love you, too, honey.

Tim cut up behind the pole barn toward the house. His sudden presence scared a deer enjoying breakfast in the clover by the barn. Over his shoulder, sunrise shaped a red crescent, turning the trees into dark pillars. Not a breath of wind.

He pulled a lawn chair out, watched the sunrise. He heard the kitchen door close behind him. He could smell the coffee before Lyn handed him his mug. She set her own down and pulled a chair up next to him. Together they watched the sun disentangle from the trees; lurch free in a hot red disc.

"Going to be a hot one today," Tim said.

"Hotter than an oven," Lyn said.

"So hot you can't breathe."

"So hot the corn's popping."

"Hot as a fiddler's bowstring."

"Hotter than a horny toad's tool."

"You've got the hottest tool in town, baby."

The weather cliché game was a ritual in town any season. Tim and Lyn started their own friendly competition on those mornings they had coffee together.

"Has it struck you," Tim said, "that we don't really know much of anything? And the cops aren't telling us anything?"

Tim stared over the rim of the cup and reflected. The day was growing hot already. Hardly 7:30. "Suffocating heat." He'd forgotten that cliché.

"I mean, what do we really know?" he considered. "It's been almost a month now since they found Rachel's body and what do we really have?"

Lyn thought about it for a few moments and then said, "The detectives did this big thing about talking with Sara in private, then she turns around and tells us everything. What do they expect?"

"So they talk with each of us," Tim said. "That's what they do on TV, right? Start with the nearest and dearest and see if there's anything screwy going on."

"More coffee?" Lyn asked.

"No, thanks. But I'm going buggy just sitting here waiting for someone to call on my days off from work. How about if we try to find this Oxford Lake by ourselves?"

"You have any idea how to get there?"

"Yes. You remember Angel, the guy Rachel told us about who gave her the pot? I was up there once with him."

"Okay, I can guess what you were doing."

"That was about fifteen years ago. We just drank a couple of beers and left. You know, that's where everything started. I'd sort of like to get a feel for it."

"And that's where everything ended, too," Lyn said.

If Newaygo roads are a maze, actually finding the place you want is an act of amazing grace. As it was, Tim and Lyn came out on the far side of the lake, opposite where the body was recovered. This suited them. The investigators had been combing the south. As far as they could tell, no one had searched here.

The grass was brown and sharp at this season, but it made searching easier. It didn't take long before they were rewarded. Two concrete blocks. Maybe something, maybe nothing. Tim could see Vande Velde's cabin in the distance. He was hardly the sort to be dumping construction trash way out here. Tim snapped a series of photographs, careful not to touch the blocks themselves.

Back at home, Tim alerted Detective Babcock about the blocks. There just didn't seem to be any good reason for them to be there. And even though he didn't know details of the blocks used to weigh Rachel down, it seemed too close a coincidence. On Thursday, August 7, he met Detective Babcock in White Cloud and drove to the lake with him. Babcock marked off the blocks with yellow crime scene tape.

At the same time, Ken Kolker of the *Grand Rapids Press* was pressing his own investigation, shuffling other pieces of the general puzzle. Rachel disappeared on June 4. She wasn't the only one. Shannon was with her.

It was well known that Rachel and the veteran Wayne Davis were friendly. She went to his trailer a lot to play cards. He always had a cold beer handy. It was well known also that Davis and Gabrion were acquainted. The *Press* reporter started putting some of the pieces together. Not the whole picture. A connection here and there.

Rachel was murdered by drowning sometime during the night of June 4. Shannon was missing. Drowned? Or sold? The market was good for healthy blonde-haired, blue-eyed babies—starting around $10,000, he figured. Maybe a lot more. At the same time Wayne Davis disappeared. As did Gabrion.

It was unlikely that Davis killed Gabrion. Davis, after all, was a scruffy little man, no match for Gabrion's strength and pure viciousness. And certainly Davis wouldn't hurt his friend Rachel or her daughter.

That left one conclusion. And it publicly appeared in the newspaper on August 8: Wayne Davis had witnessed Rachel's rape, something horrible—so dangerous that he was killed to prevent its disclosure. Later that day, in a television interview, Detective Babcock gave the official police position: "Mr. Davis, I believe, has been the recipient of foul play."

Where was Gabrion? Nowhere and anywhere.

By now Tim and Lyn were coming up with theories themselves, mostly about Marvin Gabrion. This is the thing police hate. It's an interference with procedures; an imposition upon method. By necessity, the police have to hold things back. The victim's family wants justice. Above all, they want the assurance that everything possible is being done.

And there's the heart of it. The police must build a case for the prosecutor, not for the family. So the family's need for answers for themselves intensifies. That's why most families begin to investigate themselves.

Thursday night, August 7, Tim and Lyn watched the late news with the Dave Babcock interview.

Lyn clicked off the remote. Silence.

"More beer?" Lyn asked.

"Thanks, but no. My brain's already swimming in it."

Lyn laughed.

Tim loved that laugh. It was one of the first things he had fallen in love with about her. No matter how grim things were, she didn't get angry or mean. She stayed calm. She even dared to laugh.

"I'm still writing in my notebook," Tim said. "Else it just slips out of my head."

"I know. Like each new detail pushes some other stuff out your ears. So, what do we know so far?"

"At this point, I think it's what we know and what are just possibilities."

"Okay."

"Well, first I jotted down what we learned from Sara. She knew Wayne Davis well. He was on disability and his health was poor. Seems his main occupations were drinking beer and playing cards.

"Then the Gabrion brothers. The oldest is doing a long-term stretch on a drug bust. Marv's in the middle. He was always in and out. Had a girlfriend in Las Vegas. He used to talk about a baby he had with her, from what I hear. Or that she aborted. You can never get the stories straight.

"And then there's the good ol' boy, the youngest. Rachel actually liked him, Sara said. Gave her money if she was short of it or a ride someplace. Apparently, he testified against his older brother, but his memory isn't too reliable. Big guy. He cuts firewood for a living.

"I asked my son about him too. He said that the younger brother likes to get paid for the firewood first, then often forgets to deliver it.

"Okay. That's what I jotted down about some of the main people. I'm going to type all this up and keep it in order. Somehow, all of it might lead us to the big question: What happened to Shannon?"

Lyn nodded. "That's good. Any conclusions?"

"I think Gabrion murdered Rachel. He wanted to get out of the rape charge. Probably killed Wayne Davis too. Davis was on the police report, as a witness in Rachel's rape. Maybe Gabrion thought that he couldn't afford to keep him around."

"And Shannon?"

"I don't know. My guess is that Gabrion sold her. I can't imagine he'd pass on the money and with his connections in the drug world it sure wouldn't be hard."

"That's what Grandma VerHage thinks, too. She's creating that Web site with pictures of Shannon."

"We've got to get more publicity for her. Maybe television? I wonder what the police are doing."

Lyn thought a minute. "Isn't the FBI supposed to handle stuff like that? Kidnapping?"

"Right. Can't get anything out of them either."

"What else?"

Tim got up, poured himself another and returned with his notebook. He studied it a moment then closed it.

"You know what? I'm looking at this line about Marvin Gabrion. His date of birth. Then it gives his parents' home as address of record. But didn't he live in that old store up in Altona? The one the cops had on Sara's tape?"

"The Christian bookstore? The one with no books?"

"The very same," Tim laughed. "Like to go book shopping tomorrow?"

"Sounds like a plan."

A map shows that Altona straddles 5 Mile Road in Hinton Township, Mecosta County, Michigan. Those who live in the remaining dozen or so dwelling places are scattered around the intersection of the Little Muskegon River and 5 Mile Road. Altona could be officially listed as a ghost town.

It wasn't always this way. Two intrepid settlers built a sawmill on the river back in 1868. That same year, Harrison Brown built a flour mill a little stretch away. Altona flourished to 200 people by 1900. By the Great Depression most of the people had fled, leaving their shacks for better pasture somewhere. During the 1950s most of the original houses and the flour mill were razed. Sometimes people wander the scrubland with metal detectors. They don't find anything.

Want to know what's going on in Altona? Try "Altona Sports News" in an online search engine. Nothing shows up. Or try an exciting entry, "Things to do in Altona." Blank. Nothing, because there's nothing there.

The dozen or so residences sprawl out from one two-story building, formerly a general store and previously the residence of Marvin Gabrion and his Christian bookstore.

The police had searched the building during their investigation. They came upon a book titled *The Perfect Victim*. This violently graphic true crime story starts with twenty-year-old Colleen Stan hitchhiking. After passing up one ride with two men as unsafe, she was relieved when a car with a husband and wife and their infant pulled over. It was the last relief she would feel during seven years of soul-numbing captivity.

The couple, Cameron and Janice, had reached a compromise in their young marriage. Cameron was a twisted sexual sadist who first wanted to practice on his wife. When she finally rebelled, they agreed that he could find another woman and do with her whatever his corroded mind desired. To keep Colleen available at all times, he kept her locked in a coffin-shaped box that he placed directly under the bed in their small trailer.

The Perfect Victim isn't just a book about a crime. It's a book about the viciousness and twisted mind of one demented person insisting upon domination and that person's complete willingness to satisfy his perverse desires upon another living being.

That was the only book police had found in the Christian bookstore.

As Tim and Lyn pulled their car into the lot of the faded building, Tim observed, "Five Mile Road. Due east of Oxford Lake."

Stepping out of the car, a wave of heat hit them. The kind of heat that seems to suck the air out of your lungs.

Broken-down asphalt fronted the building, weeds boldly making their presence known. To the east, a twenty-foot, well-rusted metal stanchion dangled from an iron frame with wooden slats. The faded white letters wearily announced Altona General Store. Under the sign, a blue and white payphone leaned to one side.

Or maybe it was the sign that leaned.

Or maybe everything was a bit crooked.

On the east side of the building a field of dried and rutted mud, like a drought-stricken lakebed, led to the backyard. The grass was desiccated and sparse, weeds seemed to frolic everywhere. Against an overgrown spruce stood a birch cross, ten feet tall.

Some houses and outbuildings stood a few hundred yards off. The dereliction and emptiness of Gabrion's house, its lonely remove from any neighbors, seemed profound.

The white paint had bleached and the red shutters were worn so that a gray undercoat showed in spots. Tim walked up to the pillared porch. "I wonder if the police left any doors open," he joked. He put his hand on the knob. It turned easily.

"What! Maybe we're invited in."

"And maybe you're stupid beyond belief?" Lyn asked.

"No crime scene tape."

"Still. I don't feel like doing jail time for trespassing," Lyn confided. "Besides, I imagine the search warrant pretty much scoured the place."

"We know from the transcript that his brother and that other guy were loading up Gabrion's stuff onto a truck."

Lyn laughed. "He'd be smart if he weren't so dumb."

"A twenty-watt bulb."

"Oh, don't be so generous."

"Babcock made him unload everything exactly where he got it. Two deputies watching every move."

"Did Babcock tell you if he found anything?" Lyn asked.

"What? Tell the parents who are still trying to find their granddaughter? Of course not."

"He did describe some general things though," Tim said.

"Well, it is a general store. Like what?"

"Ratty old brown sofa and chair and a table. A huge potted plant hanging from the kitchen ceiling. His American flag curtains duct-taped over the windows."

"The man does love his duct tape, doesn't he?"

They were walking across the cracked mud into the backyard. A wasteland of weeds and detritus.

"And don't forget," Lyn continued the list of what the detectives found, "they found the book. *The Perfect Victim.*"

"I was thinking of ordering it off the Internet. Published in England, so I doubt you'd find it anywhere near here. Maybe at www.psychopaths.com."

"Tell me you made that up."

He chuckled. "I did, but after reading four or five reviews of the book, that's where it would belong," Tim said as he stepped through the knee high weeds and looked down. "Well, what do we have here?"

Behind a pile of dried branches, a mound of refuse sprawled in a gray patch. All broken chunks of concrete. And several full concrete blocks.

"I wonder if Babcock saw those," Lyn said.

"I'll call him when we get back. I'm pretty sure he did. But look, they're exactly the same as the blocks we found at Oxford Lake."

They turned back toward their car. Coming up the far side of the house, they saw a sign they hadn't noticed before. It was propped up by concrete blocks. At the top, a two-by-four slat of wood, painted white, lettered in blue: KIDS. Below that a four by eight sheet of plywood, lettered at the top: WE HAVE NONE TO SPARE. And at the bottom:

PLEASE SLOW DOWN. The blue letters were uneven and faded, as if the letterer ran out of paint.

"The guy's all heart," Lyn said bitterly.

"I think we should make one more stop," Tim said after they climbed back in the car, the air-conditioning blasting. "Since we're up this way anyway."

"Where do you want to go?"

"Check out a few things on Ian Decker."

"Sure that's his name?"

"Last I heard. But I also heard he did some work here at the general store slash Christian bookstore for Gabrion."

"Slash dump."

"True. But if he did odd jobs for Marvin Gabrion and he'd been calling Rachel, I wonder what the connection was."

"Hmm. Good idea. Know where he lives?"

"I've got a fair idea. We'll start with a junkyard his uncle owns." "You know, I keep thinking about that guy from the Parents of Murdered Children meeting. He made a pretty good case for Fight Crime: Invest in Kids. We could do foster care, give some kids unconditional love, get them off to a good start."

Tim nodded. "I think we could, too, but let's wait until after Gabrion's trial."

The junkyard, in fact, once belonged to Ian Decker, inherited from his father. Before he ran it totally into the ground, not knowing and not much caring about such distractions as ferrous or nonferrous metals, his uncle purchased it from him.

After some wandering around on the angular roads, Tim and Lyn drew their car up alongside a junkyard. This one looked like a business, not just a scrap heap like the one Kenny Mochenrose had in his backyard. Two guys, about twenty years old, stood near the drive, having a cigarette. *The guys probably work at the junkyard*, Tim thought. *Enough grease and oil on their jeans and T-shirts to start an outboard motor. At least the owner's doing right making them smoke outside. Most junkyards are an explosion waiting to happen.*

"I grew up in a junkyard," Lyn said. "Leave the engine running."

"Okay." A wall of superheated air hit him as he exited the car. *Must be ninety-five degrees*, he thought. He walked over to the two men.

"Nice day, huh."

"Is if you're a bullfrog croakin' in a swamp all day," one of the men answered.

"Yeah, but bullfrogs can't smoke."

The other one took off his sweat-stained ball cap, scratched a thatch of red hair. "Hadn't thought about that," he said.

"This here the Decker junkyard?" Tim asked.

"Sure is. No need for a sign."

Past the gate, Tim saw a tall, very neat man negotiating a transaction with a driver hauling a pickup load of scrap metal. He pulled a roll of bills out of his pocket, wrote up an invoice on a clipboard and directed the driver to a distant part of the junkyard.

"You ever heard of Ian Decker?" Tim asked the redhead.

"Used to see him every day. Now he's done gone missing. Just don't see him anymore."

"Sort of disappeared all of a sudden?" Tim asked.

"You ain't another cop, are you?" asked the other man.

"No. Nothing like that. Have you had a lot of them up here?"

"Cops and reporters. They always go together. Like piggyback, you know."

"Do you guys ever get any large gas tanks?" Tim asked, thinking about dead bodies.

"We don't like them, but I'll take them from large companies. I sure don't buy them."

A wrecker towing a behemoth four-door sedan rolled into the driveway, kicking up a cloud of dust.

"That must be his uncle then?" Tim asked.

"Yeah. Ian couldn't run a business. Didn't have any sense period that I ever seen. You know he lived just down the street there. Lived with his grandma. His folks are all dead, you know. Damned if he ain't dead, too."

"Well, thank you, guys. Try to stay cool."

They crushed their cigarettes under boot heels before returning to the yard.

Chapter 11

National Attention

For Tim, the investigation was moving along at the speed of garden slugs. Days dragged into weeks then into months.

Some mornings he awakened from a restless night of tossing and turning, nearly screaming for answers. Violent thoughts rocketed through his brain, slamming at the sides of his skull. Nowhere to turn; no way to exorcise anger in one brutal storm.

Tim continued to regularly write in his notebooks:

> The discovery of Rachel's murder and Shannon's kidnapping is an ongoing emotional drain and a waiting game. Every day we wait for law enforcement, the task force, the FBI. Maybe the United States Postal Service is close to finding Shannon. We try to make jokes. It is taking so long that we are starting to think about dead ends in the investigation.

Regularly, Tim and Lyn worked through a series of phone calls: the detectives, the FBI, people who might know other people. And they received calls. *The Grand Rapids Press*, the major newspaper for western Michigan, assigned Ken Kolker, a reporter, to cover Rachel's story. It was right after Kolker published his major story, coming up with clear facts and setting them out in a compelling way in the Sunday *Press*, that some things in the investigation began to change.

To locate Shannon, Tim figured, they would need a massive public awareness campaign. A substantial cash award was collected by fellow workers at the automobile plant, all of which fattened the Silent Observer fund. Shannon's paternal grandmother began using the Internet, creating sites and eventually using age enhancing photos.

But to really get attention, what do you need? It turned out that Kolker's story spread widely on the newswire. In fact, it spread to two major television programs.

American Journal was the first television program to contact Tim's family, through Ken Kolker, in early September. The *American Journal* crew arrived at Tim and Lyn's house on September 24. Tim recorded the events in his notebook:

Elizabeth, Aiden and a cameraman were the *American Journal* team. They arrived early Thursday morning. I wasn't even dressed yet. We were immediately impressed with their professionalism. Elizabeth came in and talked, while the other two guys checked out our home and property to select locations for filming. Elizabeth seemed very well prepared. She had a lot of questions in her head, didn't use notes. Elizabeth wanted to be very sure all of the facts were right. They hadn't heard about the missing Ian Decker, but I really didn't have much information at the time. They took eleven pictures of Rachel and Shannon back to California with them.

The "America's Most Dangerous" segment of *American Journal* aired Friday evening, September 25. Elizabeth started the show with video shot outside the Newaygo County Sheriff's Department. She told the audience that Marvin Gabrion was accused of rape, kidnapping and murder. The camera did a quick cut to our front porch, where I stood. "Marvin Gabrion is a menace to society. He's a very brutal person who killed my daughter. She was a happy woman here, working and making plans to do things with her life," I said to the camera.

Elizabeth then described the night Rachel met Marvin Gabrion. The video cut to a dark forest, reported to be north of the local grocery store, near the pond. It was actually video taken on the back roads to Oxford Lake.

The camera showed clips of Gabrion's Christian bookstore in Altona. We don't know the guy, but Elizabeth got a quote about Marvin Gabrion: "The people whom I've talked to have been of the mind that there is something not quite right about him."

The video cut back to me on the front porch of our house: "He's got a reputation of intimidating people and scaring them to make them do what he wants them to do."

Returning to the Newaygo County courthouse, Elizabeth told about Gabrion's $75,000 bond and the disappearance of Wayne Davis. She used the newspaper quote: "Investigators say that Wayne Davis was last seen in the company of Marvin Gabrion."

Back on our front porch, Elizabeth described the events of June 4 and then asked me when I first realized that there was a problem. "June 15 was Father's Day," I replied. "I was worried all day, because Rachel had always found some way to get in touch with me on Father's Day. This was the first Father's Day when I had not heard from her."

The camera cut to Oxford Lake. We knew how difficult it had been for Elizabeth to do her lines at the lake. She described what happened and then cut back to our front porch. "I didn't realize how brutal some of the people are in the world."

Back at Newaygo County courthouse, Elizabeth told the audience, "The police believe that Shannon is alive and that Marvin Gabrion sold her."

On the front porch again, I pleaded, "I feel that Shannon is alive. She is out there and we want her back."

In the woods near Oxford Lake, Elizabeth gave a physical description of Marvin Gabrion and then adlibbed about his ability to live off the land. We'd never heard that.

"He needs to be removed from the freedoms that society has to offer. He needs to be locked up." The phone number for the Rockford Post of the Michigan State Police was displayed or viewers could "call your local FBI." The announcer closed the segment with, "There is nothing more important right now than finding that little girl."

After the *American Journal* story aired, news of Rachel's murder and Shannon's disappearance spread. By the end of September, it had caught the attention of the producers of one of the nation's most popular true crime shows: *Unsolved Mysteries*. A larger audience, a bigger production.

For the first time in many months, Tim's spirits lifted. In late September he wrote in his notebook:

Living at our latitude we seldom see the northern lights. Tonight they were fantastic, bright greens and whites, dancing across the northern sky. I'd spent a fair amount of time gazing off to the north the last few months. The progress with *Unsolved Mysteries* and the bright aurora borealis left me feeling quite positive.

The Saturday household chores place a constant demand on our time, but we are almost always preoccupied with Shannon. Wondering, *Where is Shannon?* If she was sold, it was probably to someone who wanted a baby very much. Someone who would value her life and raise her well. We hope that Shannon is not an angel, but that she sailed away in the arms of basically good people.

Maybe this wish was too guarded, too large. It was better than the fearful unknown. But the hope for their granddaughter's life did have an annealing effect.

Tim was sure to record the events of filming the *Unsolved Mysteries* segment in his October notebook:

On October 1, director Eric Nelson flew out to investigate and plan our *Unsolved Mysteries* show. He is a friendly guy, with plenty of humor. He has a family connection in Grand Rapids. He felt that he had wasted his time at the FBI because Special Agent Gilligan had referred all his questions to Newaygo County law enforcement.

I gave Eric plenty of background. I'm trying to get him to use Rachel's poem, maybe in the background somewhere (like on Oxford Lake).

We took the scenic back roads up to Oxford Lake. Eric was worried about getting his five-ton trucks in. We talked about needing to rent SUVs to get through the two-track roads. We also commented on the fact that the leaves would be gone by the time the whole crew came out. There were plenty of pine trees in the background, across the lake. "This is a very unique lake; we have nothing like this in California," he said.

Sergeant Miller returned my call at 9:30. "In reference to your call earlier, you are free to talk about the two letters you received from Rachel. We are calling them the 'on vacation' letter and the 'Little Rock' letter. Please don't talk about the letter to the prosecutor."

I'm thinking there were two letters to the prosecutor.

"Any questions about who Rachel left your home with should be referred to law enforcement." That works for me.

During the early days of October, plans developed for filming the *Unsolved Mysteries* program. The waiting was uncomfortable, sometimes causing a vague unease or fear. After all, the murderer had not been caught yet. Tim and Lyn joked about wanting a cop or a soldier behind every tree at night—although it wasn't entirely a joke. Sometimes they sat in long silences, as stretched and nervous as electrical wires, and agonized about Shannon's whereabouts. Restless walks. No answers.

In the October 4 edition of the *Grand Rapids Press*, journalist Ken Kolker wrote, "Murder suspect continues to elude nationwide manhunt."

Chapter 12

Captured

S herman is one of those quaint little villages that dot the Erie coast-line of New York. It has a past that no one quite remembers, but the town hangs on like a tarnished lady who still wants to be noticed. Main Street is tied together by a string of brick buildings the color of industrially begrimed red.

The first story of the buildings, running the length of the abbre-viated Main Street, is neatly painted. A storm roof, stanchioned by stout, triangular poles, drapes colorful signs proclaiming wares. The storm roof over the sidewalk is essential. In the winter the snow howls over Lake Erie and rampages through these small towns. Farmland, neatly plotted and pieced, surrounds Sherman like a dark girdle.

At the edge of town, near some woods that screen the surround-ing farmland, sits a squat, one-story building: United States Post Office, Sherman, New York. Unprepossessing, rather dowdy in its early 1970s architecture, the town soon turned explosive. All because of one small post office box.

That post office box was taken out in the name of Robert James Allen, missing since January 11, 1996. Records confirmed that Allen's social security check arrived at its regular time and was removed at a regular time. The FBI determined that it was cashed regularly. In fact, on the same January date, a checking account in Allen's name was established in nearby Jamestown, New York. Interviews with post office employees established that this "Robert Allen" did seem to look a great deal like the mug shots of Marvin Gabrion.

"Those *eyes*," one marveled. "They gave me the creeps. Evil."

The FBI had tentatively established a connection between this "Allen" and Gabrion, a connection the Timmermans did not learn about until after his arrest. Now the investigators had to figure out how to take him down.

Gabrion's long, multi-page rap sheet turned up by the FBI showed an increasing turn toward violence. During his twenties and thirties, his record was littered with DUIs and outstanding warrants in several states for failure to appear. These escalated to assault, obstructing police, burglary, larceny, assault with a dangerous weapon and felony sexual assaults. Since he randomly used eight different aliases, the cases were like shuffling cards. The wonder was how little jail time he had actually done, but anyone in the judicial system would understand. For example, you might have a trial for assault and a key witness or even the plaintiff doesn't appear. Case dismissed. Someone could have a list of DUIs twenty pages long, but they all end in suspended or revoked licenses and a couple of months in jail. The offender jumps in the car and drives off to the nearest bar.

The FBI was determined that no one would be jumping clear on this one.

On Tuesday, October 14, 1997, FBI agents staked out the post office in Sherman, New York. The day before, the FBI agents told postal clerk Rita Shaw the plan. She left a message in "Robert Allen's" post office box that she had material that would require his signature to collect. The investigators hoped that would draw Gabrion out of the secluded space of the postal boxes and into the main lobby. On that day, only Shaw remained in the lobby. Other employees were sent home. FBI agents stationed themselves in the back. Others were stationed outside the building. One witness estimated that there were "at least fifteen" federal agents.

At 11:30 Gabrion arrived. He entered the lobby, approached Shaw and signed for his material. Then something alerted him.

Gabrion was a survivalist. However low his moral capacities had sunk, creeping in that void was a primitive, nearly feral instinct for self-protection. He had been on the run for four months, always moving, setting defenses, planning the next move. He sensed it. Maybe it was the click of the walkie-talkie by the agents in back. He sensed a threat. He bolted. One of the men in back shouted into his walkie-talkie, "He's onto us" and they raced to the door.

Outside the post office, Gabrion ran up a small hill, maybe six feet away, then turned around and ran toward his car. A wall of agents met him, chasing him up the alley alongside the post office where they took him down. Five or six officers struggled with him.

Marvin was not particularly large or overly strong, but he fought with demented panic. Finally one of the officers drew his .45 gun and shoved it against Gabrion's temple. They shouted the command, "Stop resisting." They cuffed and subdued him. Three agents squeezed the shackled Gabrion into a shiny SUV and escorted him out of town.

Two blocks down the street was Gabrion's dirty blue sedan with a friendly black dog waiting in the passenger seat. A flatbed came and hauled the car away.

Incongruously, while all this was going on, two young Amish girls walked down the street. It suddenly struck the remaining FBI agents that Gabrion had been wearing an Amish style beard.

On October 14, Lyn was at home. Special Agent Gilligan called. She didn't want Lyn and Tim to hear the news first from the media.

"Lyn, this morning Marvin Gabrion was arrested in Sherman, New York."

But there was more. In March of the following year, Gabrion stood trial for social security fraud in Lansing, Michigan. At that time the full story of Gabrion's fraud emerged. It was determined that he used Allen's identification to rent the room on South Division in August several years before. He was evicted three months later for nonpayment of rent. That December he opened a bank account in Michigan using an Indiana driver's license in the name of Robert Allen. The account remained active until July two years later—shortly after Rachel's death.

In New York, he opened the post office box and checking accounts to process the social security checks. The court determined that Gabrion obtained a total of $13,945.94 by fraud.

Moreover, using Robert Allen's name, he sold a parcel of land to which he had no clear title. And, most surprising, this "Robert Allen" had purchased the Altona Christian bookstore. (Upon appeal by Gabrion in 2000, the five-year sentence stood as imposed.)

Meanwhile, the investigation into Rachel's murder and Shannon's disappearance continued.

Chapter 13

Spreading the Word

In Cedar Springs, Tim struggled with divided loyalties. He wanted desperately to fly to New York and see the man who killed his daughter put in chains. At the same time, *Unsolved Mysteries* wanted to fly out a crew as soon as possible. They wanted Tim to play himself in the production. This story would bring much needed attention to his still-missing baby granddaughter Shannon.

Unsolved Mysteries boasted a 70 percent success rate in solving its mysteries. Tim and Lyn found their own hopes of finding Tim's granddaughter rising.

On Monday October 20, *Unsolved Mysteries* began filming their segment. Tim documented in his notebook:

> The first sign of *Unsolved Mysteries* was a caterer from Grand Rapids. She got here early to set up coffee and snacks in our garage. The rest of the crew was here by eight-thirty. It was quite an entourage: a five-ton panel truck filled with cameras and equipment. Another five-ton truck was rented from Detroit. In addition, there was a passenger van, two four-wheel drive SUVs and a couple of cars.

> Mary Simmons, the producer, got things off to a good start. She said, "We will be responsible for any damages or cleaning, but here, have two hundred bucks just in case we miss something." There was an amazing number of people. We had Eric Nelson, the director, whom we've met several times before.

The weather was brisk, with temperatures in the low forties. We talked about getting acclimated to the weather. I thought that it shouldn't bother me, with my long underwear. It was supposed to be springtime in Michigan, so I tried to fake it and rolled my sleeves up.

We started out easy. They had me shoot a scene where I walked along the north side of the house. The next scene was down by the road: I get our mail from the mailbox. I thought that it was easy; they didn't ask me to do anything I haven't done before. Today I just had to do it in front of bright lights and a camera.

A young Michigan actress named Leslie portrayed Rachel and had a very strong resemblance to her. This was her first real acting job, but she has done some singing on stage, in a musical. For three days' work she will receive $1900 and her agent $100. She did a good job and was very friendly. (We learned years later that every time *Unsolved Mysteries* airs a rerun of our show, she gets a check.)

The chief electrician had to borrow extension cords and I had to help him find the newer grounded electrical outlets in our one hundred-year-old-plus home. The grips were the all-around help, setting up scenes and moving things around. There was a wardrobe lady, a makeup artist and executive assistants.

A baby actress named Michelle portrayed our baby Shannon. She came up from Grandville with her mom. There are some very strict regulations about using children in the entertainment business. A licensed social worker must be on hand to look out for the child. Mary was quite upset with the social worker she had hired from Grand Blanc, on the other side of Michigan. Michelle was dreadfully afraid of her. The social worker had never done this kind of thing before and Mary had to spend much time with her, explaining her job requirements.

We were very impressed with the amount of time and attention to detail devoted to each of scenes. The cameraman always checked the light levels before filming. His assistant made constant adjustments while filming, often with the cameraman adjusting something else.

Some of the scenes were very carefully set up. They filmed a scene of "Rachel" getting into a car and leaving our home. The camera was positioned on the north, the passenger side of the car. A large reflector was set up in front and a black screen went behind the driver. We could see Leslie well and her bright smile, but it was impossible to make out any of the driver's features.

They had an ample supply of pre-stamped space station hologram envelopes. I had to swipe one. After all, it was addressed to me. Eric asked me if I knew that they sold envelopes like these in jail. "Yes I did," I told him. "Did you know that I gave the same envelopes to the police that contained incriminating letters from Gabrion's mother to Rachel?"

I talked with Kurt Schram from the Michigan State Police; he introduced himself first. He did tell me that they were going to bring some additional charges against Marvin, more welfare fraud in Grand Rapids, not for the media. He didn't know how long it would take to extradite Marvin, but really wasn't in any hurry: "He's not going anywhere." DNA evidence is still at least six to eight weeks away. I asked him about the other evidence, perhaps fingerprints or an inside wrap of the duct tape. He said they were trying very creative ways to match up duct tape evidence, torn edges, etc. He stated that Marvin used duct tape quite a bit.

"A fan of duct tape," Schram explained.

During the filming I asked Lieutenant Schram a couple of times to get the "what and where" of his job. He works out of Grand Rapids and the way I understood him, he supervises all detectives on the western side of the state. He was at Oxford Lake for the duration and would do anything that *Unsolved Mysteries* wanted him to do to cooperate. Mary asked him for the composite sketch of the man with whom

Rachel left. He called over to Babcock, "They want a copy of the composite. Do you want to discuss it?" Pause. Dave said, "Yeah, we can discuss it." Pause. Glances were exchanged. Kurt, "You go first." Dave said, "Okay, I don't think we want to release it."

Mary doesn't take no for an answer easily. She got Eric and entered into conversation with Kurt and Dave on the two-track. I saw them talking and tried to ease up on them, but Schram warned me off, "Mr. Timmerman, we're negotiating here." I was just trying to snoop.

A police artist had come to our house, intent on making a composite drawing of the boy Rachel left with. Rose was the most helpful of us and, not knowing his identity at the time, produced a composite resembling the missing Ian Decker.

After thanks, but before good-byes, I asked if they got the composite. "Yes," said Eric. I had told Mary the story about how our daughter had worked with the police artist to produce the composite and then the police came to our house with pictures of six or eight people. To my untrained eye they all looked like the composite.

Unsolved Mysteries was still filming on Wednesday, October 22, but no scenes needed Tim. He wanted to get out anyway. On Tuesday afternoon he flew out to Buffalo, New York, where Marvin Gabrion was to be arraigned the next day at a preliminary hearing.

At this point, Tim wasn't even sure what the charges would be in Buffalo. As the jet winged eastward toward Buffalo that evening, Tim's anxiety level intensified with each mile.

It didn't stop when he landed in Buffalo, checked into a hotel and tried to sleep. When he woke early the next morning, he wrote in his notebook:

Remind me never to do this again. I couldn't fall asleep, there was nothing on TV last night, the heater sounds like a jet engine. I was wide awake by 4:00 A.M., got a drink of water, tossed and turned, tried to read, tried to rest and finally got up at 6:00. The in-room coffee is not too bad and the shower water was hot, so maybe I'll get over it.

Studying the maps, Sherman looks easier to find than the U.S. Court House. Breakfast is at 6:30; I'll be checked out and on the road to Sherman.

Sherman. That was where the take-down had happened. Tim wanted to visualize it, to relive the capture of the monster that had tormented his dreams for four months. He wanted to see him as Rachel had in her dying minutes; then see him with a .45 handgun at his temple. He imagined his finger on the trigger.

Sherman was sleepy that morning, the embrace of autumn in the air. *Almost a pretty little town,* Tim thought, *if you go for that kind of thing.* A throwback, not wholly unlike Cedar Springs. On one side of Main the covered sidewalk, like a low skirt on a wearied courtesan. On the other, an auto parts store, a car dealership, a hardware store. *All the essentials,* he thought. Even the post office looked mundane, innocuous in the morning light. He returned to the rental car and set out to find the federal courthouse in Buffalo.

Tim's notebook continues:

I got to the courthouse in plenty of time. The detail map from the hotel clerk helped, but I mostly got lucky parking next door to the courthouse. I asked the marshals about *United States of America v. Marvin Gabrion.* They directed me to the clerk's office on the fourth floor.

The clerk didn't have the papers, because the judge had them for that afternoon's court date. She was very helpful though. She sent me up to the judge's chambers. "Just ask one of the girls up there and they'll help you out." I was a little apprehensive about knocking on the judge's door, but the security guard told me to just push the buzzer. The secretary there gave me two copies.

The Marshals recommended a nearby restaurant for lunch... good food and reasonable prices. It cost me eight bucks for two tacos and a soda. I left half of the second taco. I roamed around the courthouse until almost 2:00 P.M., hoping to catch sight of Gabrion.

He was escorted in by a chunky little bailiff. Marvin was wearing a clean white shirt, blue pants and sneakers. He had a scarred face, an Amish beard with a clean-shaven chin and mustache area and curly dark hair. I never did see the eyes.

The bailiff took off Gabrion's handcuffs while waiting for the judge. Three marshals stood across the courtroom doors.

Judge Heckman, a nice looking, slim blonde judge. "Are the defense and government counsel present?"

"Yes, Your Honor."

Heckman, "I have a certified copy of the indictment that the accused falsely and with intent to deceive used a social security number. What is the maximum penalty?"

Government counsel replied, "The maximum penalty is five years in jail and/or $250,000 fine."

It was agreed to waive the reading.

Judge Heckman mentioned a recent charge.

Gabrion argued, "That was a drunk driving charge that they brought up two months after the incident; it's ridiculous. Bob Allen is here in New York. I was not drawing his SS."

Heckman responded, "You have the right to an ID hearing and a detention hearing. I've been advised of some charges in West Michigan. Authorities will have to take them up there."

Gabrion stood up to sign a form waiving his ID hearing.

He started talking about how this was ridiculous for drunk driving.

Judge Heckman interrupted him, "We can proceed with the detention hearing and you will have a seat!"

The federal prosecutor began, "We have a series of documents marked for evidence." He asked the court to look into Mr. Gabrion's criminal history.

"Numerous physical injury charges since 1974, numerous offenses, active warrant from Nassau County on an alcohol charge from May 1988."

The charge from Nassau County, out on Long Island, stemmed from an arrest of Gabrion for drunk driving and a personal injury accident on October 21, 1993. Gabrion, in his fashion, had disappeared.

The Nassau County court issued a bench warrant, but designated it as "Anywhere within New York State." This was before Gabrion was arrested for raping Rachel. When he was incarcerated in Newaygo County, nobody checked the records and he was released on bail. One wonders how things might have been different.

The prosecutor continued, "When the FBI arrested Mr. Gabrion, he had signed ID as Robert Allen. Six agents physically corralled and struggled with Mr. Gabrion."

Marvin's attorney conferred. "Mr. Gabrion agrees to be transported to Western Michigan."

"Bail can be approached at that time. I order Mr. Gabrion to Western Michigan under custody of the U.S. Marshals for further indictment. Hearings will take place then," Heckman said.

Gabrion's defense lawyer requested, "In light of publications and stories in the media, I would ask that no one in law enforcement speak to Mr. Gabrion while he's being transported."

"U.S. marshals will transport," Judge Heckman declared. "Mr. Gabrion will have no discussions with any law enforcement before meeting with his lawyer."

Tim's notebook describes the conclusion of his day at the courthouse:

After the hearing I chatted with all of the reporters and then decided to go out for some air.

Reporters were waiting in the side hallway for Gabrion to come out. So I ran up to the eighth floor of the parking ramp to get the camera. It seemed like we were waiting in that hallway forever, making conversation about my little buddy. I thought, *I'll see him coming. I have time to call Lyn for a minute.* Dialing the number, the janitor pointed out the flurry of activity outside. I ran outside and took a couple of bad shots of Marvin hiding under the hood of his camouflage jacket. But the shackles showed clearly.

A reporter caught me after Marvin's car pulled away. Did I have any statement, he wanted to know.

"I'm happy that Gabrion is behind bars." The reporter asked me why I went to Buffalo. "I wanted to see Gabrion in chains. I believe he chained my daughter and threw her in Oxford Lake. He belongs in chains." This guy gave me great directions to the airport and there I dropped off the rental car.

Later, the words "I WANTED TO SEE HIM IN CHAINS" appeared in a nearly inch-high headline above the news story of Gabrion's hearing.

Chapter 14

A Twisted World, A Monster's Mind

The focus seemed to have shifted. Tim and Lyn still hoped that somehow their blue-eyed, blonde-haired granddaughter—just learning to walk and speak her first words—was out there alive. But at this age, Shannon would be tottering along on her sturdy little legs. Her smile would be crinkled by a few baby-white teeth. Her handful of vowels arranged into a vocabulary all her own.

They ached with loneliness for her.

Tim expressed his feelings in his notebook:

November 17

"Do not go gently into that good night...

Rage, rage against the dying of the light."

Dylan Thomas

The best way out of this mystery...is through it. This [missing Shannon] is the hardest thing I've ever done, but I'm going to get through it.

Then a very odd twist occurred. Tim received a handwritten letter, return address the Erie County Holding Center, addressed to Mr. Timithy [sic] Timmerman. When he opened the hand-printed letter, all in capital letters, he read it through several times with jarring disbelief.

HI

WE ARE TRYING TO START A NON-PROFIT ORGANI-
ZATION CALLED –NO MORE MISSING CHILDREN – WE
WOULD LIKE TO USE SHANNON AS THE POSTER
CHILD. WE WOULD HAVE THE BEST COLORED
PHOTO COPIED AT A GOOD PHOTO CENTER UNTIL
THERE IS ENOUGH 10-20 TO DO A LAY-OUT ON THEIR
COLOR COPIER. THIS WOULD BE ALOT BETTER THAN
THE BLACK AND WHITE. USE SCISSORS TO CUT
APART—THEN GLUE THE PICTURES TO THE 8.5-11 IN
FLYERS, A COPY COMPANY HAS AGREED TO 50% OF
REGULAR PRICE COST WOULD BE 2-3¢ PER COLORED
PICTURES. IT WORKS GOOD.

WE   SHOULD BE ON THE INTERNET WITHIN A
MONTH.

SOME PEOPLE MIGHT THINK ME SELF-CENTERED
FOR USING SHANNON AS A POSTER CHILD.

PEOPLE WILL REALIZE SOMEDAY, THIS WAY, THAT I
WAS NOT A MONSTER. MAYBE IT IS SELF-CENTERED.
IN THAT WAY. BUT I HAVE ALWAYS BEEN DISTURBED
WHEN SEEING ALL THESE MISSING CHILDREN FLY-
ERS. I MYSELF HAVE LOST A CHILD THRU ABORTION,
I DON'T THINK I COULD TAKE THAT AGAIN. THERE
WAS NOTHING I COULD DO, BEING IN THE WOMAN'S
CHOICE AGE.

I HAVE AN ATTORNEY WORKING ON GETTING – NO
MORE MISSING CHILDREN – NON-PROFIT STANDING.

BY USING NEW D.N.A. TESTING METHODS WITH
SALIVA, IT WILL WORK, AND ITS TIME. ONCE WE GET
THE FLYERS UP AND ON THE NET IT WILL SNOW BALL.
WE CAN CLEAR THE OBVIOUS OBSTACLES OF PRIVACY
RIGHTS AND MISS-USE. PLEASE PRAY AND ACCEPT
HELP FROM OTHERS.

> GOD BLESS
> MARVIN

Stunned and confused by the audacity of the letter, Tim turned it over to Detective Miller. Tim thought he might reply to the letter, but wasn't quite certain what to say yet. How does one reason with a psychopath?

One doesn't. But can one trick and trap? Tim liked the idea.

While Gabrion was being prepared for transport to West Michigan, a flurry of investigation continued. More arrests and warrants from Gabrion's past turned up. Sara participated in a lie detector test for the state police. Clothing from a child Shannon's age was brought in for identification. It wasn't hers.

Behind the scenes, detectives and prosecutors were discussing how best to try the case. At first it seemed Newaygo County had first claim and the prosecuting attorney, Chrystal Roach, wanted the case. It was a keen intellectual challenge and a publicity jackpot. The kind of case that got prosecutors promoted to the bench if they were successful.

But here again rose that curious stickler issue of geography. Surely Marvin Gabrion wasn't aware of it when he weighted Rachel with chains and cement blocks, rolled duct tape around her head and dropped her body over the side of the boat that the spot was precisely 227 feet into federal property. In that case it should go to federal court.

The federal court, unlike Michigan, had the option of the death penalty.

In the lawyers' offices, people argued toward clarity of approach. Who should prosecute Gabrion and for what charges? In the detectives' offices, the head investigators aligned evidence. In Tim's mind, there was no order at all, reflected in his notebook entries:

December 2

"When confronted with his misconduct the psychopath has enough false sincerity and apparent remorse that he renews hope and trust among his accusers. However, after several repetitions, his convincing show is finally recognized for what it is—a show."
—Bourdin

I'm still too depressed to write much. I'm frustrated by my inability to control it. Ken K. (the *Grand Rapids Press* reporter) had called, informing us of the preliminary hearing Thursday at one. I told a supervisor at work that I'd be late for work on Thursday.

In his own desperate attempt to locate Shannon, Tim had sent Shannon's picture to all the major networks, targeting news shows, entertainment shows, anyone, including *The Tonight Show*, who might show the picture to a national audience.

December 7

Pearl Harbor Day

Not too much going on. Thursday's *Tonight Show* was pretty mainstream. "Nasty the Dominator"…a toe wrestler from England. LeAnn Rimes did a beautiful a cappella version of *Amazing Grace*. It prompted a third letter to Jay Leno. Shannon is way more interesting and important than Nasty.

I went to see my therapist Thursday morning. I complained about frustration, depression and the adrenaline rush that follows any thoughts of events that occurred at Oxford Lake. He says that I'm relatively normal. The intensity of emotions is in direct proportion to the events. Next appointment is Tuesday.

Friday… vacation day at work. Checked over the…oil, tires, coolant… Took Lyn to an inn.

Marvin Gabrion took away a mother's love for her child.

Sometimes too much loss destroys relationships with the living. During these trying months of uncertainty, Tim worked hard to maintain contact with his daughter Sara, currently enrolled in high school. He was working second shift then and, as Tim put it, "I hardly ever saw her." So he began writing notes to her to keep in touch.

Hi Sara,

Happy Tuesday!

I mailed a nice little "headline" story to the G R Press yesterday. You'll have to take a look at it. I'm working on getting publicity for Shannon, but I'm not having much luck at it. You keep working hard too, ok?

I love U,

Dad

Sara was glad for the messages and replied in turn.

Dear Dad,

When will I get to see you? I know you love me anyways. I didn't mean to sleep in. I'd love to read it. Thank you for the accounting solution; I'm glad that you remembered. I always work hard.

Love,

Sara Jane

Hi Sara,

I'm sorry I didn't see more of you yesterday. We need to take some walks to the bridge... I'm trying to keep a lot of sticks in the fire, like publicity for the search for Shannon. I haven't had a lot of visible results yet, but I'm trying. It keeps me busy. You keep busy, too, schoolwork is important, so do your best.

Love,

Me

Dad,

I try to keep busy, but oftentimes I find myself in my own little world gazing out at nothing. I don't like to walk. I'll see you soon.

Love,

Sara Jane

Hi Sara,

I've had times when I'm stuck in my own world gazing out too. It's perfectly normal, though not real comfortable. The best thing to do is talk with somebody. It's a good thing to talk about Rachel, particularly the good memories.

Love,

Dad

As he exchanged messages with Sara, Tim glanced at the second letter he had received from Marvin Gabrion, lying on his desk so that the postmark showed: December 12.

MR. TIMMERMAN,

I AM VERY SADDENED BY YOUR LACK OF HOPE.

PLEASE LOOK AT THE FACTS. THE POLICE THOR-
OUGHLY SEARCHED THE LAKE AND AREA, ACCORD-
ING TO THE PAPER, G. R. PRESS.

EVEN ADOLF HITLER DIDN'T KILL BABIES, THEY
WERE PUT IN HIS YOUTH CORE.

THE POLICE TOOK HAIR SAMPLES AND D.N.A.
BLOOD AND SALIVA FROM ME ALMOST A MONTH
AGO. APARENTLY THEY FOUND EVIDENCE ON
RACHEL.

I USED TO THINK POLICE THEMSELVES MAY HAVE
DONE THIS, BUT IF SO THEY WOULD HAVE FRAMED
ME BY NOW.

WE HAVE TO HAVE YOU BE WILLING, IN ORDER
FOR US TO HELP YOU FIND SHANNON. I PRAY SHE IS
HAPPY AND HEALTHY WHITCH SHE MOST LIKELY IS.
UPPER MIDDLE CLASS OR RICH ARE USUALLY THE
RECIPIENTS OF THESE MISSING BABIES. I READ
WHERE A GIRL WAS RAISED IN A ROOM ONLY LET
OUT TO SCHOOL. PLEASE LET US HELP. I AM NOT
LOOKING FOR ANYTHING BUT THE MISSING CHIL-
DREN PROBLEM SOLVED. IF SHANNON CAN BE
SAVED SO MUCH THE BETTER.

TO MAKE SHANNON THE POSTER CHILD WE WILL
NEED YOUR PERMISSION AND A GOOD COLOR
PHOTO.

IF YOU WOULD BE WILLING TO ALLOW A XTRA PH
LINE TO CENTRALIZE EFFORTS IT WOULD BE A BIG
HELP.

PLEASE FORGIVE ME IF ANY OF MY IDEA'S OFFEND
YOU. I AM ONLY TRYING TO HELP YOU, LIKE YOU
ASKED, TOO FIND SHANNON. ALL WE REALLY NEED
IS YOUR PERMISSION TO USE HER PHOTO. JUST FOR-
GET ABOUT THE PHONE LINE THING.

THEY CAN USE THE NEW SALIVA D.N.A. TEST TO
FIND PATERNITY RESPONSIBILITY CHEAPLY.

WE CAN SOLVE THE MISSING CHILDREN PROBLEM
THE SAME WAY. I HAVE WRITTEN GOV ENGLER, I
EXPECT POSITIVE RESPONSE.

I PRAY FOR YOUR POSITIVE RESPONSE TO OUR
HELPING HAND.

GOD BLESS
MARVIN

Tim had responded with brief, direct comments to Gabrion's
first letter. He hoped Gabrion would make a slip-up. Instead of
responding to the list of grievances, Tim kept focusing on Shannon's
whereabouts.

Dear Mr. Gabrion,

Months ago you wrote me a long letter and offered to help
me. Twice I've asked you to help me. How many times will you
deny me?

Rachel's dead body was discovered on federally owned property. The investigation of the sticky duct tape on her dead body
is the U.S. government's responsibility. I can tell them you
helped me.

Oh, do you like the picture I made? [Sparky the electric chair]
I'm a good electrician. The United States of America is investigating you. Time goes on, but life definitely does not.

Where is Shannon?

You'll feel better with God.

The last line referred to Gabrion's own signature closing, "God
Bless."

An excerpt from Tim's notebook dated January 28 captures a
report from Detective Miller:

Miller: "Gabrion likes to feel that he's in control. He's been
a manipulator and con man his whole life. He's been writing lots
of letters. We've been telling people not to write him back."

Miller added, "We know it's frustrating for the family. Nobody thought it would last this long. We're running three investigations. The disappearance and murder of Wayne Davis. The disappearance and murder of Ian Decker. And Rachel's murder. They overlap and interweave. Last week I spent two days with a guy who helped to tie it all together."

Miller stated that Gabrion has been telling everybody about corruption, a plot to kill the governor…BS stories. "Can't arrest a loony toon for being stupid."

Gabrion's response letter to Tim, dated February 2, reveals a greater shift to the bizarre.

TIM,

I AM SORRY TO HEAR THAT POLICE HAVE LATELY TREATED YOU AS A SUSPECT. I KNOW HOW IT FEELS TO BE FALSELY ACCUSED YOUR FEELING OF COURSE WOULD BE AMPLIFIED. THEY (HACKS) STOLED SOME LEGAL PAPERS, LETTERS FROM MY ATTORNEY AND THE PHOTO YOU SENT ME IN THE CHRISTMAS CARD.

I USED PHOTO TO FOCUS MY PRAYERS—FOR HER HEALTH AND HAPPINESS AND HER SAFE RETURN TO HER GRANDPARENTS WHOM LOVE HER SO MUCH.

I HOPE YOU HAVE ANOTHER ONE; I WILL KEEP IT IN MY BIBLE. BRING IT OUT WHEN I PRAY. ONLY.

I HAVE NOT WRITTEN AS I AM NOT WANTING TO HEAR TALK OF "PUTTING SHANNON TO REST" AS FACTS POINT TO HER ALIVE.

PROBABLY POLICE HASSELED YOU BECAUSE YOU OR SOMEONE TRIED TO LOOK AT FACTS OF INVESTIGATION. THOSE FACTS WOULD IMPLICATE A POLICEMAN OR A FRIEND OF ONE. I SPEAK OFTEN OF CORRUPTION IN NEWAYGO COUNTY POLICE DEPT. ANYONE WHO'S BEEN ANYWHERE KNOWS OF THE POLICE BROTHERHOOD PROTECTING EACH

OTHER. THAT CONNECTS N.C.P.D. TO NEWAYGO
STATE POLICE DEPT.

I FELT THAT YOU ARE A CAPABLE PERSON. IF I
HAVE A GOOD LEAD CAN YOU CHECK IT OUT WITH-
OUT MAKING THE MISTAKE OF TELLING POLICE. I
HAVE FACTS SUPPORTING MY HYPNOSIS OF COR-
RUPTION. I BELIEVE.
    MARVIN GABRION

As they examined the letters with Tim, the detectives felt that
sometime soon something would crack and break out. Obviously,
Gabrion felt under enormous pressure. What they wanted was a finger
pointing on the map and a voice saying "Here. Here is where you can
find Shannon."

April 10 was Good Friday. It was a good day generally. *Unsolved
Mysteries* was scheduled to air that evening. Tim and Lyn looked forward to it avidly and it was every bit as good as they hoped. The
scenes rang with chilling authenticity, the details impeccable, the
drama compelling. Most importantly, the *USA Today* Nielsen broad-
cast ratings came in at 10.3 million viewers. This was the publicity for
which they had hoped.

As the letters from Gabrion continued, a twisted inner world
unfolded. Anger and paranoia surfaced in a May 1 letter.

TIM

IAM NOW IN CONTACT WITH A POLICE OFFICER; I
WANT VERY MUCH TO SOLVE RACHEL'S MURDER.

I PRAY BUT ALSO AM WANTING TO DO SOME-
THING MORE.

A LOT OF PEOPLE GOOD AND BAD HOLD BACK
WHEN TALKING TO COPS, ON ONE HAND AND ON
THE OTHER POLICE ARE LIMITED TO STRICT MODE
OF OPERATIONS.

<u>YOU</u> BEING FATHER OF RACHEL CAN CONTACT
AND HELP EMENSLY IN OUR EFFORT. THERE ARE A

FEW PEOPLE LEFT UNQUESTIONED WHOM ARE
POLICE INFORMANT AND THEREBY ABOVE SUSPI-
CION!

IF CRAZY MEDIA STORY'S ARE TRUE YOU'VE STILL
NOTHING TO LOSE IN FACT YOU'VE EVERYTHING
TO GAIN THIS CRIME VERY EASILY COULD HAVE
BEEN DONE BY A FRIEND.

I AM NOT THREATENING YOU OR ANYONE ELSE.

I'M NOT ASKING YOU TO DO ANYTHING ILLEGAL
IN ANY WAY.

PLEASE GET YOUR HEAD OUT OF SAND—HELP ME
SAVE HER.

WE MUST WORK CONFIDENTIALLY AS PEOPLE
HIDE THINGS AND CLAM UP IF WARNED. RIGHT
NOW THEY ARE PROBABLY LOOSE LIPPED THINKING
I'M FRAMED.

SEND ME YOUR PHONE NUMBER I'LL BE IN FED-
ERAL PRISON SOON WHERE COST ON PHONE IS
CHEAP 3.85 15 MINUTTES.

IF YOU OR VERHAGE'S HAVE ANY TOYS ECT MAY
HAVE EVEN DRIED SALIVA ON IT—STATE POLICE LAB
HAS TOLD ME COULD BE USED FOR D.N.A. TESTING
BABY BOTTLE PACIFIER. PUT IN AIR TIGHT ZIPO BAG
AND FREEZE IT.

MARVIN

Again, in consultation with Detective Miller, Tim responded with a
brief note:

Marvin,

My wife and children don't want you to call my home. That's
why I have not sent my phone number.

My head is not stuck in the sand. I told you a long time ago
if you help me, I'll help you.

The government asked me what I thought about the death
penalty. I told them, if Mr. Gabrion will tell me where my granddaughter is then let's just skip it.

You're right, Marvin, I have everything to gain. I lost Rachel, I lost Shannon. I want to believe Shannon is alive. What do they do to baby killers in prison, Marvin?

You help me, I'll help you.

Tim

Sometimes it seemed to Tim that he and Gabrion were playing some kind of deadly game with these letters—one he wasn't always sure he wanted to play. Here was the question: Would Gabrion break first? Or would Tim?

In between—rising momentarily through the web of anxiety, anger and sorrow—appear those snippets of routine that remind us that life goes on. Tim fought daily against letting the events of the past two years overwhelm him. And he fought to remember the little things like birthdays, humor and the beauty of nature that undergirded the fact that life goes on.

On March 31 the family celebrated Sara's birthday. Tim wrote to her:

Sara, happy seventeenth birthday... I remember my seventeenth, the last birthday before starting our adult life.

You've been forced to deal with so many difficult things...me too. I enjoy helping you and appreciate your helping me too.

Sara, enjoy your accomplishment. Life is too short...for Rachel, let's say it was short, but, just right for her. I believe Shannon's life is "in progress."

Ours too.

Love,

Me

In his notebook Tim reflected on significant quotations:

"Murder is the ultimate act of depersonalization. It transforms a living person with hopes, dreams, and fears into a corpse, thereby taking away all that is special and unique about that person. The constitution does not preclude a State from deciding to give some of that back." —Justice Sandra Day O'Connor, *Payne v Tennessee*

"Statistics are people with the tears wiped away."—President John F. Kennedy

Tim also tried to keep the tone lighthearted with his family:
Great Morning Family,
    You can't imagine how our lives have changed. I wanted to wake everyone up, but life must go on...after taxes we've won millions...playing the lottery finally paid off! Last I heard it was 24 million, wow! NOT.
    Happy Wednesday,
    Dad

If only Marvin Gabrion would be over and done with, that might be the cautery that would heal grief and allow the family to move ahead.

A well-known trait of certain medical disorders is to associate one's actions and desires with divine mandate. Some years ago, a slogan drifted across popular culture: "The devil made me do it." With many psychological disorders, the slogan becomes "God told me to do it." The person feels he or she has a personal conduit to God, an alignment with God at his or her side.
    Diagnosis of a psychological disorder is a highly skilled, complex and intensive task. Symptoms overlap and interweave. Psychiatrists call it comorbidity: a state of primary diagnosis with symptoms of a secondary diagnosis. However competent, psychiatrists would be extremely reluctant to hazard a diagnosis without face-to-face interviews with the patient. After all, psychological signals are manifested not only in the words of the patient but also in physical mannerisms that accompany those words.
    Nonetheless, in the increasing series of letters Tim received over the spring and summer months, even the most objective of viewers became aware of two traits. One, a prophetic tone emerged, intertwined with a sense of grandiosity frequently associated with a delusional/paranoid disorder. This is the same symptomatology found in

Jim Jones, Charles Manson and others—a twisted voice conveying the bearer's belief in his or her special power and spiritual insight.

The second observable trait of the "summer letters" is a greater sense of mania. The *Diagnostic and Statistical Manual of Mental Disorders'* list of symptoms for mania or bipolar disorder is extensive, including, for example, racing thoughts, irritability and distractibility. In fact, one of them overlaps with the sense of grandiosity and special knowledge typical of the delusional/paranoid disorder (comorbidity).

The twin symptoms of divine, grandiose revelations and a sense of persecution incite a volatile psychological mixture. Both symptoms appear more pronounced in the series of summer letters. From Gabrion's June 24 letter:

INNOCENT UNTIL PROVEN GUILTY IS A CRUEL JOKE. JULIAS CESAER SAID "WORDS ARE THE WORLDS MOST POWERFUL WEAPONS." WITH MEDIA PROSECUTORS, FAMMILLY ECT PROPEGATING LIES AND REFUSING TO TELL THE TRUTH, I AM ALREADY AS GOOD AS GUILTY. TODAY YOU HAVE PEOPLE BEING PAID TO ASSIST YOU IN YOUR FALSE ACCUSATIONS SO YOU 'GOOD CITIZENS' DON'T NEED TO BLOODY YOUR HANDS WITH THE INNOCENT. LIKE YOU DID IN JESUS' DAY. YOU ARE THE SAME HATEFUL FALSELY ACCUSING MOB. JUST GENERATIONS REMOVED. I COULD FILL A BOOK WITH LIE'S TO ME AND ABOUT ME. HALF THE STORY EXPERTS WILL ONCE AGAIN FORCEABLY APPOINANT ANOTHER DO NOTHING, DISHONEST ATTORNEY. I WILL STAND ALONE WHILE POLICE, PROSECUTORS, MEDIA BRAINWASH PUBLIC WITH HALF-THE-STORY MIXED WITH FLAT OUT LIE'S. INSTEAD OF HELPING ME START A D.N.A. INVENTORY OF CHILDREN WHITCH WOULD ULTIMATELY FIND 100'S MAYBE 1,000'S OF MISSING CHILDREN, INCLUDING SHANNON VERHAGE, YOU 'GOOD CITIZENS' WOULD HATE THE LIE'S RATHER THAN LOVE THE CHILDREN WE HOPE

TO SAVE. ALLOW ME TO LEAVE YOU WITH THE
WORDS JESUS CHRIST SAID TO HIS MOB OF FLASE
ACCUSERS.
"THOU SAITH I AM"

At approximately the same time, Marvin Gabrion sent another letter to Tim's daughter, Sara. This too was full of suppositions and dis-
torted details. At one point he implored Sara to take over his hypothetical charity. At another he accused her of being addicted to drugs. In
fact, Sara had developed an abhorrence of drugs after witnessing their
effects on so many of her friends. Then, in a new twist, he introduced
his cryptograph, pairing the name Azza with two biblical passages. The
long, rambling letter can be broken down into three essential parts.

In part one, Gabrion attempted to enlist Sara's aid with estab-
lishing his hypothetical charity "No More Missing Children." As
incentive he offered her the paid directorship, with her setting her
own salary. Additionally, he made his usual protestations of innocence.
In an unusual twist, however, the letter was written in moderately
neat cursive rather than the chunky dark printing of the other letters:

Sarah [sic], I did not rape your sister, my dog bit her, she
apparently took the fake rape secret too her grave, I've read a
lot of her letters (case material) she wrote twice in the letters she
was thinking about dropping charges, letters are too friends and
family. she was growing up trying too deal with being abused as
a child. Very aware of her feelings, it is a terrible shame she died.
It would be even worse for you too abandon Shannon, you do
not know what kind of a life she is being put through right now.
Whatever it is it is the wrong life, she should be with you now!

Then, Gabrion introduced his cryptograph, which became
nearly a signature mark for him and grew increasingly convoluted.
Azza appears to be the name he gave to his child that his common-
law wife supposedly aborted. Over the course of several letters he
imparted to Sara the role of a divine conduit, speaking to him the will
of God. In the first appearance, the cryptograph appeared like this:

AZZA   Matthew 19 vs. 30   Revelation 22 vs. 13

The Matthew passage reads: "Many that are first, shall be last, and the last, first" (King James Version). The passage from Revelation 22:13 reads: "I am the Alpha and Omega, the First and the Last, the Beginning and the End" (King James Version).

Part two provided a rambling four-page description of the No More Missing Children charitable organization. Part three, however, proved a treasure trove of abnormal psychology. It had been decided that Gabrion's trial for the murder of Rachel Timmerman would be held in federal court, presided over by the distinguished juror Judge Robert Holmes Bell. Here Gabrion's loose, sprawling scrawl was replaced by a tight compression of letters, as if the printing itself would contain, somehow, the torrents of rage.

MARVIN GABRION'S STATEMENT LIFE OR DEATH, NOW! STOP WASTING TAX-PAYER MONEY ON JUDGE ROBERT BELLS FAKE ILLEGAL FORM OF SO-CALLED JUSTICE.

I AM A MEMBER OF MENZA (TOP 1% I.Q.) AND FOUNDER OF THE CHURCH OF I AM TRUTH. IF BELL HAD NOT STOLEN MY LEGAL RIGHT TOO PRESENT EVIDENCE AND WITTNESSES IN MY DEFENSE, I WOULD EASILY WIN AQUITAL. I ONCE AGAIN STRONGLY REQUEST TO CHANGE MY PLEA. EIGHT MONTHS AGO I WROTE BELL, PROSECUTOR TIM VER-HEY, AND SO-CALLED DEFENSE ATTORNEYS CHRIS YATES OF FEDERAL PUBLIC PRETENDERS 616-742-7420 COCAINE AT LAW, PAUL MITCHELL DICK UP HIS ASS AT LAW 616-456-7831—AND DAVE STEBINS MORATI-CIAN/VULTURE AT LAW 614-224-7291. ALL IGNORED! WHY? NEPOTISM AND GREED, THEY STOLED $20-30,000 TAXS JUST SINCE THEN. 200,000 TOTAL 47,600 TO MITCHELL ALONE, (15,000 MITCHELL TO BELL) MONEY STOLEN BY THESE CORRUPT, LAW-BREAKING ATTORNEYS COMES FROM BOTTOM OF AMERICA'S FINANCIAL FOOD CHAIN, UNBORN CHILDREN OF POOR AND WORKING CLASS PEOPLE. PARENTS TRUE CHOICE? YOUR TAXES GOV. ABORTION/MURDER

DOC. OR THEY (666) TAX YOUR WHOLE FAMMILLY INTO STARVATION. MY WIFE MELANIE TRAMMELL TRAPHAGEN Gabrion ROSHETTE FROM DALLAS TX. NOW ORLANDO, CHOSE MURDER FOR MY DAUGHTER AZZA BELL AND HIS ILK SATANICALLY GAVE HER THE RIGHT TO CHOOSE BASED ON SEX OF CHILD! MY DAUGHTER WAS TORTURED, QUARTERED, MUR-DERED, HER BODY PARTS USED FOR LONGEVITY, MEDICINE, BEAUTY CREMES, ECT. MAINLY SERVING ULTRA RICH. GOD CREATED AZZA BELL AND HIS ILK SANCTIONED HER <u>MURDER</u>! I AM BEING TORTURED, TORMENTED AND HIGHLY ILLEGALLY TREATED HERE AT CALHOUN CO. JAIL, WITH BELL'S ENCOUR-AGEMENT. BELL FEARS THE TRUTH. BELL PURPESILLY KEPT ME FROM MILAN, MICH. FEDERAL DETENTION CENTER, HIGHEST SECURITY INSTITUTION IN MICH, WHERE I BELONG. WHY? MILAN HAS A FULL LAW LIBRARY, TYPE-WRITERS, AND JAIL-TAUGHT LAWYERS. BELL AND HIS ILK FEAR FALSELY ACCUSED GETTING ACTUAL ACCESS TO LAWS. INSTEAD WE ARE "SACRIFI-CIAL CASH COWS" FOR BELL AND HIS CO-CONSPIRA-TORS, CASH COW MITCHELL'S WORDS. CALHOUN JAIL SPITS IN MY FOOD, POISENS IT (SO THEY SAY) DENY'S ME ANY MEDICINE PER LT. ADOLPH ISHIAM 616-969-6339, FOR PAINFUL BLOODY SORES CAUSED BY THEM NOT ALLOWING ME TOO WASH! CONGRESS, TOP LAWMAKERS, ORDERED FOR PHYSCHOLOGICAL REASONS—1 HR OUT OF CELL PER DAY, AND T.V., RADIO OR NEWSPAPER FOR SOCIETAL CONTACT, OR LOSE YOUR MIND! HEALTH REASONS—3-SHOWERS PER WEEK MINIMUM. C.C.J. [Calhoun County Jail, a tempo-rary holding] HAS THREATENED TO KILL ME, HAS BEAT ME, PURPOSSILLY STEAL ALL HUMAN RIGHTS AND DINGNATY WITH BELLS ENCOURGEMENT. CALL BELL 616-456-2021 WRITE BELL-FED. CRT. HOUSE RM 402.

CALL BELL 110 MICHIGAN N.W. G.R. MI. 49503 BELL
HAS FAX NO. UNKNOWN COURT CLERK 456-2381. TELL
BELL 1. STOP TORTURING MARVIN Gabrion 2. STOP
WASTING TAX-PAYER MONEY ON FAKE JUSTICE 3.
ACCEPT Gabrion PLEA CHANGE AND FIRING OF ALL
THREE ATTORNEYS 4. BELL TO DECIDE LIFE OF
DEATH, AS IS Gabrion's LEGAL RIGHT NO 5-10,000 FOR
JURY TOO HEAR BELLS AND ATTORNEYS LIES. CASE
NO. 199 CR76 NEXT CRT. DATE 5-23 10 A.M. U.S. MAR-
SHALLS BARBARA LEE ALSO ENCOURAGES MY TOR-
TURE, 616-456-2438

SHOULD BELL THE CONSTITUTION DESTROYER
AND TORTURER DECIDE DEATH, DON'T CRY FOR ME!
I WILL BE IN HEAVEN, WITH RACHEL TIMMERMAN,
READING THE BIBLE TO AZZA   AS I USED TO ON
EARTH. WHEN G D, THE TRUE JUDGE, SENDS BELL TO
HIS DAMNATION FOR MURDERING MARVIN Gabrion BY
EXECUTION. TAKE THIS, COPY, SPREAD BELL'S LATEST
LUDACROUS JOKE "YOU WILL GET A FAIR TRIAL" NO
ONE IN AMERICA GETS A FAIR TRIAL. THE ATTORNEYS
(PROSECUTORS, JUDGES ECT.) PURPOSILLY SEND
THOSE REPRESENTED BY COURT APPOINTED ATTOR-
NEYS TO JAIL OR PRISON OR DEATH. INNOCENSE OR
GUILT NO DIFFERENCE PROOF O.J. SIMPSON, PATTY
RAMSEY, JOHN DUPONT, JOHN HINKLEY. ALL PAID
EXTORTED BLOOD MONEY. (BLOOD AND MISERY OF
INNOCENT POOR) SO BELL AND CO-CONSPIRATORS
(MOST ATTORNEYS) GET RICH. SHOULD BE NO POSSI-
BILITY OF BACK DOOR MONEY. TO JUDGES, ALL CON-
TACT BETWEEN JUDGES AND ATTORNEYS SHOULD BE
OPEN TOO PUBLIC AND ALL MEDIA, SECRECY HAS
BRED THESE HIGHLY CORRUPT, GREEDY, IMMORAL,
BABYKILLING, CO-CAINE USING DEMONS LIKE BELL
AND MOST ATTORNEYS. CALL BELL MAKE HIM STOP
HIS THIEVERY IN MY NAME. SHOULD I DIE? SO WHAT!

STOP THEIR THIEVERY SO 1, 2, OR MORE OF <u>OUR</u> INNOCENT UNBORN MAY LIVE!

KEEP AT BELL! AZZA   MATTHEW 19 VS 30   REVALATION 22 VS 13
Marvin Gabrion

Fearing the complete unraveling of the monster's mind, Tim wrote one last letter to Gabrion, hoping to win by reason what his earlier pleas had failed to gain. His only goal now was information on Shannon.

Marvin,

It is difficult to reply to your letters. You say that you want to help me, yet nothing happens. Please put yourself in my point of view.

I procreated, producing my firstborn, Rachel. She was a cheerful, fun child.

She was more difficult as a teenager. She told me, as did Wayne Davis, that you violently raped her when she was but a child. Are you comfortable with the DNA evidence of the rape?

Did you know that the authorities removed all of the duct tape from Rachel's body? Did you get any hairs on it? You put duct tape on my Rachel, also chains, locks and cement blocks. Do you have the keys to those locks or do the police have them now? Did the cops in Buffalo remove your hair? [Gabrion shaved his entire body when he learned that a hair was found on Rachel's body.]

I saw Shannon with an Amish couple. They had gray hair, a dark brown horse and a black buggy. [A false sighting Tim had on a bike ride.]

The FBI has talked to me. If you check it out, Rachel's body was found on federal property. Federal law will allow the death penalty. What do you want, Marvin?

What went wrong? Did you think you were smarter than Bob Allen, Wayne Davis, Ian Decker, how many more?

Shannon can save you.

The truth will set you free.

Tim

Several allusions in Tim's letter are significant. First, a key taken during the search warrant served in Gabrion's Altona Christian bookstore fit and opened the handcuffs on Rachel's body.

Second, the cement blocks weighing down Rachel's body were consistent with those on Gabrion's Altona property.

Third, Rachel's blocks had been partially painted with pink spray paint. A can of pink spray paint at the Altona Christian bookstore proved an identical match to the blocks chained to Rachel.

Fourth, like many prisoners, Gabrion sought out pen pals. It just so happened that one of those responding, briefly, was the daughter of a state cop. In one such letter, Gabrion had drawn a remarkably accurate map of Oxford Lake. He included the two-track road and the rise of the hill above the landing and marked the spot below as "Canoe Landing."

Thus far, the map would only indicate that he was familiar with Oxford Lake. But he added more details by drawing the island in its proper topographical spot and the line dividing federal from private water. And just north of that line, he placed three X marks with the caption:

Body Found, 1 of 3

The problems: How did he know the body was found there? His location was indeed slightly incorrect. If he placed bodies just north of the federal line, Rachel's body was recovered 227 feet south of it. Bodies do not shift in a stagnant lake, especially when weighted with sixty pounds of cement block. The only reason Rachel's body surfaced was because of the effect of natural decomposition gases acting with a balloon effect.

Furthermore, what did he mean by one of three bodies recovered? Who were the others? Two of the others he had murdered in his trail to cover his crimes? Or, the thought thundered like a nightmare of noise, could one be Shannon?

Nonetheless, if he was working by night, it would have been nearly impossible to pick out landmarks without an aerial survey map or specific topographical markers.

In his notebook, Tim jotted these lines:

> Should I be content knowing that Shannon is safe, clean and well cared for? I miss those blue eyes and loved the gentle, sweet, high-pitched "hi." I want my Shannon back.

Time does not completely heal a broken heart; it only teaches you how to live with it.

At this point, believing that Shannon had been adopted and not murdered was Tim's only comfort.

Chapter 15

Dredging the Pit

Not knowing was a trial itself for Tim and Lyn. Gabrion was being held in a Michigan prison, serving five years on the social security fraud case involving Robert Allen's identity. His letters and comments had degenerated to self-serving and paranoid rants. Clearly, there would be no bargaining with him—nor any help from him.

Tim believed that his own investigation and contributions to the detectives had been essential. His photos of the concrete blocks at Gabrion's Christian bookstore in Altona and those he found at Oxford Lake proved to be a crucial match, for example. So, too, was his analysis of Rachel's presumed letters between her death and discovery. Undoubtedly she had been forced to write them before being murdered.

A series of police actions focused on Oxford Lake. Two months after Rachel's body had been found, divers undertook the first systematic search of the lake. Conditions were nearly impossible. Every motion seemed to stir up silt and nothing else. The cadaver dogs that searched the lake found very little as well. Repeatedly they signaled in the area where Rachel's body was found. They aggressively signaled three spots in the lake, but each was impenetrable. The lake was searched again in April, but the conditions were no clearer. Divers attached themselves to weights approximating the two cement blocks attached to Rachel. They sank into thick muck and held at fifteen feet.

With the revelation of Gabrion's letter pinpointing three bodies in the lake, authorities decided to dredge the mapped area.

On April 28, 2001, Tim drove north to Oxford Lake where welders were beginning work on the pilings. One of them observed, "There are two feet of clear water and sixty feet of silt."

Tim asked them what they were going to do with forty-five foot pilings. "Weld them together," a worker said, "and go down ninety feet."

It took a long time to set up the dredging operation. The state police had wanted to do it for some time but they were hindered by the cost. Their budget could spare only $120,000 of the nearly $300,000 needed. After it had been declared a federal case, the United States Department of Justice stepped in to pay the rest of the cost.

Detectives already had Rachel's body pinpointed to the location. They would try the case on that. But there were too many mysteries, too many unknowns. Primarily Shannon. Was her small body buried in the silt? And the others? Ian Decker? Wayne Davis? Robert Allen? With the financial help of the Department of Justice, the operation proceeded in the spring.

The first challenge was to provide access through the primitive landscape to the lake itself. A hiker would get tired out by the trek. A four-by-four could follow the twisted two-track in low gear. But how could they get the heavy equipment for dredging in there? Authorities found a ready supply of cheap help in their own jails. Armed with shovels and power saws instead of guns and knives, a group of jail trustees labored each day, clearing trees and brush, widening and leveling the two-track, backing in and spreading loads of gravel over the low spots.

Stacks of heavy eight-by-eight timbers were delivered and lined the rise of the hill above the lake.

By mid-May the heavy machinery arrived.

The great yellow boom of the crane rose above the quiet shoreline waters like some prehistoric creature, dragged up through the slime. Its rollered feet clambered aboard a thick wooden barge over two long ramps. The ramps bent under the enormous weight.

The surrounding area, now overgrown once again, lay ripped

and scarred in the wake of the monster. This lake was not meant for such beasts. It is a lake of small things. It is a lake of horrors that chill the bones. That is why the monster has come—to probe the horrors. The barge moved slowly out over the lake, towed by a powerboat. It was David dragging Goliath, one weary footstep at a time until it stopped.

A second barge emerged, carrying a white-cabbed truck that housed the boom swing for the suction hoses and the powerful suction pumps.

The boom crane began swinging sheets of metal for the pilings. The clamor of the hydraulic jack that slammed them down through the silt reverberated across the marsh and forests. Birds disappeared. Small creatures retreated to their dens. *Wham*! The metal pilings sank. As they did, welders blazed the sections together. Each length of metal, welded together, shaped a box. It would descend directly over the indicated Xs on Gabrion's map.

They began to find some solid ground. Finally the slam of the jacks paused. The birds returned.

On the rise of the shoreline hill stood another structure, wholly out of place with nature. Nature is all curves. It flows. Nothing is angular or perpendicular. Nature always rises, yearning toward the sun. Nature resists flat things. Fallen trees, leaves, old growth it devours, feeding the never-ending cycle. Yet, this object would make use of one natural force—gravity.

This is the collection screen for the suction pump. Built on the rise of the hill out of the same heavy timbers, and covered by a trampoline-like membrane, the rectangular structure received debris and permitted the water to flow through, back into the lake.

It was a good idea, an engineering trick designed to reveal the hidden, to disclose mysteries held in the lake's cold heart. The powerful suction pump roared into life. Water flowed to the screening station. Then nothing. A piece of metal left inside the coffer dam had blown a pump. They tried again with a new pump. The same thing happened. Then again.

The awful truth surfaced. The welders, instead of throwing their spent rods outside the coffer dam or returning them to the barge, had dumped them inside the dam itself.

Hopeless. They could blow pumps all day and still find no answers. Three hundred thousand dollars and hundreds of hours of labor sucked up in human error.

They dismantled the pumps, towed the crane barge back to shore and offloaded the monster. It disappeared on the back of a flatbed truck. The pumping barge was towed back, dismantled, hauled out. The screening station, so strange and so useless now in the unnatural setting, was torn down, the heavy timbers trucked out.

Within a year, brush overgrew the scars. Saplings arose where trees were felled. Once again, it was a place of small things. And quiet.

Part 4

The Trial

Hotspur:
And I can teach thee, coz, to shame
the devil—
By telling truth. Tell truth and
shame the devil...
O, while you live, tell truth and
shame the devil.

William Shakespeare
Henry IV

Chapter 16

The Evidence Speaks

Spectators enter courtrooms with different expectations. This was especially so during earlier years when the courthouse was the centerpiece of town, a large brick or stone building, floors of worn marble and walls of dark paneling. Since then, of course, crime has exploded. To handle the burgeoning loads, new courthouses, with sterile chambers of light wood and white marble and industrial gray carpeting, have sprung up like monolithic spires of justice across the face of the nation.

Maybe spectators during those earlier times, slouched on the wooded benches of the old courthouse, expected the defendant to suddenly break down and through a torrent of tears confess to crimes charged and perhaps to others unknown. Or perhaps they awaited viewing a defendant who goes wild and lies twitching under the weight of three deputies. Such spectators were adrenaline junkies. They lived in their imaginations when they were not lulled to a stupor no modern taser can touch.

A certain percentage of spectators in a courtroom still come to see an unending parade of the underbelly of human nature. Each defendant is different, enabling the spectators to believe they are better than many in this sordid world.

Other spectators are legal junkies, They run the show in their grandiose imaginations with superior knowledge of little known technicalities and intricate legal terms. They throw out their renditions of motions *ad limine*, their pursuants, their *Diaz v Hooperstein* 73 F.3rd at 627s with fluent grace. They imagine wearing designer suits, expensive shoes and French silk ties. In reality, some lawyers are duller than dirt and not nearly as smart. Most of the smart ones are practicing in corporate law and they're charging $500+ per hour. If committed to prosecutorial or defense law, they might be very intelligent and skillful but are probably wearing suits off the rack.

Some spectators enticed by the promise of courtroom drama come anyway. Modern courtrooms are relatively small and similar in décor. Gone are the days of the deep rooms, long aisles, ceilings hung with chandeliers and dark paneled walls. Everything is tight, squeezed together. Theoretically, all citizens have a right to attend, from retired millionaires to street people trying to get warm or sleep. That's theoretically. Practically, there just isn't room for them all in the modern courtroom.

Some come leaving their flights of fantasy elsewhere. They are the realists. They are family and friends of the members involved, carefully arranged on each side of the aisle. On the prosecution's side sit those desperate for answers. They want to know "Why my kid, my husband, my wife? What happened in the missing pieces of the crime?" And on the defendant's side there are the unspoken questions also: "Did he really do this? Will he be acquitted?"

If the trial is an important one, like this one, the spectators come early to secure seats, along with reporters and sketch artists. No room for anyone playing imaginary games in *The United States of America, Plaintiff, v. Marvin Gabrion, Defendant*, File No. 1:99-CR-76. The spectators came out of love, out of despair, out of hope or final loss of hope. The courtroom was full.

Representing the prosecution were United States Assistant Prosecutors Timothy VerHey and Don Davis. The defense was represented by Paul Mitchell and David Stebbins.

In a courtroom, before a witness enters, the spectators study the attorneys, analyze them, make a series of notes in a mental file. Who looks confident? Who looks honest? Are they disheveled or styled according to *Gentleman's Quarterly?* All these are discrete signals that will influence their opinions. They go beyond evidence to that subterranean vault of personal judgment. The attorneys know the game. It is precisely one they play with the jury also, playing it out like a well-staged and choreographed drama. They are uniformly polite and consummately professional.

Presiding over the court for this case was the Honorable Judge Robert Holmes Bell of the United States District Court. Appointed to the position by President Ronald Reagan in 1987, Judge Bell had served with distinction—that rare person highly respected by prosecutors and defense alike. When the State Bar of Michigan named him one of its five "Champions of Justice" for 2002, it noted Bell as a "just, compassionate and giving individual."

The first activity in the total scope of the trial included the judge's decisions on pretrial motions, argued in January 2002. Perhaps the most interesting one, in retrospect, was a motion submitted by the defendant "to engage in allocution before the jury during the penalty phase of the trial without subjecting himself to cross-examination." As the judge patiently pointed out, the defendant thoroughly misunderstood "allocution."

Rule number one for the defense team usually is to keep the defendant off the stand. Once there, he is defenseless. Gabrion had been contentious with his lawyers from the start. He believed they were in cahoots with the prosecution. He believed they were incompetent. To tell the full range of his story, he pled for allocution.

Allocution, however, has nothing to do with taking the stand during the trial. Rather, it is an opportunity for the defendant to express remorse and plead for mercy during the penalty phase of the trial. As the judge ruled, "Allocution...will not be permitted for the presentation of evidence or controverted factual issues. A statement of apology, of remorse or a plea for mercy...is not evidence. That is what allocution is about."

It was unpleasant news for Gabrion, who wanted a major part in running his own defense. Tension seethed between Gabrion and his lawyers. At times he acted strangely disconnected, picking his nose and examining the excavation like a little boy bored in church. Often he simply put his head on the table and feigned sleep. Other times he bristled with angry tension, glaring at his attorneys, glaring at the audience.

After the motions, hearings on evidence followed. Then as the time for opening arguments approached, Tim felt a melancholy tension settle over him. After five years of looking for answers, it would come down to the next few weeks. Tim noted:

February 24

It turned into an incredible, unseasonably warm February Sunday. I busied myself with chores and getting things squared away to be at trial for the next couple of weeks. I made some notes about the day sitting outside in the sunshine without even needing to wear a coat.

As before a loved one's funeral, the day was filled with a pensive melancholy. Time seems to slow, but thoughts and feelings continue intensely. We've been told that a murder trial is difficult. Events and emotions that have dimmed in the past are brought to the surface once again. I'm hoping I'm strong enough. Sometimes the negative energy can be so strong. I know that Rachel's murder has changed my whole life. Fighting back and not losing control of my life is a continuing task.

Despite the abundance of emotion and trepidation, one thing can't be denied. It is a fine thing to sit outside in the sunshine with a fine cigar.

For the next several weeks, that was the last moment of relaxation and peace Tim experienced.

Juries are entities unto themselves, like a twelve-celled organism. Yet, the modern *voir dire*, or jury selection process, tries to ensure that each cell in that organism is different. Independent intellects rather than emotional imaginations. Diverse backgrounds rather than one class stratum. The accused, after all, has a constitutional right to a jury of his or her peers.

Rachel Timmerman and her daughter, Shannon, smile for the camera.

A teenage Rachel pretends to drive her favorite truck.

Baby Shannon frolics in her grandparents' backyard.

Three generations of Timmermans:
Grandpa poses with his granddaughter, Rachel,
and great-granddaughter, Shannon.

Shannon plays in her grandparents'
living room.

An envelope featuring the space station hologram in question during the hunt for Marvin Gabrion.

A diver prepares to search
for clues of Rachel's murder.

The post office in Sherman, New York,
where Marvin Gabrion set up a PO box to receive
Robert Allen's social security checks.

This is the cinder block Marvin Gabrion used to drown Rachel.

The Christian bookstore location in Altona, Michigan, that was previously owned by Gabrion.

Tim Timmerman stands in front of the eerie sign created by Marvin Gabrion.
"KIDS
WE HAVE NONE TO SPARE
PLEASE SLOW DOWN"

The dredging of Oxford Lake for clues begins.

Marvin Gabrion is led away in shackles from his arraignment in Buffalo, New York.

This is an artistic rendering of Marvin Gabrion's mug shot.

MARVIN GABRION's STATEMENT.
LiFE oR DEATH, NOW! STOP WASTEing
TAX-PAYER MONEY ON JUDGE ROBERT BELLS FAKE
ILLEGAL FORM OF SO-CALLED JUSTICE.

I AM A MEMBER OF MENZA (TOP 1% I.Q.) AND FOUNDER OF THE CHURCH OF TRUTH. IF BELL HAD NOT STOLEN MY LEGAL RIGHT TOO PRESENT EVIDENCE AND WITTNESSES, IN MY DEFENSE, I WOULD EASIIIY WIN A ACQUITAL. I ONCE AGAIN STRONGLY REQUEST TOO CHANGE MY PLEA. EiGHT MONTHS AGO I WROTE BELL, PROSECUTORS CHRYSTAL ROACH AND TIM VERHEY, AND SO-CALLED DEFENSE ATTORNEYS CHRIS YATES OF FEDERAL PUBLIC PRETENDERS 616 742-7420 COCAINE AT LAW, PAUL MITCHELL DICK UP HIS ASS AT LAW 616-456-7891 AND DAVID STEBBINS MORATICIAN/VULTURE AT LAW 614-224-7291, ALL IGNORED! WHY? NEPOTISM AND GREED, THEY StOlED $20-30,000 TAXS JUST SINCE THEN. 200,000 TOTAL 47,600 To MITCHELL ALONE, (15,000 MITCHELL To BELL) MONEY STOLEN BY THESE CORRUPT, LAW-BREAKING ATTORNEYS COMES FROM BOTTOM OF AMERICA'S FINANCIAL FOOD CHAIN, UNBORN CHILDREN OF OUR POOR AND WORKING CLASS PEOPLE. PARENTS TRUE CHOICE? YOUR TAXS PAY EV, ABORTION/MURDER DOC. OR THEY (666) TAX YOUR WHOLE FAMMILLY INTO STARVATION, MY WIFE MELANIE TRAMMELL TRAPHAGEN GABRION ROSHETTE FROM DALLAS TX. NOW ORLANDO. CHOSE MURDER FOR MY DAUGHTER AZLA♥, BELL AND HIS ILK SATANICALLY GAVE HER THE RIGHT TO CHOOSE BASED ON SEX OF CHILD! MY DAUGHTER WAS TORTURED, QUARTEAed, MURDERED, HER BODY PARTS 'SED FOR LONGEVITY, MEDICINE, BEAUTY CREMES ECT. MAINLY SERVING, ULTRA RICH,

I AM GOD CREATED AZLA♥ BELL AND HIS ILK SANCTIONED HER MURDER! BEING TORTURED, TORMENTED AND HIGHLY ILLEGALLY TREATED HERE AT CALHOUN CO. JAIL, WITH BELL'S ENCOURGEMENT. BELL FEARS THE TRUTH. BELL PURPOSIILY KEPT ME FROM MILAN, MICH. FEDERAL DETENTION CENTER, HIGHEST SECURITY INSTITUTION IN MICH, WHERE I BELONG. WHY? MILAN HAS A FULL LAW LIBRARY, TYPE WRITERS, AND JAIL TAUGHT LAWYERS. BELL AND HIS CI'' FEAR FALSLY ACCUSED GETTING ACTUAL ACCESS TO LAWS, INSTEAD WE ARE SACRI-F. AL CASH COWS" FOR BELL AND HIS CO-CONSPIRATORES, CASH COW MITCHELL'S WORDS.

CALHOUN JAIL SPITS IN MY FOOD, POISONS IT (SO THEY SAY) DENYS ME ANY MEDICINE PER LT. AdOLPH ISHAM 616-969-6339, FOR PAINFUL BLOODY SORES CAUSED BY THEM NOT ALLOWING ME TOO WASH! CONGRESS, TOP LAWMAKERS, ORDERED FOR PHYSCHOLOGICAL REASONS - 1 HR OUT OF CELL PER DAY, AND T.V., RADIO OR NEWSPAPER FOR SOCIETAL CONTACT, OR LOSE YOUR MIND! HEALTH REASONS - 3-SHOWERS PER WEEK MINIMUM. C.C. JO. HAS THREATENED TO KILL ME, HAS BEAT ME, PURPOSSIILY STEAL AIL HUMAN RIGHTS AND DIGNATY WITH BELLS ENCOURGEMENT. CALL BELL 616-456-2021 WRITE BELL: FED. CRT. HOUSE RM 402

CALL BELL 110 MICH' ' ALW. G.R. MI. 49503 BELL HAS FAX NO. UNKNOWN COURT CLERK 456-2381
TELL BELL ① STOP TORTURING MARVIN GABRION ② STOP WASTING TAX-PAYER MONEY ON FAKE JUSTICE ③ ACCEPT GABRION'S PLEA CHANGE AND FIRING OF AIL THREE ATTORNEYS ④ BELL TO DECIDE LIFE OR DEATH, AS IS GABRIONS LEGAL RIGHT NO 5-10,000 FOR JURY TOO HEAR BEIL'S AND ATTORNEY'S LiES. CASE No. 199 CR 76 NEXT CRT. DATE 5-23 10 A.M. US. MARSHALLS BARBARA LEE ALSO ENCOURAGES MY TORTURE, 616-456-2438

SHOULD BELL THE CONSTITUTION DESTROYER AND TORTURER DECIDE DEATH, DON'T CRY FOR ME! I WILL BE IN HEAVEN, WITH RACHEL TIMMERMAN, READING THE BIBLE TO AZLA♥ AS I USED TO ON EARTH. WHEN GOD, THE TRUE JUDGE, SENDS BELL TO HIS DAMNATION FOR MURDERING MARVIN GABRION BY EXECUTION. TAKE THIS, COPY, SPREAd BELL'S LATEST LUDACROUS JOKE" YOU WILL GET A FAIR TRIAL" NO ONE IN AMERICA GETS A FAIR TRIAL. THE ATTORNEYS (PROSECUTORS, JUDGES ECT. PURPOSIILY SEND THOSE REPRESENTED BY COURT APPOINTED ATTORNEYS TO JAIL OR PRISON OR DEATH, INNOCENSE OR GUILT NO DIFFERENCE. PROOF? O.J. SIMPSON, PATTY RAMSEY, JOHN DUPONT, JOHN HINKLY, AIL PAid EXTORTED BLOOD MONEY (BLOOD AND MISERY OF INNOCENT POOR) SO BELL AND CO-CONSPIRATORES (MOST ATTORNEYS) GET RICH. SHOULD BE NO POSSIBILITY OF BACK DOOR MONEY TO J ES, AIL CONTACT BETWEEN JUDGES AND ATTORNEYS SHOULD BE OPEN TOO PUBLIC AND ALL MEDIA, SE   CY HAS BRED HIGHLY CORRUPT, GREEDY, IMMORAL, BABYKILLING, CO-CAINE USING DEMONS LIKE BELL AND MOST ATTORNEYS. CALL BELL MAKE HIM STOP HIS THIEVERY IN MY NAME.
SHOULD I DIE? SO WHAT! STOP THIER THIEVERY SO 1/2, OR MORE OF OUR
INNOCENT UNBORN MAY LIVE! amga MATTHEW REVALATION   Marvin Gabion
KEEP AT BELL!   A22A   19 VS 30   27 VS 13

One of the many letters Marvin Gabrion sent to Tim Timmerman from prison.

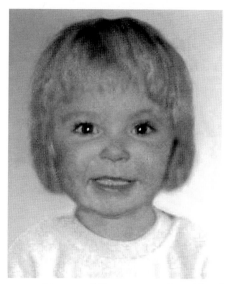

A computer-generated image of Shannon, produced by the FBI in 1998, showed her as she would look at two years of age.

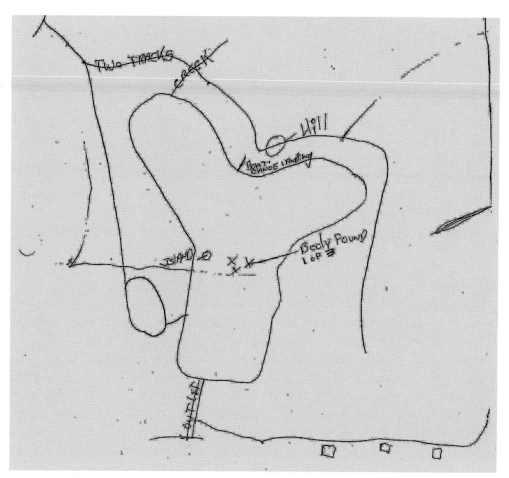

The telltale hand-drawn map of Oxford Lake created by Marvin Gabrion.

A Google Maps image of Michigan's Oxford Lake, where the body of nineteen-year-old Rachel Timmerman was found, bears a remarkable resemblance to the map drawn by Gabrion.

What does this mean when applied to a Marvin Gabrion, accused of crimes so monstrous they make a rationally and emotionally stable person shudder? By the same principle of *voir dire*, attorneys have varying ideas of the opening statement. Some feel it is relatively useless, a mere formality—that the case will be won or lost on the preponderance of evidence alone. On the contrary, some attorneys believe that the opening and closing arguments are the opportunities to win the jackpot. It is all drama where even the most minuscule item of evidence takes on world-shaking relevance.

That is the way movies have it, anyway.

In real life some attorneys present a smooth and compellingly eloquent statement—a perfect appeal to reason and emotion. Truly also, some fumble with a sense of grammar as twisted as a new language, with a progression of ideas as lurching as a centipede and a self-assurance as firm as gelatin. Sometimes they win by a sympathy vote. But not often. In both cases, however, prosecution and defense share similar roles. One outlines the crime, the evidence and why this one individual should be found guilty of that crime. The other, for whatever reasons, answers that his client couldn't possibly have done it. These can range from the so-called mental incapacity test (Gabrion had been examined three times since his arrest and been deemed competent to stand trial in each instance) to the infamous SODDI (Some Other Dude Did It) defense. Bereft of the first alternative, Gabrion's case headed in the latter direction.

The courtroom was busy when Tim and Lyn arrived on that first Monday, February 25. Marvin Gabrion shuffled into the courtroom, shackled at the wrists and ankles, taking careful twelve-inch steps within the fourteen-inch ankle chain. He had perfected the jailhouse shuffle: shoulders bent forward, head twitching back and forth, eyes peering for any threat. Often he caught the gaze of a spectator in the audience and held it with his malevolent glare.

The prosecution opened its case by taking the jurors back to the calm and lovely afternoon of July 5th—five years earlier at Oxford Lake. A tranquil lake, until Rachel's body was spotted through the lens of binoculars.

But how did this story start?

"Let me tell you how the story started," began the prosecutor Don Davis. "On August 7, 1996, Marvin Gabrion raped Rachel Timmerman. She reported to the Newaygo County Sheriff's department and to Gerber Memorial Hospital. Marvin Gabrion was charged with this rape and was scheduled to stand trial on June 5, 1997. Mr. Gabrion didn't want to stand trial, but the only way to avoid it was to get rid of Rachel Timmerman. He had to kill her. The government of the United States will prove that Marvin Gabrion murdered Rachel Timmerman.

"Marvin Gabrion put these handcuffs on Rachel Timmerman." He slammed the handcuffs down on the prosecutor's table. "After he had Rachel Timmerman restrained, he covered her eyes and mouth with duct tape, but didn't cover her nose. Marvin Gabrion wanted her alive a little longer, so she could feel his torture. She couldn't fight back anymore as he used chains…"

KWHAM filled the court room as he slammed the chains down.

"Marvin Gabrion used this very chain and these locks—" he slammed the locks down, a little less loudly, "…to attach these cinder blocks—" he whipped a blue cloth off the cinder blocks, "—to Rachel Timmerman's body. Then he put her in a boat, rowed several hundred feet out into the lake and threw Rachel Timmerman to her death in the murky bottom. Rachel Timmerman was nineteen years old when she was murdered by Marvin Gabrion." He pointed his finger at Gabrion and continued to do so whenever he said Gabrion's name.

"Now let me take you to the tiny town of Altona, where Marvin Gabrion lives. It's June 6 at four in the morning. A neighbor saw Marvin Gabrion grinding the serial numbers off a boat. Marvin Gabrion was seen about this time with bruises and scratches on his face. Rachel Timmerman had fought back; indeed she had fought for her life.

"The Michigan State Police obtained a search warrant for Marvin Gabrion's residence in Altona. Officers found cinder blocks about the property that are identical to the blocks used to murder Rachel Timmerman. Some of the blocks have paint on them— we found the paint cans. Some of the blocks had tar on them—the tar matched. These locks that Marvin Gabrion used to attach the chains and cinder blocks to Rachel Timmerman will be opened by keys found at Marvin Gabrion's residence."

Gabrion's eyes grew deader and colder, like the surface of Oxford Lake. What mysteries lay coiled behind them in the folds of his brain?

As the prosecutor displayed a large map of Newaygo County, he pointed out Oxford Lake and Hungerford Lake, six miles to the east.

"At the time Marvin Gabrion murdered Rachel Timmerman, he had a campsite at Hungerford Lake. Here we found an empty duct tape package. At his campsite we found baby items and a girl's hair clip. Rachel Timmerman was at this campsite before she died."

"Lies, lies!" Gabrion kept muttering.

"The government will prove to you beyond any reasonable doubt that Marvin Gabrion killed Rachel Timmerman, as he threatened he would, to prevent her from testifying against him in a rape case."

The defense attorney's statement was brief, simply calling into question the nature of the evidence and circumstances since no one "saw it happen." His course was set then: the evidence would all be circumstantial, therefore insubstantial to convict his client.

The time arrived that Tim had most anticipated and most feared. He was called as the first witness. He was a stranger to courtrooms. Would he help or hurt the case? He felt exposed, unprepared except for all his fears and memories of five long years. He reflected on his testimony in his notebook later:

Nobody reminded me about the swearing in part of testifying. Judge Bell stopped me before I could sit down and had me swear. "Do you swear to tell the truth, the whole truth and nothing but the truth, so help you God?"

"I do."

My testimony for the government was exactly like my phone conversation with the prosecution the day before. I told the jury that my legal name was Luverne Timmerman, but everyone called me Tim. I stated where I worked and my address and telephone number. I testified that I was absolutely certain on what day I had last seen Rachel, because I had fractured my finger the day before. Rachel and Shannon had been living with us and after this day I never saw them again. This testimony was good enough that Lyn did not have to testify that she saw the girls leave our home.

The prosecutor asked me if I'd received any letters from Rachel. I stated that I had. "The first letter was postmarked June 4, from Cedar Springs, Michigan. The envelope was a pre-stamped space station hologram."

I was asked about the contents of the letter. "It just didn't make much sense to me. It didn't sound like Rachel writing. She said goodbye to me just the day before and she started the letter apologizing for not saying goodbye." I told the jury that I'd received one more letter, postmarked Little Rock, Arkansas, about June 16. Both letters were entered into evidence.

Cross-examination by the defense was a little unnerving. As anticipated, the defense attorney asked me about Rachel's incarceration. "I don't think I've ever been told the whole story about it. I believe it was for a probation violation."

"But are you aware, Mr. Timmerman, that to get jail time there must be an underlying felony conviction?"

I replied, "I've heard something about a small amount of marijuana, a couple of joints, but I'm not sure."

Mr. Mitchell asked about Liz's House, but I had no idea what he was talking about. Lyn told me later that Liz's House is a halfway house program. Lyn had taken Rachel there, as one of the conditions of her probation, but it had been an unworkable program for her. My time on the witness stand was over, for the guilt phase of the trial.

After testifying, one is never quite sure what was said or, in fact, left unsaid. But Tim had fulfilled his role in the drama. The letters were indeed critical evidence, showing that Rachel had been forced to write the first immediately upon her capture—an attempt by Gabrion to forestall suspicion. The second letter could have been written near the same time, but was mailed, as nearly as could be determined, by Gabrion from Little Rock. The purpose was to explain the disappearance. Tim also added to his notebook that he was done "for the guilt phase of the trial." Far more difficult for him personally would be his Victim's Impact Statement during the sentencing phase.

George Vande Velde entered the witness stand to describe his experience of discovering the floating body five years before. His testimony was brief, solely to establish the sequence of events. When he was excused, a lovely young woman with long black hair rose from her row to meet him. She held out her hand for his. Together, they exited the courtroom.

Immediately outside the courtroom, Vande Velde sank onto one of the hard chairs. He shook his head.

"There's Rachel's dad. I'm going to go talk to him a minute." He stood.

"Mr. Timmerman," he said approaching Tim, "I have to tell you how sorry I am for you. After the dreams I've had, I can only imagine how you must feel."

"Thank you, sir. It hasn't been easy."

"Gloria, I need some coffee," George said to his companion.

"There's a cafe around the corner," Gloria said.

He nodded, didn't move.

"I can't get that picture. . . that monster . . . out of my mind." George tried to explain.

Gloria squeezed his hand.

"The papers," George said, barely audible, "say he has blue eyes. They're not blue. They're . . . murk. Like swamp mud. There's nothing behind them. Like . . . he has no soul."

"Everyone has a soul, George," Tim said gently. "It's what they do with it that counts."

George shook his head. "If that man has a soul, it's the color of night."

"What do you mean?"

"I'm not sure myself. Night has no light, so it has no color, no life. That's what I saw sitting at that table."

When Sergeant Richard Miller, a twenty-plus years' member of the Michigan State Police, took the stand, Tim and Lyn began to see just how carefully the detective had organized the case. His testimony was specific, detailed and reassuring of just how meticulously he had worked.

His testimony began with a description of the shallow, marshy, murky lake. A videotape was played of the drive through two-track roads back into the lake area. Sergeant Miller paused the videotape so he could show the jury where a piece of duct tape had been found. The government introduced the "Marvin Gabrion map" of Oxford Lake. The large reproduction of this map was displayed on an easel in front of the jury for most of the next week. Mitchell rose to object to the map, but Judge Bell responded, "Your objection is noted, but overruled."

Sergeant Miller testified that "we were unable to get real close at first. Because of the weed mass, we had to go south first, then back north. This weed mass clogged the lake; the outlets from the lake basically disappear in all of the weeds. The Michigan State Police took this picture of Oxford Lake." It was entered into evidence.

Sergeant Miller always talked directly to the jury. He continued his description of the lake. "There are approximately two feet of water. Underneath is muck, silted material. This muck is quite deep. We found hard pan eighty-five feet down."

More photographs were introduced. These included progressively closer pictures of Rachel's body and the more benign aquatic vegetation. Sergeant Miller testified that "The bottom block was in the mud." The judge recessed the court for lunch.

After lunch, the prosecution returned to the subject of Oxford Lake and the recovery effort. Sergeant Miller stated that "approximately one third of the bottom block was still in the mud. The chains appeared to be new. There was no sign of oxidation on them."

The Newaygo County Sheriff Department's dive team pulled a mesh trampoline mat underneath Rachel's body then secured it with a rope into a bundle. A truck on the shore was used to pull the package most of the way across the lake.

Sergeant Miller brought the remainder of the physical material into evidence. "There were two padlocks. They gave the appearance of being new. The chain was ten and one half feet long. The blocks were secured with three spring-loaded, nickel-plated clips. These clips appeared to be new; they still had barcodes on them. We also removed duct tape and a pair of white metal handcuffs. We sent the duct tape to the FBI. We did not find any hair, fiber or DNA connected to the defendant."

The government went over the timeline for the record. The first news release was on July 8. Sergeant Miller was informed of the tentative identification of the body on July 11. Identification of Rachel's body was confirmed on July 14. Sergeant Miller stated that "Sergeant Babcock and I first went to Altona on July 12 to attempt to interview Marvin Gabrion. We couldn't find him, but we did speak with Gabrion's neighbor."

The blocks removed from Gabrion's yard were identified with a tag, initials and complaint number. A search warrant was obtained for his bookstore and home in Altona, Michigan. The searching officers saw that Mr. Gabrion's improvised red, white and blue curtains were installed with duct tape.

Sergeant Miller stated that "we seized quite a number of items. There was only one book in the house—*The Perfect Victim.*"

Sergeant Miller opened the locks from Rachel's body with the keys found at Gabrion's house. There were two keys and both keys opened both locks. Gabrion muttered loudly that they were Ian Decker's keys.

A prescription pill bottle was entered into evidence. Mr. Mitchell wanted to see it and he conferred with co-counsel David Stebbins. We later learned that the only significance was the name on the bottle. The medication was prescribed for Marvin Gabrion. The keys and prescription bottle were in a wooden bowl that had not left the premises.

The officers also seized two aerosol spray cans of paint. These were sent to the FBI crime lab for analysis. After the police left their search, Tim and Lyn brought a sign to Sergeant Miller's attention. Tim and Lyn had walked down the road a bit and saw two cinder blocks around a sign Gabrion had erected. The sign read "Slow—Children...we have none to spare."

After the break Mr. Mitchell began his cross-examination. He had many questions about the lake and he wanted to know about water flow and drainage. Sergeant Miller had done his homework on the hydrology of Oxford Lake. Mr. Mitchell asked, "Three stakes were placed in Oxford Lake for reference point. Other than the number, the quantity of three, the geometric pattern of the stakes does not match with the three Xs on Marvin Gabrion's map of Oxford Lake?"

"That's correct."

The second day of the trial was when the direction of the prosecution case emerged: What happened? How did it happen? Who did it? What links the three?

Dr. Cohle, the forensic pathologist, testified to the cause of death. The defense crossed, raising certain hypothetical causes. "Yes, that could have happened," Dr. Cohle responded, "but in my opinion it didn't."

An entomologist from a major university next testified about how long Rachel was exposed to air by analysis of blowfly larvae. He concluded that the body could not have been exposed to air prior to July 1, but most likely on July 2 or 3.

A third significant witness was FBI Special Agent Gilligan, but here again her testimony focused on forensic details. She testified that the total weight placed on Rachel's body was 63.26 pounds. She related that on June 13 two years after Rachel's body was found, she went to Oxford Lake with a diver. The water depth was measured at two feet, two inches. Wearing a surface air supply dive suit, the diver grasped sixty pounds of weight. He plunged to a depth of twelve feet and remained there unmoving for five minutes. The diver himself followed on the stand to corroborate the testimony.

After a break, a series of witnesses testified to Rachel's fear of Marvin Gabrion.

The third day of the trial, February 27, opened with four witnesses who testified they had seen Marvin Gabrion's pickup truck in the vicinity of Oxford Lake on the day of the murder. One witness was quite specific. She said a truck slowly passed her home on a one-lane bridge. Inside were two men and, in the middle, a girl with long blonde hair. She was specific on the date: June 5, 1997.

Putting an "in custody witness" on the stand carries risk. After all, any prosecutor dreams of witnesses who are good citizens, intelligent, confident and articulate. So far these prosecutors had been successful. The defense attorney had nibbled at their testimony, but had been unable to take a bite out of them.

An "in custody witness" immediately carries a certain amount of suspicion walking to the stand. They are, first of all, convicted criminals—so-called bad boys. Nor does it help if one shuffles into the courtroom dressed in an orange jumpsuit, the other, now released, squirming in an ill-fitting suit.

There was nothing funny about their testimony, though. The first was incarcerated with Gabrion at Milan State Penitentiary. Another inmate had asked Gabrion, "We know you killed that girl, but what did you do with the baby?" The inmate then testified to Gabrion's reply: "I killed the baby, because there was nothing else to do with it."

Gabrion, meanwhile, was putting on his own show, alternately growling comments at his co-counsel or simply leaning back in his chair, letting his eyes drift lazily about the courtroom. He acted as if he had the secret weapon, the hidden truth that would destroy all this bother. A magician's trick: bring out the wand and it would all disappear. He wanted to take the stand. And at intervals he muttered the same refrain: "Lies, lies."

The afternoon testimony focused on the smaller but essential links in the chain of evidence: Gabrion's aluminum boat and his camp at Hungerford Lake, near Oxford Lake.

Jenny Bingham came to the stand. She had been camping near Gabrion's camp at Hungerford Lake, due east of Oxford Lake. She testified that she had seen Gabrion with an aluminum boat. When asked if she'd noticed anything unusual about his appearance, she replied, "Yes, two things. He looked like he'd gotten beat up in a fight and although the weather was quite warm, he was always wearing gloves."

The final witness for the day was a unique individual, John Cornelius. He came across as a really nice guy, without a care and wearing worn clothing. John had known Gabrion nearly his whole life. On the night in question, he had gone to a local convenience store. As John was leaving, he saw Marvin Gabrion walking toward him in the parking lot. "Hi, Marv, how ya doing?" They had a conversation and he passed Gabrion an innocent remark, "Well, I just got rid of my girlfriend. We broke up."

Gabrion then told John, "I just got rid of my girlfriend, too. Permanently. I bound her with chains, locks and cement blocks and threw her into a lake."

"I went home and told my mom about it," John testified. "I didn't know what else to do."

Paul Mitchell questioned every nuance and fact. He theorized that this conversation might have happened in July after television news about the body found in Oxford Lake aired. John was sure it had happened in mid-June. John's mom corroborated John's testimony with a deathbed deposition.

On Thursday, February 28, a parade of FBI agents testified that while Sergeant Miller had been putting the case together in Michigan, FBI experts had focused on two things. First, they determined the trail that Gabrion followed from Grand Rapids to his arrest in New York. Gabrion was indeed a master of identities, having traveled through Kentucky to Virginia, where he worked on a tobacco farm, to New York, all under assumed identities. The second focus was forensic evidence. This evidence ranged from the padlocks, an expert witness on concrete blocks and the matching tar deposits on the blocks which an FBI chemist testified about. A paint expert testified that the paint on the blocks matched the paint found in Gabrion's Christian bookstore. Another testified about trace material left on Rachel's body and the duct tape. All these FBI experts, under the skillful direction of the prosecutor, constructed a wall of insurmountable evidence.

The prosecutor reviewed Gabrion's arrest in Sherman, New York, on October 14. One could feel the objections as to relevance coming. Not so. The police had in their possession at the time a hair caught on the duct tape attached to Rachel—a hair that was not hers.

A subpoena had been issued and served to obtain a hair for DNA testing from Gabrion while he was in custody. When the FBI went to serve it, Gabrion had painstakingly shaved every hair from his body, even his feet. "It's good hygiene," he told the FBI.

After testimony about the link between Gabrion's Altona property and Rachel, the prosecution rested.

The judge turned to Gabrion, "How are you doing, Mr. Gabrion?"

"I'm doing pretty good, Your Honor. I want to be the first defense witness."

"Listen to your lawyers, Mr. Gabrion."

The defendant stared at him unbelievingly, arrogantly.

It was time for the defense, time for Marvin Gabrion to go digging in his little black bag of magical tricks.

Chapter 17

Evidence of Guilt

U sually it is a defense attorney's worst nightmare: The defendant wishes to take the stand. However, if the defendant appears to his attorney to be truthful and innocent, if he appears intelligent and confident, if his story is consistent and compelling, countering the prosecutor's case, the defense might go with it.

If, on the other hand, the evidence of guilt is as overwhelming as several granite mountains and if the defendant is unstable, prone to emotional outbursts and disconnected thought, the attorney wants him nowhere near the witness stand. Nonetheless, at 9:09 A.M. on Friday, March 1, Marvin Gabrion was sworn in to testify on his own behalf. It didn't begin in the most auspicious manner.

"I have a prepared statement, a narrative for the jury, and I have—if I could, I'd like to read that at the present moment," Gabrion began. "Ladies, gentlemen—ladies, gentlemen and citizens. I have numerous police reports and documents proving the facts I will relate presently to you. Respectfully, I have no choice but to offend some of you, as I am the speaker of the truth. Bear with me and we will get to the truth, good for one and all."

At that point, Gabrion began reading from a list of police reports, disputing the evidence entered into court. The prosecutor objected:

"Your Honor. He's just reading police reports. He's supposed to be testifying about facts he knows. I'm not objecting to the form of the inquiry, although it is objectionable. But that doesn't give him free reign to talk as long as he wants about whatever he wants to talk about. It still has to be relevant. It isn't."

The judge observed, "Yes. Stay on the relevance of this case if you would, please."

Gabrion broke in. "The police reports aren't relevant to the case, huh?"

He then continued at length explaining how two other individuals, whom he named, had carried out the murder. They had framed him by taking materials from his Altona house and planting evidence. From the start, it was clear Gabrion's intention was to follow the SODDI defense. He stacked name upon name, freely fabricating connections. More than once he got caught in an outright lie, as helpless as a naked man in a blizzard. The pattern started quickly with his fabrication of Rachel's "suicide note."

Davis, at this juncture, had just been objecting a second time to Gabrion's reading of police reports. "If the defendant is testifying from his own knowledge, I certainly don't have objection. If he's testifying about what he's read someplace or what somebody else told him, I do. Lack of foundation for what he's doing now."

Judge Bell nodded. "You're to testify what you know about this case. Not what you've read, but what you know about this case, as with every other witness, what they know about the case, what they know about the facts of the matter, if you wish."

Gabrion went on. "They met with a man named Eddie Start and proceeded—"

Davis raised a hand. "Your Honor—"

Gabrion was not to be stopped. "—to Eddie's cabin."

Davis frowned. "He apparently is ignoring both my objection and the Court's ruling."

Judge Bell shook his head. "Is this—I'm not sure whether he's testifying himself or whether he's testifying over something he read."

Davis sighed. "Then I object to the lack of foundation. I would ask that the witness explain how he knows what he's testifying to."

"Well, you can cross-examine on that." Bell turned to Gabrion. "Continue as to what you know and what's relevant to this case."

Gabrion's voice rose. "Ms. Timmerman, Ms. Timmerman wrote a note. This is how I know a lot of the facts that I've already been trying to say. I do not want Shannon abused by my dad, my mom and Shannon's dad. Typed suicide note addressed to Marvin Gabrion. The men, Ian and Eddie, tried to assist her death by chaining blocks to her that one of them got from my roadside sign which read: Kids, we have many, none to spare, please slow down. Ms. Timmerman authored a six-page goodbye note which was delivered to me at my campsite on the Big Muskegon River in Mecosta County."

Davis stood. "Objection, Your Honor. If Mr. Gabrion is referring to a note, I'd like to see the note."

"You can cross-examine on this. This is coming in as a narrative about this witness's knowledge. You can cross-examine," Judge Bell stated.

Davis asked, "May I inquire, is the Court instructing me not to object?"

Judge Bell shook his head. "No, no. But the objection as to something that was done and said you can cross-examine on. I'm assuming—"

Davis nodded. "I understand, Your Honor. We have made a Rule 16 discovery of the defense. We have not obtained any such discovery materials. He is now referring to a note. I'd like to see the note and then I can comment as to whether or not his testimony is objectionable as to this supposed note."

Bell's voice hardened. "I don't want to be arbitrary here."

Mitchell broke in. "We have no note, Your Honor. We have not."

Following Gabrion's prepared statement, it was time for the prosecutor's cross-examination of the witness. Calmly Don Davis stepped to the podium, studying Gabrion. The murky blue eyes glared back at him like those of some prehistoric reptile. Davis started at the beginning.

Q   Mr. Gabrion, I would like to take you to the night of August 6, 1996, the night that you raped Rachel Timmerman.

A   The night of the fake rape, yes, sir.

Q   Fake rape?

A   Yes.

Q   What do you mean by fake rape?

A   It was make-believe. It was fake, so it's a fake rape.

Q   You mean you weren't there?

A   There was no rape, so it had to be a fake.

Q   You're saying it was some kind of romantic encounter that you had with Rachel Timmerman?

A   It could be more accurately considered a date rape than a rape, but it definitely was nothing romantic involved about it.

Q   It wasn't romantic?

A   No.

Q   Please explain.

A   Have you read the five-page—

Q   Please explain. It's not rape, it's not romantic. What is it?

Mitchell intervened. His voice rose. "Your Honor, Your Honor, excuse me."

Judge Bell would have none of it. "Calm down. Calm down. Just answer his questions."

Mitchell stiffened. "I must object."

Gabrion asked in a singsong voice: "It's what? It's not rape, it's not romantic, then what is it?"

Davis continued his questioning:

Q   That's the question.

A   It was a nineteen-year-old prostitute trying to sleep with a fourteen-year-old boy and I got caught in the way. That's what it was.

Q   You were dating her, weren't you?

A   Incorrect.

Q   You wrote a letter to Mr. Timmerman and you referred to that night as "the night we dated, Rachel tried to sell me LSD and marijuana." The night we dated. That's your letter. Were you lying to Mr. Timmerman?

A It's probably not my writing.

Q Oh, it's not your writing?

A Right. Roberta Gilligan come over to the Sheriff's Department and tried to charge me for writing letters to the governor and threatening to kill him. The governor helped me start an organization to save babies.

Q That night that you raped Rachel Timmerman, do you recall telling her that if she told the police, that you would kill her, but not before you killed Shannon and made her watch? Do you remember telling her that to keep her from going to the police?

A Of course not. It never happened either.

Q Do you recall biting her on the nose?

A No. But she was pushing the car out of the—out of the sand and fell down and hit her nose on the bumper. That might have caused the bleeding on her nose or she sat on top of my dog. It could be either one. My dog was midnight black.

Q She sat on your dog?

A Right, when she—

Q That was the night that you were playing cards with a bunch of individuals, weren't you?

A 'Til about midnight.

Q And you went out for a ride?

A Right, in the convertible.

Q With all of them?

A Right.

Q And you told all the other passengers to get out of the car?

A Incorrect.

Q Didn't you?

A She did. She told everyone to get out. She said, "Take me down by the river and I'll suck your dick."

Q Now, Mr. Gabrion, what is it that made you so immediately irresistible to Rachel Timmerman that night?

A   She said she thought I was extremely powerful looking for
     a man—for a white man or something like that is what she
     said. She was extremely drunk.

Gabrion insisted that the dog had been with them that night.
He named a list of witnesses at the card-playing party who had seen
it. Unfortunately the prosecutor had already checked with those presumed witnesses—at least the ones still alive. Not one of them had
seen Gabrion with a dog. The defendant grew shriller by the moment,
as if he could convince the jury by his own insistence.

Finally the prosecutor had to remind Gabrion of the basic way
a court works:

Q   Mr. Gabrion, this trial consists of testimony from that wit-
     ness stand and evidence that's been admitted. I'm asking
     you to tell us what witness testified there was a dog?
A   It was in the police report. That should be considered evi-
     dence and proof. But it isn't.
Q   But it isn't.
A   Well, that's your rule.
Q   You don't like our rules, do you?
A   Not when they're wrong, when they're purposely framing
     people for crimes they didn't commit.
Q   One of those rules permits you to subpoena witnesses. Were
     you aware of that rule?
A   Yeah. That just makes people show up in court. That's a
     good rule, probably, good law.
Q   You should make yourself avail—avail yourself of it.

For a long while it was difficult to tell exactly where the cross-
examination and the testimony were going. Gabrion changed directions so often the jurors could have gotten whiplash. Several times
the judge reminded him to answer the question. Then the prosecutor
slowly asserted control and steered the cross-examination back to the
murder of Rachel. This is where he wanted the defendant and most
certainly not in a maze of secondary issues. He began by referring to
an earlier witness.

Q Let me ask you this. Do you remember a witness telling us
that you told him the way to get rid of people is to bind them
in chicken wire, put chains around them and blocks and put
them in muck lakes; that he said that you said that multiple
times? Were you paying attention when he said that?

A I heard something of that nature. I heard his testimony was
similar in that—similar to what you're saying. But there's a
lot of differences.

Q I see. Rachel Timmerman was not bound in chicken wire,
was she?

A flurry of motions by the defense. The prosecutor picked up
the thread.

Q The way that you told your fourteen- or fifteen-year-old
neighbor that you'd get rid of bodies. Is that how you help
people find the truth and find the right way in their lives, by
telling them that?

A No, I give them a good job and I didn't kill Rachel Timmerman.

Q You didn't bind Rachel Timmerman in chicken wire, sir.
That's the difference; isn't that correct?

A Why would I take two blocks from my own sign and put it
on a girl and put her in a seventy degree lake knowing full
well she's gonna come to the surface?

Q When you did that, sir, you didn't know that she would
come to the surface, did you?

A Well, of course I would. The chicken wire is—

Q That's right. You've told us you would because you have
quite an interest in people being bound with blocks. You
were able to recite in your direct testimony—

A What?

Q —a number of instances of people being bound with
apparently more foresight and enough blocks. You're aware
of that, weren't you? You follow that closely, don't you?

A What, somebody being bound in blocks? Oh, you're talking
about the people I read about in the newspaper, you mean?

Q You seem to be somewhat of an expert in that field.

A The floaters that came to the top of the lakes and rivers
   because people didn't put enough blocks on 'em. There was
   a man who jumped off a bridge down here by the main post
   office. He had four blocks on and he came to the surface
   down by the Grand River in Grandville, okay.

Q Mr. Gabrion, the newspapers are full of people—

A Like that, right.

Q —who didn't use enough blocks, aren't they?

A Right. That's what I'm saying. I've read all these and I can
   put the dates down to them and everything. So why would
   I put two blocks on a 220 pound fat girl, seventy degrees,
   middle of the summer in warm water and throw her in a
   shallow lake? You know, that doesn't make any sense.

Q Mr. Gabrion, you're a smart man, but you made a mistake,
   didn't you?

A No, I didn't make a mistake. The killer made the mistake.
   He couldn't find the two blocks, so he took the two blocks
   from my sign and put them on the girl.

The prosecutor maneuvered back to the night of the murder.
Several earlier witnesses had testified about the bruises and abrasions
on Gabrion's face. One commented that she saw hair torn out.

Q And when you returned to the campsite on the Little
   Muskegon River and you saw, you had bruises on your face,
   you had scratches on your neck and you were missing hair.
   Rachel struggled, didn't she? Rachel scratched you, didn't
   she? Rachel tried to live, didn't she?

A Wrong.

Q She didn't try to live? She passively sat there while you
   bound her mouth and bound her eyes and bound her body
   and threw her in the lake? She didn't scratch?

A I didn't bind her at all.

Q She scratched you, didn't she?

A I didn't bind her at all. They bound her 'cause she kept
   talking and talking and talking. Eddie, Eddie bound her

because she kept talking and talking and talking to the police. She was a snitch.

When Tim heard these last few words, he involuntarily trembled. Whenever Rachel became emotional or wanted something very much, she repeated "please" three times, very rapidly, like "pleasepleaseplease."

Building on previous testimonies, the prosecutor turned suddenly to the boat itself. It was the necessary link between Oxford Lake, the Altona Christian bookstore and Gabrion's campground site where he had asked a camping neighbor to store the boat for him.

Davis, his face and voice tight and serious, continued.

Q On June 6, 1997, what numbers were you grinding off of your boat?

A It's illegal to take the numbers off of a boat in Michigan. There's 10,000 lakes, rivers and streams and a million boats. It's illegal to take the numbers off any of 'em. I was not taking any numbers off any aluminum boat. A metal grinder would eat a hole in an aluminum boat. It would not take the numbers off.

Q Well, what were you grinding off the boat?

A I wasn't grinding—oh, I had a steel brush taking the paint off to paint it. You paint the bottom blue so you can sneak up on the fish, blue and green.

There was a short pause in the courtroom. Then, perhaps envisioning all those fish staring up at the sky, a number of spectators began to chuckle. Mr. Davis pressed the point.

Q And the paint you were taking off just happened to be on the bow?

A On the bottom, right.

Q On the bow where people would put numbers?

A The numbers are not always on the bow to begin with. It's on the stern or the bow. I've owned probably fifty different aluminum boats, fishing boats.

Q Do you remember Chad Kwiat asking you where the numbers were on the boat?

A   Yes, sir.

Q   You got angry. You got angry at him and you particularly got angry at his wife, didn't you?

A   It never happened. That never happened.

Q   Should I add them to the long list of people who are lying about you?

A   Yeah.

Q   Okay.

A   Apparently.

Q   Did you get that grinder from your neighbor?

A   The grinder I got from him had a short in it and when you used it, it would give you a big jolt of electricity.

Q   So you used a different grinder?

A   It was a drill with a steel brush attachment that I used on the boat.

At 10:17 A.M., Judge Bell called for a short recess.

Chapter 18

A Murder Suspect Speaks

U pon return to the court, Mr. Mitchell voiced objections. Judge Bell quickly got to the point. "Okay. Back on record. Mr. Mitchell, you had something you wanted to place on the record?"

Mitchell nodded. "Yes, Your Honor. The Court may have noted that I was making several objections previously. I misspoke myself on one of the objections. I meant to say 404 (b), not 403 (b) and that was my objection to going too far afield in this case.

"We're getting—in our opinion, Mr. Davis is going too far in terms of facts and getting into areas that they had already told us previously that they did not intend to bring in. I realize it's cross-examination, but that is not a free warrant to go ahead with anything they want. They have to remain within the confines of this case and the relevance of this case and no more.

"So I object to anything regarding Ian Decker or Mr. Davis that would leave the impression with the jury that somehow this defendant is responsible for the disappearance of those people. Also Mr. Allen and those—we haven't gotten into that area, but who knows if we will at this point.

"I also wish to put on a continuing objection to Mr. Davis's argumentativeness. Mr. Davis is assuming facts not in evidence and the—his testimony—the testimonial nature of his questioning. Thank you."

Davis countered the blows and his voice rose with emotion. "As to the first objection, Your Honor, we intended to stay a long ways away from the disappearances of Wayne Davis, Bob Allen and Ian Decker. However, Mr. Gabrion chose to introduce that subject into this record, claiming that they are the keys to this—the—his innocence, if you will. I think that fair inquiry would allow me to go far, far further than I have gone. I have restrained myself in discussing the disappearance of Mr. Decker and Mr. Davis. I didn't open the subject.

"As to the facts—"

Judge Bell interrupted. "Okay. Let me go to that."

Davis nodded. "Yes."

Bell zeroed in. "I haven't heard anything yet that I thought was out of the bounds of relevancy either from that which has already been presented from the witnesses or that which has been inserted for the first time by Mr. Gabrion in this matter. 403 is probative—prejudicial versus probative— and I think so far has been probative and, obviously, anything in a criminal case is prejudicial. So the weighing obviously has to be done and I think the weighing is on the probative side. It is cross-examination.

"Now, I'm more concerned with the objection as to the allegation of either assuming facts that aren't yet in the evidence or assuming it in an argumentative fashion. I think there's some validity to that and I'm not trying to circumscribe you, Mr. Davis, nor am I telling you that you should not be vigorous. I think there were several questions that in fact were somewhat prompted by Mr. Gabrion.

"If the question's a yes or no—"

Gabrion was visibly agitated. "Say yes or no."

Bell frowned. "Is it daytime or nighttime, it's daytime. Just answer it. It moves along much quicker. It makes your task easier and it makes Mr. Davis' task easier and we all get done sooner if we do it that way. Otherwise, if you answer with a long narrative and open up a whole group of things, then you give Mr. Davis that much more ammunition to come back and question you."

Gabrion's tone was terse. "Okay."

Bell sought calm and to move on. "We all set on that?"

"Yeah," Gabrion said.

Bell nodded. "All right."

Davis said quietly, "Your Honor, the record should also reflect that I appreciate Mr. Mitchell and the Court's comments about the nature of the tone of my voice. I will try to restrain my true feelings to the extent possible.

"However, I should also say as to the questions themselves, I have asked not a single question that I don't have a good faith basis to ask and I am prepared and willing to put on the record at any time the good faith basis for every one of my questions. Mr. Gabrion can either deny or he can agree with my leading questions. The choice is his. I have a good faith basis to ask every one of them."

Bell was brisk. "Okay. We're all set?"

Mitchell nodded. "Yes, Your Honor, as long as I don't have to object anymore. I've objected to the continuing nature of this. I just think that having to get up every five minutes is not—is burdensome on the Court."

Bell interrupted. "Wait a minute. Make it very clear I'm not asking you to stay seated. If you think something is clearly impermissible or out of bounds, please say so. I certainly won't inhibit you in any way from doing that."

Mitchell sounded frustrated. "I'm having a hard time being heard, between Mr. Gabrion and Mr. Davis. My voice has to be raised to a decibel level beyond the norm."

Bell sighed. "All right."

"Thank you." Mitchell stated flatly.

"Understood." Bell nodded. "We'll let the jury—have the jury come back in and we'll continue."

The jury entered the room at 10:39 A.M.

Bell stated. "You may be seated, ladies and gentlemen. We're continuing with the cross-examination of Mr. Gabrion. Mr. Davis, you may continue."

Once again Davis took up his passionate arguments:

Q Mr. Gabrion, we were on June 6, 1997. Can we at least agree that at 4:00 A.M. on that day you were grinding something off your boat?

A   I heard testimony that—

Q   We all heard the testimony, sir. Can we—

A   It was—

Q   Can we agree that you were grinding something off your boat that day or do you dispute that?

A   That's what I read in my statement—

Q   Mr. Gabrion, my question.

A   Okay.

Q   Were you grinding something off of your boat at 4:00 A.M. on the morning of June 6?

A   Maybe.

Q   I'll take a maybe. We also heard that in addition to grinding things off your boat that you were loading objects out of your boat and then back in, objects such as a chain and three blocks. Mr. Gabrion, we know where two of the blocks are. Tell us, please, where the third block went.

A   The date was June 4 according to the witness, not June 6.

Q   It was June 6, sir. But my question is not about the date.

A   Well, it makes a lot of difference.

Q   It was June 6, sir.

A   On or about June 2—

" Excuse me." Bell said.

Davis turned abruptly. "Mr. Gabrion—"

Bell's voice hardened. "Answer the question."

Davis continued:

Q   Mr. Gabrion, the witness testified that on the morning of June 6, 1997, he was awoken about 4:00 A.M., heard you grind—heard you drag a boat across gravel, take the boat into the garage and grind something off it at the bow. Before you did that you took three blocks and a chain out of the boat, later put them back in and took off in your pickup truck. My simple question to you, sir, is we know where two of the blocks are. They're government Exhibits 17 and 14. Where is the third block? What did you do with it?

A There was no three blocks in my boat, period, ever.

Q Just two.

A Never, no blocks in my boat.

Q No blocks?

A No blocks.

Q Mr. Gabrion, that boat, those blocks and that chain went to the shores of Oxford Lake. Do you recall seeing Kay Haveman there and asking her about the fishing?

A Incorrect.

Q You don't recall that? She wasn't there?

A I wasn't there. It was Eddie and Ian Decker.

Q They were there?

A Correct.

Q And they told you about Kay Haveman?

A Incorrect.

Q They told you about Roseanne Schuette?

A Roseanne Schuette was never there, probably.

Q Probably? You didn't see her?

A No.

Q She was still at—she stayed in the car. You didn't see Roseanne Schuette; is that correct?

A I didn't see her 'cause she wasn't there.

Q You only saw Kay Haveman. But now you're telling us that it was somebody else who saw them?

A I never saw either one of them. I said they told me that they seen them at the lake.

Q And also, sir, Rachel Timmerman was on the shores of Oxford Lake on that day alive, unbound. My question to you, sir, is did you suffocate her on the shore or did you take her into the lake and drown her?

A I never killed Rachel Timmerman, period. I didn't have anything to do with it. I was nowheres near around when she expired either. I know Fast Eddie and Ian Decker were and that Eddie had planned on killing her. I know exactly where Eddie's cabin is if you care to know where that is so you can go—

Q   Remember telling—

A   —check it out.

Q   After you used the boat to take Rachel out into that lake,
    after you bound her mouth because she was talking too
    much, after you bound her eyes and after you threw her into
    the lake alive and watched the bubbles rising, you took that
    boat someplace where you didn't think it could be found,
    didn't you?

A   You're trying to say that I took the boat to my Christian
    bookstore in the broad—with a neighbor watching me and
    now you're trying to say I hid the boat, too?

Q   You took the boat on the afternoon of June 6 to the Little
    Mus—

A   There was supposed to be a yes or no answer to that?

Q   You took the boat—why don't you let me finish. You took
    the boat on the afternoon of June 6 to the campsite of Jenny
    Bingham on the Little Muskegon River, didn't you?

A   No, I didn't.

Q   And you didn't want that boat at your campsite just a tad
    up the river —

A   I didn't have a campsite on the Little Muskegon River.

Q   After three weeks of storing your boat on the Little
    Muskegon River, you thought you'd gotten away with it,
    didn't you?

A   I always owned a boat. I told you I've always had a fishing
    boat.

Q   Is there something—

A   So why should I be hiding a boat?

Q   Is there something about my question you don't under-
    stand? After three weeks—

A   I never hid any boat. That's the thing I don't understand
    about the question.

Q   After three—I didn't even talk about hiding the boat. I asked
    you, after three weeks you thought you had gotten rid of—
    gotten away with it, didn't you? No body surfaced, did it?

A   No, I don't—I never thought that I ever did any murder, so why would I think that I had gotten away with it?

Q   What? Do you think what you did to Rachel Timmerman is justified and not murder?

A   No, I don't think what you did to her is justifiable at all. I think what you did is you forced her to testify in a case against a person, lying in a case which forced her to become a victim to a crime, you and these prosecutors and the police. You know what you did, she knows what you did, and you're gonna pay for it at God's judgment, period.

Q   She got what she deserved, didn't she?

A   From you. From you.

Q   Rachel Timmerman got what she deserved, didn't she, and haven't you told that to a lot of people?

A   Wrong.

Q   And after three weeks you thought you had pulled it off. You thought you had gotten away with it. And then you thought, "Why let a good boat go to waste? Might as well— why leave it—"

Mitchell rose. "Objection. Is there a question mark at the end of this two-sentence—"

Bell ruled quickly. "Sustained. Rephrase."

Q   Did you think, did you think, "Why let a good boat go to waste?"

A   What boat are you talking about, sir?

As Mr. Davis intensified the pressure and focus of his questions, Gabrion grew increasingly disturbed and angry. He had chosen to take the stand. Nearly every person in the courtroom was wondering why. The prosecutor's questions consistently narrowed. The tangled fabric of Gabrion's lies was being dismantled.

Q   The boat that you used to take Rachel Timmerman into the middle of the south portion of Oxford Lake alive, the boat that you used to murder Rachel Timmerman, that boat. The boat that you stored away from your campsite on the Little Muskegon River, the boat that you ground the numbers off of, the boat that you put two and maybe three cement blocks and chain in that boat.

Gabrion wouldn't let it go. "Is there more than one boat involved in this case?"

Q You asked me, sir, what boat. I told you what boat. You thought at the end of three weeks you might as well sell the boat, didn't you?

A Where did I sell it at, then, if you're so know-it-all?

Q This is just—

"Excuse me, excuse me. Answer the question yes or no if you can." Bell ordered.

Gabrion stammered. "Can you repeat the question, please?"

Q Yes. After three weeks, sir, you thought you'd gotten away with it. You thought, "Why let a good boat go to waste" and you tried to sell it, didn't you? You brought it back to your store, the store, your home in Altona and put a for sale sign on the boat, the murder weapon, didn't you?

A Incorrect.

Q You didn't put that boat for sale?

A Right.

Q The Kwiats [neighbors] weren't driving down Five Mile Road and saw a "for sale" sign and stopped to talk to you about it?

A About some boat, but not *the boat*.

Time halted for a beat as Gabrion tried to recover. Every eye met every other eye, wordlessly communicating, "What did we just hear?"

Q The boat that you used to kill Rachel Timmerman was a different boat?

A There was no boat used to kill Rachel Timmerman to begin with.

Q How did her body get out in the middle of the lake?

A By you and that state police helicopter.

Q And where did I and that state police helicopter remove her body from, if you know and you apparently do?

A From the north side of the private lake where you put the blocks on her. Where do you think? Where you and Tim Timmerman put the two cinder blocks on her.

Q How many blocks were on her before that?

A The two that you put on her.

Q How many before—you're claiming that I put two blocks on her?

A That's correct.

Q With Mr. Timmerman's help.

A That's right. Then you used a state police helicopter to put her in the water.

Q Did I first put her in the north end of the lake?

A Right over there where you put your thick fat finger.

Q I put my fat finger on the north end of the lake—

A That's right, right there. See where the island is? That's where you dropped her.

Q I dropped her here?

A No, that's—that's where the—if you take your pointer down to the, down towards you, towards your waist, down towards your waist. Move your pointer towards your waist from where you had it originally. Take the pointer and move it from—you're just doing it on purpose because you don't want to know exactly where the cabin is or what actually happened on purpose.

Q Mr. Gabrion, when I and Tim Timmerman dropped her at some portion of the north end of the lake, how many blocks did we put on her?

A   You put two of them, two blocks in the woods and then later
    on you picked her up with a helicopter and put her right out
    there in the water.

Q   Were you watching from someplace?

A   Yeah, from where God always watches people like you.

Q   You, God, were watching from someplace?

A   That's right.

Q   Where?

A   You know where.

Q   Tell me.

A   You know where.

Q   Tell me.

A   You know where.

Q   That's not an answer.

A   Yes, it is.

Q   You're referring to yourself as God?

A   I'm referring to myself as what I am and who I am.

Q   God?

A   What I am and who I am.

Q   Is that with a capital "G"?

A   It's not starting with a "P" like "prosecutors," that's for sure.

Q   Capital "G". When you portray yourself as God, do you ever
    draw pictures of yourself as God?

A   No. Do you?

Q   Do you put three eyes on your God?

A   No.

Q   Do you call yourself Azza?

Mitchell's voice rose again. "Your Honor, excuse me. I object
to this."

"Sustained. Sustained," Bell retorted.

The spectators' eyes were riveted on the witness. The three-eyed
god derived from a portrait of his presumably aborted daughter that
Gabrion drew in his correspondence to Tim. The name he gave to this
daughter was Azza. The prosecutor took advantage and steered the

questions in a slightly different direction, designed to further test Gabrion's credibility.

Q Did you ask your mother to send your brother over to the house in Altona to clean it out to get rid of evidence?

A I'm not sure if I ever did that. They really cleaned it out good. They took the chain saws and a whole bunch of stuff, so if I did, they did their job well.

Q Did you accuse anyone of planting evidence at the Altona store?

A Well, they—

Q Did you accuse anyone of planting evidence, yes or no?

A Yes, because they did.

Q You accused your mother of planting evidence, didn't you?

A Maybe.

Q And if you had written that in a letter, "my mom apparently planted it," referring to evidence, you wouldn't disagree with me, would you?

A I can't disagree or agree with it because I can't see it.

"May I?" Davis said turning to the judge. The document was then provided to the witness.

Q Number 3.

A That's the one that Sergeant Miller left on the table, *The Perfect Victim*, about a girl being held underground.

Q Yes, the book *The Perfect Victim*. In a letter—

A Right. My mom left it in the Christian bookstore.

Q In a letter to Kim VerHage, Shannon's grandmother, you accused your mother of planting that book, didn't you?

A Did you hear what I—I just said *The Perfect Victim* book was left at the Christian bookstore by my mother.

Q "My mom apparently planted it at my Christian bookstore."

A Well, you call it what you want. It's planted or left there.

Q It's not what I call it, sir. It's what you wrote to the grandmother of Shannon.

A   Tomato to-mah-to.

Q   In addition, sir, middle of July 1997, you were burning evidence in your stove on Altona Street, weren't you?

A   (Laughing) No.

Q   You think that one's funny, too?

A   Because it's ridiculous. I had a garbage burner in the yard. Why would I burn garbage inside my house? And I was actually in Fort Wayne, Indiana, and using the phone making long distance calls on that day.

Q   Is that where you were hiding?

A   Timothy VerHey [U.S. Prosecuting Attorney] represented the prosecution in a case where I was using the phone from Fort Wayne, Indiana, from a motel in a social security fraud case, same day, July 14.

Q   And, sir, the purpose—

Irritated, Gabrion made hand motions.

A   Thank you.

Q   Are we waving at one another?

A   (Laughing) No.

Q   And, sir, *The Perfect Victim* was not the only evidence found at your house. In fact, sir, you left the keys that fit the locks on Rachel Timmerman, didn't you?

A   Those chains are smaller than the ones that the dude said I put in my boat, so how would the small chains get onto Rachel Timmerman?

Q   You're quibbling, sir. We're talking about your keys fitting the locks on the chains—

A   They're not my keys or my locks.

Q   Mr. Gabrion, where did you learn how to get the information that you got from Ed White [a driver's license used by Gabrion in New York] to get his identification? That was pretty slick. How did you learn to do that?

A   I learned to do that when I was a kid. I been using false identification all my life. CIA trained me to do it.

Q The CIA trained you?

A That's right. I took all the training for the CIA, the SEALS, the Rangers, how to use false identity.

Q I have in a letter that you claimed in 1972 and '73, the winter and the spring, that you worked covertly as a CIA agent, no heroic deeds, just low personal risk stuff in Tucson, Arizona. Is that your CIA training?

A That was for the DEA, for busting five pounds of cocaine for the DEA.

Q That must have been a misprint when you wrote it, then. You wrote CIA. You also claim that you were out arresting bank robbers in 1974. Do you remember that?

A Yeah. Strong-arm rob—strong-arm citizen arrest, bank robber, gun-wielding. He had a gun in his hand.

With Gabrion's lack of credibility well established at this juncture, the prosecutor began to list the people that Gabrion had accused of the crime of murdering Rachel, attacking the SODDI defense. It grew to an extensive list. Gabrion had accused twelve people, either directly responsible for the crime or closely associated with it. Twelve names. Tension increased with each one. Davis systematically destroyed the credibility of each charge. Gabrion was visibly upset, his answers increasingly strident. Finally it boiled over.

The hot point occurred when Davis questioned Gabrion about Shannon. Davis referred to a letter Gabrion had written to Detective Miller, in which he stated that he knew the whereabouts of Shannon.

A That's not the words I used. Why do you continually put words in people's mouths that aren't there? I said that he could be a hero by doing the right thing. He wasn't, so he isn't.

Q In fact—

A He's the heel.

Q In fact, sir, at that same time—

A Just like you.

Q At that same time when you were holding out that carrot to all these people, at that same time you were telling an earlier witness "they'll never find Shannon", didn't you?

A   You're talking about a bank robber, dude.

Q   Didn't you?

A   You're talking about a multiple bank robber who stalked a woman in Lansing who's doing life in prison for threatening to kill the president.

Q   Didn't you also say that "she's not in the lake because I didn't drown her"? You killed her another way, didn't you?

A   I don't know what you're talking about now.

Q   Shannon is not in the lake because you didn't drown her. How did you kill Shannon?

A   Shannon's not dead.

Q   And lastly, sir, you heard an earlier witness testify that you told him that you killed the baby because there was no place to put it. Was that your motive to kill Shannon, because there was no place to put it?

A   Is that the character of the witnesses you're going to keep repeating the testimony of?

Q   You won't answer that question, will you? Will you, sir? You won't tell this jury, you won't tell anyone that the reason that you killed Shannon was because you had no place to put her?

A   You're a liar.

Q   That's the reason that you—

A   What more can I say? You're just lying and you keep lying and lying and lying, so what can I say?

Q   Is that the reason—

A   Except that you're lying.

Q   Is that the reason—

A   Yes, you're lying.

Q   Is that the reason you killed an eleven-month-old, because you had no place to put her?

A   Incorrect.

Q   Then why did you kill her?

A   I didn't kill her.

Q   Why did you kill her mother?

A   I didn't kill either one of them, never. Thou shalt not kill.
Q   You killed her mother—
A   Two wrongs do not make a right. Thou shalt not kill.
Q   You killed her mother—
A   Thou shalt not kill.
Q   Be quiet. You killed her mother—

The defense objected. "Neither is on course here."
Gabrion was furious. "Make me."
Mitchell tried to keep his strong convictions bottled to be quiet, firm. "That question was answered."
Bell moved it along. "Next question, please."

Q   You killed her mother because she was going to testify against you, didn't you?
A   Incorrect.
Q   And you put her body—
A   I never killed either one of them. It's thou shalt not kill. Two wrongs don't make a right.
Q   And you put her body—
A   Live it, learn it.
Q   And you took her alive with tape across her mouth because she was talking too much—
A   No, someone else did that.
Q   And you put her in Oxford Lake and watched the bubbles rise, didn't you?
A   Wrong.
Q   And you enjoyed seeing the bubbles rise, didn't you?
A   No. Never happened.

Davis said forcefully. "I have nothing further."
The damage had been done. There was little the defense could do. One could imagine a loud flushing sound as their case went down the toilet.

The defense had additional witnesses the following Monday, March 4, before the close of the trial. The first was an FBI fingerprint expert who testified that "I found no latent prints on the duct tape removed from Rachel Timmerman. I found no latent prints on the duct tape from the Hungerford Lake campsite."

He also examined ten sheets of paper with Rachel's known handwriting. On these, sixty-two prints were identified, with thirty-nine identified as Rachel's. It was noted that the fingerprint treatment affected the color of the paper, turning it grey or purple.

Don Davis cross-examined: "Isn't the chance of finding fingerprints substantially lessened if the person is wearing gloves?"

The next witness worked for the padlock company in Wisconsin. Mr. Larry Fields explained the mathematics of producing locks and keys. The locks Mr. Gabrion used on Rachel were inexpensive. The serial number showed that they were produced in 1993. That year the padlock company produced 1,700,000 locks. Defense attorney Stebbins churned some numbers: from 1993 to 1997 thirteen million of these locks were produced, with only forty different keys. "Doesn't that mean that there are well over three hundred thousand keys out there that will open this lock?"

"Yes, sir, that's correct."

Tim VerHey queried, "Mr. Fields, your company sells security, doesn't it?"

"Yes, sir," the witness replied.

"Isn't the mathematical chance of any key fitting any lock less than 4 percent?"

"Yes, sir," he said matter-of-factly.

"I have no further questions for this witness."

Mitchell said quietly, "Your Honor, the defense rests."

Judge Bell informed the courtroom, "The proofs are concluded."

Chapter 19

Wrapping Up

The courtroom was so packed Tim almost lost his seat for the closing arguments.

Articulate, serious and committed to his case, prosecutor VerHey began forcefully. "When we began this trial we posed three questions. First, whose body was it? We now know that Rachel Timmerman's body was discovered floating on Oxford Lake.

"The second question was who killed her? You now know the answer. Marvin Gabrion murdered Rachel Timmerman. He handcuffed her, bound her with chains, locks and cinder blocks. But he still wasn't finished with her. He covered her eyes and mouth with duct tape. Marvin Gabrion put Rachel Timmerman in a boat, rowed the boat out into the lake. Then Marvin Gabrion murdered Rachel Timmerman: he put her in the murky waters of Oxford Lake and she died.

"The third question was why was she killed? You know the answer." VerHey displayed the large picture of Rachel and Shannon. "Mr. Gabrion murdered this young mother because he did not want to face a rape charge.

"The government has proved beyond any shadow of doubt that Marvin Gabrion murdered Rachel Timmerman. He acted with malice and forethought. Marvin Gabrion deliberately murdered Rachel Timmerman.

"It is now up to you to decide. Using your common sense of everyday experience is not just okay, we insist on it.

"You have seen evidence that the defendant, Marvin Gabrion, is one person that benefitted from Rachel Timmerman's death. You have seen the facsimile that Marvin Gabrion sent to Detective Sergeant Babcock about the rape. The Newaygo County prosecutor told you that she charged Marvin Gabrion with raping Rachel Timmerman. The Newaygo County sheriff's department arrested Marvin Gabrion for the rape on January 20, 1997. Marvin Gabrion made bond on February 3, 1997.

"Rachel Timmerman wasn't perfect; in fact, she was in jail for a probation violation from January 8 to May 5. This explains why Marvin Gabrion's rape case took such an unusual path through the Newaygo County courts. This did two things: it delayed the trial and kept Rachel Timmerman from testifying under oath about the rape charge. The rape charge was dismissed on June 25. That is enough evidence right there, but there is more.

"Rachel Timmerman's father, Tim Timmerman, received two letters. Chrystal Roach received a letter, written by Rachel Timmerman. Why did Rachel follow the script, word for word, of what the defendant says happened? Why do the pre-stamped envelopes matter? Because Marvin Gabrion himself was writing them. We showed you that he used the same pre-stamped envelopes to mail his letters in June of 1997. Marvin Gabrion testified that he knew where to get the envelopes. These letters show all by themselves that Marvin Gabrion had Rachel Timmerman in his clutches. The letters are enough evidence for you to find Marvin Gabrion guilty of murdering Rachel Timmerman, but there is more."

His strong measured words conveyed his convictions. "Marvin Gabrion drew a map of Oxford Lake: body found here, one of three. Marvin Gabrion told the jail trustee that he drew that map. Jenny Bingham told you that she saw the defendant the evening of June 6. She testified that Marvin Gabrion looked different. She said the defendant told her that he'd got in a fight. She also told you that on this warm summer evening, Marvin Gabrion was wearing gloves."

Gabrion seemed to be paying close attention now. He was rubbing his chin, giving many in the courtroom a one finger salute and animatedly looking about the crowded courtroom.

"Sam Franklin testified about what he saw Marvin Gabrion doing with the boat at four o'clock in the morning of June 6. Ladies and gentlemen, Marvin Gabrion's actions with the boat are enough to convict him of murdering Rachel Timmerman. But there is more.

"When Marvin Gabrion was arrested near the post office, in Sherman, New York, he was using the name of Robert Allen. Marvin Gabrion had a valid driver's license in that name. In Marvin Gabrion's wallet was another driver's license. This one was from Virginia, in the name of Ed White. This piece of proof shows you that Marvin Gabrion is guilty. The telephone calls and conversations that Rachel Timmerman had telling people about his threats are enough to convict Marvin Gabrion of murder."

Gabrion was now digging somewhere deep in his mouth. It appeared he had found a hair and he was using it for good oral hygiene. He was flossing vigorously. Many assumed he was trying to appear nonchalant for the jury.

"On Friday Marvin Gabrion said that you could call it a date rape. Remember the testimony of John Cornelius. He said that Marvin Gabrion told him how he got rid of his girlfriend. This alone is enough to convict the defendant of murdering Rachel Timmerman."

Gabrion was sneezing loudly, throwing tissues on the floor. Judge Bell, high up on his bench, issued stern looks his way.

"None of us will ever think about blocks the same way again. We have analyzed paint on blocks found on Rachel Timmerman's body. We found blocks with paint on them in Marvin Gabrion's yard. We even found the spray can the paint came from. The FBI paint expert told you that he can't tell them apart chemically. These blocks had tar on them. The FBI expert can't tell them apart chemically. The defendant admits the blocks on the sign are his. The blocks alone are enough to convict Marvin Gabrion of murdering Rachel Timmerman, but there is more.

"The keys found in Marvin Gabrion's residence open the locks found on Rachel Timmerman. The keys are enough to convict the defendant of murdering Rachel Timmerman.

"Putting all of these pieces together, there is no doubt. Put them all together, the letters, the blocks, the chain. The keys and the locks.

The boat, the handcuffs and the duct tape. Ladies and gentlemen, there is no doubt."

At this point, Marvin Gabrion was smiling brightly, looking about the courtroom. Tim thought he was putting on a pretty brave front, while knowing inside he was screwed.

"Ladies and gentlemen, now you know what the facts are. We, the government of the United States, are asking you to return a verdict of guilty."

After lunch Paul Mitchell, the defense attorney, seemed to Tim to be visibly nervous, moving his papers around this way and that. He checked his water supply and adjusted the placement of his cup. Finally he spoke.

"Good afternoon, ladies and gentlemen. Quite frankly there are some very real problems with this case. There is a total lack of direct evidence connecting my client to this crime. No scientific evidence whatsoever connects my client at all with Rachel Timmerman. There is no evidence beyond reasonable doubt where it occurred.

"We have heard a collection of people tell conflicting stories about what they think they saw around Oxford Lake. We have Amy Kwiat who said it was a black, full- size pickup. She said the interaction lasted two or three minutes and her husband said it was almost instantaneous. She didn't realize the identity of the man in the truck until after Mr. Gabrion was arrested in Buffalo. The TV news had pictures of my client covered with a coat. Later the television news produced a picture and then she recognized Mr. Gabrion as the man driving the truck months before.

"Kay Haveman can be totally disregarded. On November 27, she was interviewed by the police. She told them she didn't see anything. She said she was at the lake for a breath of fresh air. She is confused about what vehicle she was driving. The bugs weren't bothering her.

"I believe this last-minute witness brought in to bolster this testimony is not believable. She claims to have heard nothing in the news about a body in a lake two miles from her home. The witnesses are simply parroting one another. We say that what the government calls valuable information is unbelievable in a capital murder case.

"Chad Kwiat saw a full-size black pickup truck. He said that he went to Oxford Lake five or six times a year. You've heard time and time again that my client had a small red pickup. Isn't it likely that these witnesses saw him at Oxford Lake?

"Sam Franklin's testimony must be disregarded. There is a complete lack of detail to the first police officers responding to his complaint. It was too dark to identify all of those items. He is simply embellishing his testimony. Use your common sense.

"John Cornelius, a sad person. Why would Mr. Gabrion come out of a store and tell his story to this man? He's a paranoid schizophrenic. Is that the kind of witness you want to hang your hat on in a capital murder case?"

Mitchell went on to list several other witnesses he deemed as unreliable. He then turned the jury's attention to evidentiary matters, again calling their impact into question.

"We've heard a lot of testimony about boats. Vee bottom, flat bottom, silver color or dark. The government has not shown us any boat.

"There are very clear problems with this case; there are inconsistencies. The physical evidence: there are numerous items, yet there are no fingerprints. There is not one hair. No scientific evidence tying the defendant to the victim. There was one hair on Rachel Timmerman, but no DNA testing was done on this hair. No duct tape from Rachel's body matches any duct tape found anywhere else.

"The possibility of another key fitting the locks is out there. It is reasonable to doubt. I wonder if likely in your mind is beyond reasonable doubt. The locks are a red herring."

Mitchell walked over to the map of Oxford Lake. "The pink areas are the boundaries of the National Forest. Mr. Gabrion is not confined by these boundaries." Tim wondered what that meant.

"I want to remind you that there was no mud found in the body. There is no proof beyond a reasonable doubt. There is only the likelihood. I'll leave it up to you."

Tim VerHey, a maestro of the courtroom, finished up for the government. "You have heard Mr. Mitchell attack the credibility of our witnesses. Last Friday I kept track of people Marvin Gabrion accused of drowning Rachel Timmerman."

He went on to specify the list. Next he defended the integrity of the witnesses, who had testified despite their fear.

"When judging the credibility of the witnesses, ask yourself about Sergeant Miller's credibility," he added.

"Kay Haveman didn't want to testify, but she did."
Mr. Mitchell rose and objected. Judge Bell stared him into sitting down.

Tim VerHey continued talking about Kay Haveman. "Should she have been frightened, based on what you've heard?

"The defendant, Marvin Gabrion, told you that Ian Decker and Fast Eddie helped Rachel Timmerman commit suicide. Then they delivered a six-page suicide note to Marvin Gabrion. Is this credibility?

"I would like to remind you of the forensic pathologist, Dr. Cohle's testimony. He concluded that Rachel Timmerman was most likely thrown into Oxford Lake alive.

"Mr. Gabrion taunted Rachel Timmerman's family. He sent letters to her father, Tim Timmerman, and to Shannon's grandmother, Kim VerHage."

Mr. Mitchell objected that it was beyond the scope of redirect. Judge Bell ordered Mr. VerHey to wrap it up. By then Gabrion had slid his chair all the way to the far end of the table, distancing himself as far as possible from his lawyers and the jury.

Tim VerHey did wrap it up. "Ladies and gentlemen of the jury, this has been a difficult case. We have been dealing with a sadistic, cruel individual. This man did intentionally, in cold blood and against our law murder Rachel Timmerman. You know who is guilty. Find the defendant guilty."

Judge Bell gave final instructions to the jury and sequestered them for the weekend. It extended into Monday. Then into Tuesday. At ten o'clock on Tuesday, March 5, 2002, Tim and Lyn were downstairs at the courthouse, trying to relax. One of the marshals found them and told them to head for the courtroom.

"Do we have a verdict?" Tim asked.

"Something's happening. You better get up there."

The courtroom remained locked until all arrived. The marshal asked Tim to identify family members. They entered first.

Marvin Gabrion sat at the defense table, still trying to look defiant. He had penned "AZZA" across his forehead. To the spectators, he seemed oddly deflated.

"Ladies and gentlemen of the jury, have you reached a decision in this matter?"

Not a sound in the courtroom.

The jury foreman stood and replied, "Yes we have, Your Honor."

Tim's adrenaline rushed like someone entering combat. Not knowing from which direction the attack will come. Hyper-alert, fearing the worst.

The jury foreman read the decision. "Guilty."

The jurors were polled. Twelve times "guilty" fell into the silence. At a minimum, life behind bars with no parole.

When the verdict was read, Tim simply felt limp, trying to find a zone of neutral buoyancy. He penned just three words in his notebook: "What a relief."

Chapter 20

The Monster Exposed

A prosecuting attorney works like an engineer, a construction expert. He attempts to take blocks of evidence presented during the trial, link them and then cement them together in a concrete tower called "Beyond a Reasonable Doubt."

On the other hand, the defense attorney attempts to expose any weak links or cracks in the mortar. Some other dude did or could have done the deed. Too much doubt to convict.

Once the verdict is handed down, in this case a unanimous guilty verdict, the strategy changes dramatically in the sentencing phase. Some people, like Marvin Gabrion for example, believe that guilt is still an issue of discussion. It isn't. Both prosecution and defense accept the jury's decision. Yet each side has its own strategy.

The prosecution approaches this phase by revealing the guilty party's character through select witnesses and events. The defendant's attorneys work in the sentencing phase to create some sympathy in the minds of the jurors by demonstrating mitigating circumstances.

Gabrion's lead attorney and co-counsel argued for life in prison because a brain disorder had driven him to kill Rachel Timmerman. Where had the brain disorder come from? Before the trial, Gabrion's mother had claimed it followed a motorcycle accident; when broached in court it was listed as the result of an automobile accident. The second factor was growing up in a dysfunctional home. The third factor was his use of drugs, beginning with sniffing glue as a teenager and moving to hard drugs as an adult. According to the defense, all these factors rendered Gabrion incapable of making rational judgments. Or, in other words, they made him kill Rachel Timmerman.

In many respects, the sentencing phase was the most shocking of the trial, both for the actions of the defendant and the information brought before the jury regarding his character. Many of the restraints of the guilt phase disappeared. Witnesses could testify to unpleasant, even hideous experiences with Gabrion. A more powerful furor, however, arose from the possible penalties that could be decided by the jury. Here again the case drew national attention. Since the crime had been committed on federal property and was tried in federal court, the death penalty could be decided. If Michigan law had been followed, the maximum penalty was life in prison without parole.

Michigan outlawed the death penalty in 1846, only nine years after achieving statehood. The only exception was "treason against the state." Certain federal crimes, however, override state statutes, regardless of the state in which they occur. Thus, the last execution in Michigan was in 1938, in the case of a gunshot from a botched bank robbery striking and killing a bystander. The defendant was hanged on July 8, 1938.

Advocates of both sides of the death penalty rallied to their perspective bandwagons. In this case, though, the jurors had the clear and succinct guideline delivered by Judge Bell from the relevant federal statutes.

On Tuesday, March 5, 2002, the sentencing phase opened. Prior to the jury's entrance, the defense counsel drew the court's attention to a motion it had filed:

"Your Honor, I filed a motion to limit victim impact statements. Victim impact weighs heavily with the jury. We must respect Mr. Gabrion's right to a fair trial."

The matter would never fly. As the prosecuting attorney put it: "Shouldn't these people be allowed to tell the jury about how the loss of Rachel Timmerman has impacted their lives?"

The jury entered the courtroom at precisely 9:30. Judge Bell cautioned, "It is imperative that you follow and apply the law." Then he delivered the death penalty guidelines, should that be the decision. These guidelines had been drafted by United States attorney Phillip J. Green and prosecuting assistant attorneys Timothy VerHey and Donald Davis. They were then submitted to the office of John Ashcroft, Attorney General of the United States, and prepared for trial. They were now delivered to the jury:

Amended Death Penalty Notice

Phillip J. Green, United States Attorney for the Western District of Michigan, joined by Timothy VerHey, and Donald A. Davis, Assistant United States Attorneys, notifies the Court and the defendant pursuant to 18 U.S.C. §3593(a) that the United States believes the circumstances of the offense charged in the indictment are such that, in the event of a conviction, a sentence of death is justified under Chapter 228 (Sections 3591 through 3598) of Title 18 of the United States Code.

The government proposes to prove the following factors as justifying a sentence of death.

Statutory Proportionality Factor Enumerated Under 18 U.S.C. §3591(a)(2).

Intentional Killing. The defendant intentionally killed the victim, Rachel Timmerman. 18 U.S.C. §3591(a)(2)(A).

Statutory Aggravating Factors Enumerated Under 18 U.S.C. §3592(c).

Heinous, Cruel, or Depraved Manner of Committing Offense. The defendant committed the offense in an especially heinous, cruel, and depraved manner in that it involved torture or serious physical abuse to Rachel Timmerman. 18 U.S.C. §3592(c)(6).

Substantial Planning and Premeditation. The defendant committed the offense and caused the death of Rachel Timmerman after substantial planning and premeditation. 18 U.S.C. §3592(c)(9).

Other, Non-Statutory, Aggravating Factors Enumerated Under 18 U.S.C. §§3592(c) and 3593(a)(2).

Future Dangerousness of the Defendant. The defendant is likely to commit criminal acts of violence in the future which would be a continuing and serious threat to the lives and safety of others. In addition to the capital offense charged in the indictment, and the statutory and non-statutory aggravating factors alleged in this Amended Notice, this factor is supported by the following:

A continuing pattern of violent conduct against others.

A continuing pattern of threatening violent conduct against others.

Claims and admissions by the defendant relating to violent acts committed by him in the past, and violent acts planned in the future.

The risk that the defendant will escape from custody.

See, Simmons v. South Carolina, 512 U.S. 154, 2193 (1994).

Victim Impact Evidence. The defendant caused injury and loss to the victim, Rachel Timmerman, and her family. The personal characteristics of Rachel Timmerman and her uniqueness as an individual human being were such that her death has resulted in a loss to society, and has caused injury and loss to her family. 18 U.S.C. §3593(a)(2); Payne v. Tennessee, 501 U.S. 808 (1991).

Death or Disappearance of Shannon VerHage. In addition to causing the death of Rachel Timmerman, the defendant caused the death or disappearance of Rachel Timmerman's infant daughter, Shannon VerHage.

Obstruction of Justice. The defendant committed the offense with the intent to prevent Rachel Timmerman from, and retaliate against her for, providing assistance to law enforcement authorities in regard to the investigation and prosecution of another offense. See, United States v. Edelin, 134 F. Supp. 2d 59, 77 (D.D.C. 2001).

For their final deliberations, the jury received yes or no forms for both statutory aggravating factors and also mitigating factors. Since the guilty verdict had already been passed, the mitigating factors were headed by careful instructions:

Instructions: For each of the following mitigating factors, indicate, in the space provided, the number of jurors who have found the existence of that mitigating factor to be proven by a preponderance of the evidence.

A finding with respect to a mitigating factor may be made by one or more of the members of the jury, and any member of the jury who finds the existence of a mitigating factor may consider such a factor established in considering whether or not a sentence of death shall be imposed, regardless of the number of other jurors who agree that the factor has been established.

Responses to the twelve mitigating factors varied widely under the terms of "preponderance of evidence." For example the jury unanimously found: "Defendant has features of several personality disorders, including histrionic personality disorder, narcissistic personality disorder and borderline personality disorder." This very point, well established during the trial, spoke to the stipulation of the death penalty that the defendant was a clear and present danger to others.

On the other hand, not a single juror responded to the point: "Defendant committed the offense under severe mental or emotional disturbance." This was probably primarily because the guilty verdict had established that the murder had been a premeditated act.

Marvin Gabrion shuffled into the courtroom. He wore a new pose that day. Usually sneering and glaring at the spectators, that day he looked around with a superior smile. He seemed to convey the attitude of being above all this nonsense of small-minded folks. The marshals seated him next to his co-counsels, Mitchell and Stebbins.

Don Davis made his opening statement for the prosecution. "Ladies and gentlemen of the jury, you have both an opportunity and a responsibility. We don't undertake this task lightly. The government has very specific penalty phase procedures. The age of the defendant is a factor; they must be over eighteen. Mr. Gabrion is forty-eight.

"The government will prove that Marvin Gabrion murdered Rachel Timmerman after substantial planning and premeditation."

Gabrion yawned loudly and grinned as Don Davis stared him down.

"The government will prove that Marvin Gabrion did murder Rachel Timmerman in a heinous, cruel and depraved manner. The government will prove that Marvin Gabrion will be dangerous in the future."

Davis showed the photograph from the trial book of Rachel's recovered body. Tim felt his insides recoil with anger and nausea.

"It is no theory that what happened to Rachel Timmerman was for refusing to be raped in silence.

"Wayne Davis helped Elaine Gabrion make bond for Marvin Gabrion on February 3. On February 13 Wayne had to go to jail on a drinking offense. He never made it. He was last seen alive in the company of Marvin Gabrion. We will show that Marvin Gabrion pawned Wayne Davis' stereo equipment.

"Ian Decker was last seen alive in June of 1997. He was in the company of Marvin Gabrion. Marvin Gabrion says that Ian Decker was going to Texas. No one has seen Ian Decker since June 1997.

"In May 1995, Bob Allen was last seen alive in the company of Marvin Gabrion. What Marvin Gabrion called his Christian bookstore, in Altona, Michigan, is actually registered to Robert Allen. Bob Allen's social security benefits have been unclaimed since October 1997, when Marvin Gabrion was arrested. In 1998 ,Marvin Gabrion was convicted of social security fraud. He was collecting the disability payments that the government was sending to Robert Allen.

"The government believes that Marvin Gabrion did cause the death or disappearance of Rachel Timmerman's infant daughter, Shannon Dale VerHage.

"The government will show you a fake gun Marvin Gabrion carved out of soap. Marvin Gabrion impersonated a Michigan state senator. Even behind bars Marvin Gabrion is a clear and present danger. We will bring some of the corrections officers to testify who have to deal with Marvin Gabrion.

The court then adjourned for lunch.

After the lunch break Stebbins made the opening statement for the defense. During the guilt phase, the defense plan seemed to be the SODDI (Some Other Dude Did It) defense. That no longer applied. Rather the defense now focused upon three things: damage to the frontal lobe of the brain, extensive use of drugs and early childhood trauma were influences upon Gabrion's behavior. They were inescapable influences and therefore a sentence more lenient than the death penalty was called for.

He began, "We do not contest that Mr. Gabrion is dangerous. The federal government can deal with dangerous individuals. If they misbehave, their world gets smaller and smaller. You will hear new testimony today. We need you to use your common sense and values.

"What you will hear, it's not a pretty picture. Marvin Gabrion's life history. We are going to show how he got to be the person he is. There is no smoking gun. There is no one event that created any of this.

"Marvin Gabrion was in no trouble at all through high school. In fact he did quite well there. He participated on the track team and testing placed him in the ninety percentile range. He graduated from high school in 1971.

"Marvin Gabrion started inhaling glue. In fact he did this so often that the local hardware store would not even sell him glue anymore. This is where his brain damage began.

"In 1976 Marvin Gabrion went out west, living in Arizona and California. He had several car accidents; in fact he suffered a series of head injuries. As a result of one accident, Mr. Gabrion was hospitalized for several days. In the early 1980s, Mr. Gabrion returned to the White Cloud area. His acute paranoid behavior began. Mr. Gabrion had additional accidents. His escalating confrontational behavior caused him to be barred from bars.

"There is brain damage here. There is something wrong with

Marvin Gabrion. There is irregular electrical activity. It was controlled by medication, but by 1995, when his prescription ran out, Mr. Gabrion started drinking more and his problems escalated.

"Mr. Gabrion has not always cooperated with testing. His brain damage is in the area of restraints, the knowing of right and wrong. Ladies and gentlemen of the jury, we will show you a lot of small factors, but they come together to explain Marvin Gabrion."

At 11:01, the government called its first witness: Dr. Stephen Cohle. The forensic pathologist had testified during the trial about the evidence he had found. This time he testified to a different effect—what happened physiologically and psychologically to Rachel as she faced and endured her death. In his calm, practiced way, Dr. Cohle described the stages of terror: the escalated heartbeat, the fight or flight chemical rush, the futility of holding her breath, a natural instinct, as long as possible.

Marvin Gabrion grew more agitated. The spectators heard him repeatedly muttering, "Lies! Lies!" to his attorney. Stebbins did his best to ignore him.

Al Young, a neighbor in Altona, told a story about being on his lawnmower. When Gabrion came up to him yelling, swearing and attempting to pull him to the ground, he had to defend himself. Al was a tough guy who worked hard all of his life. "I had to keep hitting him, because he kept getting back up."

The next witness filled in on personality details the court hadn't heard before and with a special poignancy since she was a family member. She commented on Gabrion's violence and danger as well as harassment and arson incidents. Gabrion wanted Stebbins to object, but Stebbins didn't.

Suddenly, a loud smack cut through the courtroom. Almost falling from his seat, Stebbins held up a hand to protect himself. Gabrion was standing, looming over him.

A second blow from Gabrion came down on the frightened man, hard and flush on Stebbins' cheek and the attorney hit the ground. Twenty minutes before the punch, Stebbins had said Gabrion's behavior could be controlled with medication.

Within seconds two burly marshals rushed Gabrion from the rear, picked him up and threw him facedown on the defense table. It was a beautifully efficient and well-practiced maneuver.

Immediately Judge Bell ordered the jurors out of the room. Tim and his son reacted instantly, leaping to their feet, ready to help if necessary. Just as quickly Sergeant Miller pointed at them and motioned them to sit down. They did. Stebbins, meanwhile, had crawled past the front of the defense table to the side wall.

Two more marshals raced from the front of the courtroom, throwing their weight on the struggling Gabrion. When they had Gabrion under control and cuffed, they carried him facedown out of the court, depositing him in the holding cell.

The court broke for noon recess. When Tim and Lyn emerged from the courthouse, television news crews surrounded them, asking them to describe the "incident." They shook their heads. They felt, if anything, the "incident" would confirm in the minds of jurors the sudden, irrational violence of the defendant.

It wasn't the first time Gabrion had acted up. In an August hearing, he had been hauled out of court after calling the judge an "evil Hitler." He had written Judge Bell to ask for the dismissal of his lawyers. The reason? He accused Mitchell of having had a hand in the theft of a Rembrandt painting. But, then, he also accused the judge of participating in the theft of Queen Elizabeth's diamond ring.

He had played the role of an incompetency defense well, even though three psychiatric exams found him competent. But this morning had no role-playing. The very real viciousness of the killer had erupted.

Chapter 21

Random, Heinous and Violent

After the lunch break Marvin Gabrion remained shackled in the holding cell. In court, motions flew back and forth. Defense Attorney David Stebbins put forth three motions: a motion for mistrial, that he be permitted to withdraw as counsel and that another competency exam be given. He had visited Gabrion during the lunch break and found "that his condition is deteriorating."

Tim VerHey, the prosecutor, argued against each point.

The judge systematically denied each motion. In fact, he defended Gabrion's right to attend his own trial and stated that he would be brought back into court the next day, fully manacled and chained to the table.

Through the afternoon, the prosecution character witnesses continued.

The owner of a seven-bedroom house rented rooms individually, one of which Gabrion rented. Another renter reported that Gabrion threatened to beat him up, because he had caught Gabrion exposing himself to the owner's twelve-year-old daughter.

The next day the owner caught Gabrion in the same act, outside his daughter's bedroom window. He went inside and began throwing Gabrion's belongings out the window.

Gabrion stormed inside, claiming a right to a thirty-day eviction notice. According to the witness, Gabrion "took a kitchen knife and told my wife that he was going to kill her. He told me that he would kill me and throw me in the river so they could never find me when he got done. He said I wouldn't be the first."

The owner grabbed a baseball bat to help Gabrion make up his mind to leave. Once he left, they started cleaning out his room, uncovering "large amounts of pornography, adult books, pictures of preteen girls."

The prosecutor asked the owner how he had been paid. Some cash, he said, and "a signed social security check in the name of Robert Allen."

The tumblers began to click into place for the jury.

The second afternoon witness was a neighbor of Gabrion's at the Altona Christian bookstore. The witness, a cement finisher, had been accosted by Gabrion as he was completing some cement work. Gabrion was drunk when "he kept putting his hands in the wet cement."

The witness was working with some friends and together they hustled Gabrion off the property. As he left, Gabrion shouted, "You're all dead. You're all fucking dead." Fifteen minutes later, shots were fired at them and they called the police.

A Mecosta County sheriff's deputy was sworn in to corroborate the story. He testified, "Mr. Gabrion was passed out or sleeping when we arrived at his residence. We observed spent cartridges outside. There were casings and loaded shells on the truck and on the ground. A twenty-two caliber rifle with a scope hung on a wall inside. We confiscated his gun and the other evidence. We took him into custody. I believe he only spent one night in jail on this charge. He did write me, asking for his gun back."

The final witness for the day spoke to an event occurring on January 16, 1997. "I was walking home from the grocery store and that man [pointed at the defendant], he said his name was Marvin. He stopped and offered me a ride home. I invited him in to play some cards. My uncle stopped the game to get his pills; he's got a heart problem. Marvin got upset, he wouldn't give him the pills. He would just let him die.

"Marvin accused me of kicking his dog, but I didn't do it. Marvin took our collie and threw her against the wall. Then he started choking me and kicking me in the ribs. He was shouting, 'I'll kill you, I'll kill you and nobody will ever know about it.' My wife and son tried to help. The beating went on for at least ten minutes. When Marvin laid down on the couch, we went out to call the police. The pay phone wasn't working when we got there, so we didn't know what to do. We saw Marvin drive off, so we went home and locked the doors. We called the police the next day."

His wife was then called to corroborate the story and also his ten-year-old son. Clearly the event traumatized the boy; he could remember little, except this: "I hit him in the back with a battery charger, but all it did was make him madder and he threw me again."

After the jury left for the day, unfinished business remained. What to do with Marvin Gabrion, who was locked in a holding cell throughout the afternoon? The judge wanted to see him in court the next day. He went on record: "I want to get this on the record now. I know five years from now somebody is going to take a look at this and I want it to be perfectly clear. The court ushered Mr. Gabrion out after he struck his attorney several times. There is a constitutional right for Mr. Gabrion to face his accusers. This court has repeatedly warned Mr. Gabrion that his continued bad behavior could include sanctions. I have often used the 'zip up' signal to try to get him to be quiet. That signal doesn't appear on the transcript, but I have used it repeatedly. Events this morning came after many warnings. At all times Mr. Gabrion could see the witnesses and hear what was going on in the courtroom. His antics in front of the jury clearly prejudice him. His calculated behavior creates a dilemma solely of his own making. We'll try again tomorrow and see if Mr. Gabrion can handle it. I am also advising hepatitis C precautions for the marshals."

As they left the courtroom, Lyn observed to Tim that the defense team was using words that were too sophisticated for some of the witnesses. "It just confuses what's being asked."

Tim agreed. "It's better low-key," he said. "But maybe they don't know how to talk backwoods talk."

"Doesn't mean you have to talk like an idiot," Lyn said.

"No. That's like the rich white boy talking ghetto talk. Draws attention to itself. They should just use plain everyday language. These people will know the difference between yes or no. Sometimes the defense seems to be talking down to them, trying to make them look stupid."

They approached their purple car, a sedan with too many miles on the odometer. Driving it forty miles round trip to Cedar Springs each day, though, saved a lot of gas money. Their newer truck stayed in the barn.

"Getting late," Tim said. "Want to grab a bite to eat?"

"Sounds good. You name the place. I'm too tired to think."

When court resumed on Tuesday, March 12, Gabrion's defense attorneys asked to leave him temporarily in the holding cell and to bring him in later in the day when the jury was absent.

Judge Bell agreed. "Okay. Sometime today we'll bring him down, out of the presence of the jury." He assigned a marshal to watch Gabrion.

The first character witness of the morning was another neighbor of the Altona store. According to the witness, the event began innocently enough. Gabrion had stopped by to borrow a few tools and asked for permission to burn some trash in his fire pit. The trouble started when the "trash" included cans of old paint, sending up a dark cloud of soot over the neighborhood. The neighbor's wife went outside and ordered Gabrion out of the yard.

He returned a bit later with a golf club. Belligerent. According to the witness, Gabrion shouted, "I can see the whole neighborhood from my upstairs apartment. I can snipe from up there. Do you want to come over and see my arsenal collection? Remember, I can dust that bitch [the wife] any time."

The threat infuriated the neighbor. He attacked Gabrion, hitting him repeatedly until he got out of the yard. By then so much black smoke funneled up that someone had called the fire department. The fire chief threatened to fine them for creating a hazard.

Later in the day the neighbor heard a rifle shot. He looked up and saw the muzzle flash at Gabrion's window as he fired a second time. He called the police to arrest Gabrion and was left with a slug in the side of his house.

The next witness was a Mecosta County sheriff's deputy who had responded to a report of threat and intimidation by Gabrion in August 1996. As he arrived at the Altona house, the deputy heard two quick shots. He called in and requested bullet-resistant jackets. Gabrion suddenly walked out the front door, holding a shotgun. Officers managed to tackle and arrest him for discharging a firearm.

But that wasn't the end of it.

In the deputy's words, they found a surprise: "We did not have a search warrant, but we did want to make sure his residence was secured before taking Marvin Gabrion away. We were shocked by what we saw upstairs. It was a large, open room. There was a mattress lying on the floor. A large bullfrog was lying on its back, spread eagle, fastened to the mattress. It appeared to be covered with both dried and wet bodily fluids."

Tim looked at Lyn and muttered, "The guy had sex with a frog?"

"A bullfrog, no less," she said.

The defense did not care to cross-examine the witness.

Following witnesses testified to Gabrion's often violent and bizarre behavior. The prosecution moved forward to Gabrion's time in the Calhoun County Jail and the Milan State Prison. His brief stay at Calhoun was a study in how quickly an inmate can lose privileges.

Testimony about events during Gabrion's temporary stay at the Calhoun jail elicited additional questions about the quirks of his personality. Arriving at the witness stand was Captain Glen Slater, a well-dressed professional who was the administrator of the jail. At issue was a phone call that Gabrion made on March 9, 2001.

Captain Slater pointed out, "We housed Marvin Gabrion at our facility. We have a contract with a provider for phone service. It is a computer system that monitors and records all calls. We don't listen to them all, but they are all recorded."

The government had a tape of the call and proposed entering it into evidence.

Judge Bell agreed, "We are entering into evidence Exhibits 89 and 89t. You may listen to the tape and compare it to the transcript. The transcript has only been prepared to assist you. The cassette tape is the exhibit."

Mr. Slater's testimony continued. "Marvin Gabrion was assigned to the administrative segregation area. Prisoners there receive only one hour out of their cells per day. This phone call occurred when Mr. Gabrion was the only one out of segregation. Marvin Gabrion was calling the Milan federal penitentiary."

The government played the tape recording. On it, Mr. Gabrion claimed to be the clerk of the federal court in West Michigan. Mr. Gabrion wanted to talk to the warden, in reference to moving an inmate. He was trying to arrange his own transfer from Calhoun County Jail to the Milan federal penitentiary. "Just fax something to Judge Bell, okay?"

Davis asked, "Mr. Gabrion didn't like it at your facility, did he Mr. Slater?"

"I can only guess why Mr. Gabrion wasn't happy there. When he first arrived at our facility he had access to pencils and paper during his hour out. Mr. Gabrion earned his placement in our super max facility. His bad behavior caused him to lose his rights and privileges. In fact, his behavior caused his world to become increasingly smaller."

"Isn't it true, sir, that Marvin Gabrion even managed to misuse the crayons you gave him, didn't he?" Davis asked.

"Yes, sir."

Furthermore, in a shakedown of Gabrion's cell on January 1, 2001, guards found a cavity in the block wall behind Gabrion's bunk. Inside was a nail clipper—potentially one of the most versatile tools in imprisonment. They can be filed down to be used as anything from a weapon to a handcuff key.

But Gabrion didn't stop there. Virgil Smith, a former state senator who was at the time the Division Chief of the Wayne County Prosecutor's Office, took the stand. He testified to another recorded phone message from Gabrion, left on the voice mail of United States attorney Michael Detmer on December 12, 2000. From a transcription of the recording, the message was:

> Mike Detmer, this is Senator Virgil Clark Smith and, uh, the governor and I are concerned that, uh, you are seeking the death penalty in the case, the Gabrion case and, uh, I'm on vacation right now, but I would like to speak with you. We're concerned about, uh, the State of Michigan judge cited lack of evidence and refused to issue a warrant and then federal interests materialized after that time and we're concerned because Oxford Lake is clearly an innavigable lake according to the laws of the State of Michigan. Therefore it would be exclusive jurisdiction of the State of Michigan trying to twist things around to say that the girl died in the bottom of the lake in the mud. I'm just concerned. I'm a member of the Michigan coalition against the death penalty and, uh, I will, uh, have the Governor's office arrange a conference call with your office so that we can talk about this further. Thank you.

Davis asked, "Tell us, Mr. Smith, is that your voice on the tape?" Smith replied, "No, sir, it is not."

Following was an in-custody witness who testified, "Marvin Gabrion talked about escaping all of the time. He kept chicken bones to make them into a shank. He talked about injuring inmates and corrections officers. He especially didn't like female corrections officers; he threatened most every woman. He did not react well to receiving instructions from any woman.

"Marvin Gabrion cut himself and collected the blood in a cup, to use as a weapon. I asked him why he had to kill the girls. He said he had to take care of business."

Incidents at Milan State Prison were no better. On July 30, 2001, a guard asked Gabrion to submit to restraints so he could be moved. "Instead, he threw feces and urine at me," the guard testified. "He then started a fire in his cell."

VerHey inquired, "As a consequence of this event, were you tested for any infectious diseases?"

"Yes, sir, I have been tested for Hepatitis C; so far the tests have come up negative."

"Thank you."

For the rest of this Tuesday and in the continued absence of Marvin Gabrion, witnesses filed in and out, testifying to similar incidents. There were several escape plans, one of which involved a bar of soap carved into the surprisingly realistic shape of a handgun and died black with newspaper ink. From a distance it looked real enough; Marvin Gabrion was only two doors away from freedom.

As the day closed, the judge gave the marshals a heads up for Wednesday. Gabrion might be ready to rejoin the courtroom.

Testimony had been elicited thus far to show the heinousness and randomness of Gabrion's actions and to show that his violent nature was a threat to others and himself. The primary aim of the testimony on Wednesday, March 13, was victim impact statements—a long-awaited moment for Tim. But, in prosecutorial terms, it also drew together the two main points.

It didn't start out as smoothly as planned, however. Marvin Gabrion was in the courtroom. It was the defense's turn to call witnesses and the prosecution to cross-examine. Gabrion wanted to be first.

"Your Honor, I'd like to make a statement, on the record, so that everyone understands. I want to address issues. I have constitutional rights, this allocution thing."

"I'm not sure you understand allocution, the parameters. Allocution is typically a plea for forgiveness, for mercy from the jury. You can say something to the jury. But what do you want to talk about?"

"I want to speak in the first person, talk about some of the issues concerning the crime."

"The issues of the crime are behind us. You were found guilty. The only issue now is why to not impose the death penalty. I'm talking about allocution. This is a plea for leniency, asking for mercy and showing remorse. Facts are under oath, on the witness stand and subject to cross-examination."

"Yes, sir."

Chapter 22

Victim Impact

The prosecutor's office had collected the victim impact statements as it prepared its case. It was now time for Tim, as well as other family members, to deliver their statements. While the five victim impact statements were being presented, Gabrion sat at the defense table, deliberately ignoring them.

Perhaps no other part of the ordeal had caused Tim more stress. How does one weigh the emotional grief, the loss that would never be restored, in a page of typed statement? Tim had written, in his own words, literally dozens of drafts, agonizing over the right words for a grief that went so deep. He was the first and the last witness in the trial. Afterward, he had no memory of standing before the jury that last time, delivering the words he had written:

How were you affected by this crime?

I could fill many additional pages and not begin to describe adequately all of the effects of having my daughter murdered and of Shannon's disappearance. I lost a daughter, the first child I ever watched emerge from the womb, and my only grand-daughter. I gained some things. My life now has new things; pain, anger, frustration, depression. I tried everything I could think of to find Shannon, always wondering if I did enough, but what more could I do?

I lie in bed, late, very late, unable to sleep. My mind is filled with images of handcuffs and duct tape, with questions, what ifs. I try to slow my mind down, to fill it with beaches or scuba diving vacations.

Sometimes, on a good night, I fall asleep peacefully, only to awaken cold, wet with sweat, bound and gagged, unable to see or move, absolutely terrified. I am a large, hard-working man, not typically scared of anything. My Rachel learned to swim early and easily; she loved being in water. The method of Rachel's murder was so cruel, yet how ironic, considering her love of the water. This premeditated action has filled my mind with vivid images that devastate my ability to enjoy the human requirement of sleep.

The Michigan state police have assured me that Oxford Lake has been searched very thoroughly. The Federal Bureau of Investigation works at getting Shannon's picture all over America, lending hope that my granddaughter is alive. Was she sold? Nobody in our government can give me information about Shannon's whereabouts. Then, last week, the Newaygo County prosecutor tells the *Grand Rapids Press* that she thinks Shannon is still in Oxford Lake. It's difficult to describe how these mixed messages affect me. I am not privy to any of the information my government has...who am I to believe? Should I believe Mr. Gabrion when he sends me letters stating that Mr. Babcock, assistant Newaygo County sheriff, did the crimes?

If my government believes that my little granddaughter is in Oxford Lake, then let's find the remains. Allow the family a memorial service, closure and the opportunity to go on with our lives without the hole in our hearts of the "missing."

In conclusion: I have been involved with the self-help group "Parents of Murdered Children." The intensity of emotions that I feel is common, but difficult for anyone who hasn't been there to imagine. A successful prosecution and time are said to alleviate some of the intensity of the pain and anger.

Ink and paper are ineffective tools to describe the effects of having Rachel Helena Timmerman drowned in that beautiful part of the Manistee National Forest, of having Shannon's whereabouts be "missing." The pain, the anger, the terrifying fear that came into my life years ago exist only in my mind, coming out onto paper as a mere trickle from the vast ocean inside.

When Tim finished his victim impact statement, it was break time.

After the break the defense countered the victim impact statements by calling specialists to the stand. It seemed, at first, a bit off-track or an effort to acquaint the jury with the horrors of the prison system. But it eventually led to their defense argument that Gabrion's frontal lobe injuries rendered him incapable of full control of his actions. The first specialist was Dr. Mark Cunningham, psychologist. David Stebbins opened the questioning.

Stebbins queried, "Dr. Cunningham, have you prepared some demonstrative exhibits for the jury?"

There was a slide presentation showing custody options in the federal system. Starting at minimum security and continuing on through special security arrangements.

Davis countered, "I object. This is double hearsay."

Stebbins replied, "Your Honor, the witness is only trying to explain the federal system."

Davis was not about to let that stand. "I object, Your Honor, irrelevant. Information about other sentences imposed is irrelevant."

Judge Bell intervened, "We talked about this, Mr. Stebbins. Keep it very brief."

Dr. Cunningham continued, "At the penitentiary level inmates spend much of their days in various programs. The super max facilities are much different."

A new slide displayed the super max cell. Dr. Cunningham went on to describe it. "The super max cell is seven feet by nine feet. It contains a stainless steel shower, so the inmate doesn't need to leave his cell to wash. The bed, stool and table are all concrete. There is a stainless steel combination sink, toilet and drinking fountain. The inmate is handcuffed and his legs are shackled whenever the inmate is out of his cell. All the inmates get one hour out of their cells per day for exercise. If an inmate kills another inmate they get a minimum of seven years in the control unit. Right now the federal government has five cells that are unused, allowing minimal contact with staff. The inmates' communication is limited if they cause death, physical harm or property damage."

Tim wondered about the damage caused to him. Davis stood up for the cross-examination.

"Tell us, Mr. Cunningham—" He was interrupted by the witness on the stand.

"Excuse me, it is Dr. Cunningham, not mister," Dr. Cunningham explained.

Davis nodded. "Excuse me, Dr. Cunningham. Mr. Stebbins forgot to ask you about your qualifications, did you study prison regulations for your doctorate?"

Dr. Cunningham stated dryly, "Actually I received my doctorate in adolescent epilepsy."

Davis went on, "Isn't it true, Dr. Cunningham, that you've worked your way up from epilepsy to now doing this specialized presentation for death penalty cases often, and I don't mean every time, but often earning twenty to thirty thousand dollars per case and in fact last year you earned over two hundred and fifty thousand dollars doing this particular risk assessment testimony?"

Dr. Cunningham frowned, "Well, I do still see some patients."

Davis pressed, "But you earn most of your money in the courtroom, don't you?"

Dr. Cunningham nodded, "Yes, I do."

Davis glared at the jury one by one. Then stated, "I have nothing further for this witness."

The following witness, brought in from Columbus, Ohio, specialized in neurological behavioral disorders. After reviewing the medical record on Gabrion and attempting to interview him in prison (Gabrion refused to meet with him), he concluded that Gabrion had suffered brain damage from multiple automobile accidents. The testimony proceeded at a glacial pace, as if length would create credibility. Stebbins asked the witness, Dr. Chiari, about his credentials.

Dr. Chiari testified, "I earned my doctorate in neurological behavioral types of problems. I only know Mr. Gabrion from reading his records. I read social history data, a letter from Dr. Majors, information from Pine Rest Hospital, White Cloud Hospital Records, Hackley Hospital records and counseling agency records."

The solemn witness spoke dryly. "It is quite evident that Marvin Gabrion had a change in his personality due to brain damage. Parts of his brain are dysfunctional. I like to always do a face-to-face interview to examine the individual. I drove up from Columbus, but Marvin Gabrion refused to see me at the prison.

"It is my opinion that Mr. Gabrion's brain damage is most likely the result of multiple automobile accidents. Substance abuse, such as sniffing glue, is also a factor."

Stebbins queried, "This frontal lobe disorder, does that mean the front of the head?" Stebbins touched his forehead every time he said frontal. Stebbins went on, "So, Dr. Chiari, what you're saying is that frontal means the front?"

The judge dismissed for lunch.

Following the break, the prosecutor cross-examined the witness. Tim VerHey discussed with Dr. Chiari the 1992 auto accident. Using CAT scans and X-rays, the radiologist had concluded that all tests were normal. The logical conclusion was made. VerHey stated quietly but firmly, "So, if you are abrasive, you have brain damage?"

The afternoon seemed to be a steady flow of expert witnesses testifying to the same thing. Marvin Gabrion had suffered, somehow, organic brain damage. The question in the minds of the jurors had to be: *Does this excuse or mitigate the horrible deeds of which we found him guilty?*

To Tim and Lyn, the jury seemed far from convinced of that.

Gabrion sat in his customary place on Thursday, March 14, complaining loudly that his restraints were too tight; he couldn't write. "I want to script the questions for my evil shyster lawyers to ask me in rebuttal testimony," he spat out.

Judge Bell's manner was tough but composed. "I'm still not sure that you understand, Mr. Gabrion. Allocution is a short statement to the jury about punishment and remorse."

Gabrion jumped in. "My lawyers aren't coming by me anymore, Your Honor. Maybe the statement isn't even necessary. We can just go into Mr. Davis harassing me."

Judge Bell's voice was icy. "Truth, Mr. Gabrion. What does it mean to you?"

Stebbins interjected. "Your Honor, we are recommending against it. Mr. Gabrion has not presented any subject matter to us to which he wants to testify. Mr. Gabrion does have the right to allocution, but at this time we question Mr. Gabrion's competency. We also cite his failure to communicate with us. We recommend against it."

Since the prosecution had brought strong witnesses to testify about Gabrion's bad character, the defense tried to undo the damage. They began by bringing in members of Gabrion's own family. It climaxed with Gabrion himself returning to the stand. The judge reminded Gabrion that he was still under oath.

Gabrion stormed, "You on the jury have a job to do. My testimony should be weighed appropriately. I have worked for the CIA; I know how these things work. I have offered to take sodium pentothal, a truth serum, to prove the truth. To prove the facts you've heard concerning Wayne Davis. He helped bond me out of jail when I was arrested.

"The officers' statements about the frog, the allegations about what the police officers claimed to see at my Christian bookstore are lies, told to discredit me. I have lied about my neighbors in Altona, because they believe in pedophiling their children. Tim Timmerman didn't deserve to have Rachel, because he was pedophiling her."

The three marshals were standing very close to Gabrion now. They were ready for an explosion.

"My upbringing, my Christian camp to help kids stay off drugs, my childhood was no worse than any other average poor, white, rural person. My shyster attorney, Paul Mitchell, absconded with my medical records, but I can prove that I will die in five years. This will save the government the two million dollars it would cost to have me executed. I guess I'll have to subject myself to Mr. Davis' abuse, I mean cross-examination."

It was indeed the time for the cross-examination by Tim VerHey, who was handling the sentencing phase.

VerHey began quietly but firmly. "Mr. Gabrion, do you remember sending a letter to a reporter in New York when you were arrested in New York, on the social security fraud charge?"

Gabrion loudly objected, his eyes narrowed to slits. "I wasn't arrested for the social security fraud. That's a lie the government perpetrated against me. I was arrested for drunk driving in New York."

VerHey, taking it down a notch or two, went on, "Didn't you set up a charitable trust fund for No More Missing Children?"

Gabrion spat his next words out. "Mr. Stebbins did that. He got approval for it."

VerHey kept pressing. "Mr. Gabrion, a few minutes ago you made a comment about Tim Timmerman. You accused him of, how did it go now, pedophiling Rachel. Why did you say that?"

Gabrion shook his head vehemently. "I wasn't there. Rachel told me her dad abused her."

VerHey moved to a different tack. "Mr. Gabrion, in 1987 you were arrested in California. You gave the police a false name. You even had identification in that name. Can you tell us what happened?"

Gabrion sputtered: "That was a bad time for me. I drank a lot. I was arrested for assault with a deadly weapon, other than a gun. It was a car. The only witness against me was a heroin addict."

VerHey stared at the glowering witness. "The defense called Dr. Cunningham yesterday. What did you think of his testimony?"

Gabrion's voice was like a staccato beat. He observed wryly, "The slide show was interesting and depressing. The jails serve you these tiny little European portions. You'll never get a visit from God."

There were murmurs in the courtroom. The jury was taken out of the courtroom for a moment while Gabrion was moved to the defense table. Then it was back to business.

The prosecution followed with some of its own expert testimony regarding Gabrion's state of mind. One of these experts had attempted to do an interview with Gabrion twice. During the first, he observed Mr. Gabrion's thoughts ranged so widely and tangentially that he couldn't do a proper interview.

He tried again a week later and described for the court: "When I attempted to do a second interview, Mr. Gabrion said that he didn't remember me. Some of his behavior seemed practiced. I believe at least some of his behavior was malingering, deliberately not telling the truth. Mr. Gabrion wanted to complain about lawyers and the legal system. He became angry and the interview had to be terminated after about forty-five minutes."

After additional time on medical testimony, a livelier witness entered. He appeared disabled, but it was definitely not "frontal lobe syndrome" as the medical experts had been attributing to Gabrion. This witness's memory was sharp and clear as crystal.

He described how his relationship with Gabrion began in 1992, when Gabrion gave him forty dollars for a round trip ride to Indiana. Gabrion requested a ride a second time, but this was on the back roads of Newaygo County.

"Gabrion asked me about insurance," the witness began. "Was the car insured? I told him I had insurance. He had me turn a hundred different ways and I wasn't sure where we were. All of a sudden he grabbed the steering wheel and swung us off the road.

"Neither one of us was injured that I could tell, but I was surprised by Gabrion's actions. He was running around, banging himself into trees, just running into them. When the state police arrived, Gabrion requested an ambulance. The police brought me home. Later I went into a diabetic coma. I was unconscious for five days in the hospital. Gabrion visited me in the hospital and proposed a scheme to defraud the insurance company and split the proceeds, fifty-fifty. I had my sister's boyfriend remove him from the room.

"The bottom line was that Mr. Gabrion sued me and the uninsured motorists fund. He received a judgment against me for $38,000. I am paying it back at twenty-five dollars a month."

For much of the testimony on Thursday, Marvin Gabrion had his head down on the desk, apparently napping. He used his Bible for a pillow.

Friday, March 15, began with more medical experts, in this case a clinical neurological psychologist testifying for the prosecution. He spoke primarily about memory tests administered to Gabrion, specifically a test of symbol recollection designed to show malingering or internal fabrication. The cross-examination by the defense was tedious and protracted. Once again, as with many of these experts, the courtroom fell into a near stupor.

The jury was dismissed while certain procedural motions were discussed. The defense had brought thirty-three mitigating factors. Judge Bell whittled them down to twelve. Furthermore, he added, "I am going to throw out one factor you have listed. I don't want any lingering doubt about jurisdiction. That issue has been decided. I also don't want any reference made about Mr. Gabrion's behavior in the courtroom. I think it's in the defendant's best interests to bring the number of mitigating factors down to something an educated jury can handle."

The jury returned. Judge Bell gave the final instructions on procedure: "We are going to have four more speakers. Mr. Gabrion will make his allocution. The government and the defense will make closing arguments and the government gets the final word."

Gabrion's allocution was preceded by Judge Bell's announcement: "Ladies and gentlemen of the jury the evidence in this case has been concluded."

Gabrion took the stand. "Ladies and gentlemen, I am confined to specific matters of remorse and punishment. You have been presented a completely false version of the truth in this case. Rachel Timmerman came to Jesus while she was in the Newaygo County jail. She was a good woman, refusing to sell Shannon for ten thousand dollars.

"It is imperative that you remember this. I am returning to heaven, a continuing erotic dream, which I can control. May God have mercy on your souls."

Flipping some pages on the podium, Gabrion didn't want the marshal's help. "I've got some more controversial stuff here, but I was afraid you'd stop me. Rachel's one fear was that Tim Timmerman would abuse her."

Gabrion concluded his allocution with, "I don't care if I live or die."

Silence filled the courtroom.

Chapter 23

The Prosecution Ends

After a short break, court reconvened at 10:08. Tim VerHey stepped forward to make his closing argument for the prosecution. Probably no one was quite prepared for the legal tour de force that it turned out to be, a masterful recapitulation of the trial and a forceful directive toward conviction. A large picture of Rachel and Shannon stood in front of the podium; pictures of Wayne Davis, Ian Decker and Robert Allen rested on easels behind it.

"Ladies and gentlemen," VerHey paused for a moment to look at the jury members then he went on. "You know that the defendant, Marvin Gabrion, has committed a shocking murder. It was not quick, it was not merciful.

"Ladies and gentlemen, when we talked to you first in this case last week, we told you that we would show you by the end of the evidence the answer to three questions that relate to this case. Question one was: Whose body was it that was found in Oxford Lake on July 5, 1997? Question two was: Who killed her? Who killed that person? And question three: Why was she killed? Now that you've heard all the evidence in this case, you know the answer to those three questions.

"First of all, you know who the person was that was found dead in Oxford Lake. It was Rachel Timmerman, a nineteen-year-old girl who was just starting her life, her new life with her infant daughter Shannon VerHage.

"You know why she was killed. She was killed only because she was trying to bring someone to justice for committing a crime against her.

"And you know who it was who killed her. The defendant, Marvin Charles Gabrion. You know that he murdered her intentionally and in cold blood.

"How does that relate to what you now have to do as jurors? How does that relate to the task that's before you? When we're done with the arguments here this morning, you're going to get jury instructions from the Court. The judge is going to read to you the rules that you have to follow in evaluating the evidence and answering certain questions. The defendant here has been charged with murder on federal property. So you're going to have to look at each of the elements or questions that go into what makes up the crime of murder on federal property.

"You're going to hear a jury instruction that says you have to be satisfied beyond a reasonable doubt about the following things. First, you're going to have to conclude that the victim named in the indictment is dead. Is Rachel Timmerman dead? Second, you're going to have to consider whether the defendant caused the death and whether he did it with something called malice aforethought.

"Well, nobody goes around talking about malice aforethought. What does that mean in everyday words? Malice aforethought is defined as doing something deliberately, on purpose, not by accident. That's an intentional killing. So when you hear the words 'malice aforethought,' and I believe you'll get written versions of these jury instructions, that's what you have to conclude.

"You also have to find that the defendant killed Rachel Timmerman with premeditated intent, with premeditation. What does that mean? Well, again, you're going to see a definition in the jury instruction that tells you to kill with premeditation means that a person didn't do it on an impulse all of the sudden; that he did it after thinking about it, planning it. That's what makes a killing a premeditated murder.

"What else are you going to have to find? You're going to have to find that the defendant murdered Rachel Timmerman on federal property. The statute, the murder statute says that you have to find that the killing occurred within the special maritime and territorial jurisdiction of the United States. You'll hear what that means. It has to be on federal property, land or water.

"Another part of the jury instruction that you're going to hear from the Court talks about your common sense and everyday experience. Many of you have not been jurors before and so many of you may wonder, *What do I do? I mean, how do I do what I have to do? Can I use my common sense and everyday experience? Is it okay?* It's not only okay; we insist on it. The Court will tell you to bring your common sense and everyday experiences to the decision you have to make and when you evaluate each piece of evidence that you've heard in this case and seen in this case, use your common sense and everyday experience.

"The evidence you heard in this case over the last week tells you who the killer was and proves to you that it's Marvin Charles Gabrion. Each piece sheds light on who the killer is and each piece points only to one person: the defendant. Independently, they all point to the defendant.

"Let's talk about each piece of evidence one by one, because we want you to be absolutely satisfied that you know who killed Rachel Timmerman in June of 1997. The first thing, the first piece of evidence that you heard in this case is that the defendant had the motive to kill her. He's the one person who benefited from her death.

"How do you know that? You know that in August of 1996 Rachel Timmerman charged the defendant, Marvin Gabrion, with raping her. She said he raped her one night when he ran into her at a card party and then took her after the card party to a remote area nearby and then repeatedly raped her. Her statement to Mr. Babcock, now Undersheriff Babcock, then Detective Babcock of the Newaygo County sheriff's department was, 'He forced me to have sexual intercourse. I didn't consent to it and he even bit me on the nose during the attack.' That was her statement to Detective Babcock. You also heard that from Nikki Wilson, the social worker to whom Rachel Timmerman talked after the attack.

"Now, you also heard Detective Babcock went to Marvin Gabrion, or at least tried to contact Marvin Gabrion, to get his version of what happened. You also heard Detective Babcock didn't tell the defendant all the details of Rachel Timmerman's statement. He just said, 'She's charged you with raping her. What's your side of the story?' And you heard from Detective Babcock that the defendant faxed him a written version of what the defendant said happened that night. It was introduced as Exhibit 46. You can read it when you go back and start your deliberations, but let's summarize it right now. What did he say in his side of the story?

"The defendant says Rachel Timmerman wanted to have oral sex with the defendant. She asked him, 'Let's go somewhere and I'll perform oral sex on you.' The defendant says Rachel Timmerman then did perform oral sex on him. The defendant says that when he ejaculated, Rachel Timmerman placed with her hand some of his semen in her vagina. The defendant says that Rachel Timmerman then asked him for sexual intercourse and he refused. He said he didn't want to get her knocked up. And the defendant says that the reason that she had an injury to her nose was that she sat on his dog and he bit her. That's what the defendant said about that rape charge.

"Well, what else did we hear? We heard that the defendant was charged with this rape by Newaygo County Prosecutor Chrystal Roach on October 31, 1996. The defendant was arrested January 27, 1997. We've got a timeline here, Exhibit 81, which helps you remember these dates. The defendant was arrested January 20, 1997. He made bond February 3, 1997. Remember John Cornelius said, 'I grew up with the Gabrion family. I have known Marvin Gabrion since we were kids. The defendant asked me to help him make bond.' Cornelius said he thought it was a drunk driving charge. Turned out to be this rape charge. In any event, the defendant makes bond February 3, 1997.

"You also heard that during this time when the defendant was brought into court and put in jail for the charge, Rachel Timmerman had herself been put in jail for a marijuana charge and she was in jail from January 8 to May 5, 1997. Why does that matter? Well, we know it matters because when the defendant got out of jail and knew that he had been charged with this rape, he did not have a way to get to Rachel Timmerman. She was in jail. She was safe from him until she got out.

"Why does that matter? Well, it explains why his rape case had such an unusual journey through the Newaygo County court system which Chrystal Roach told you about. Remember she told you that in state court in Newaygo County, usually what happens is somebody comes in on the charge, the person gets arraigned in district court, there's a preliminary exam in district court and then the person goes over to circuit court for his trial.

"She said in this case that didn't happen in the way it was supposed to. This case flip-flopped back and forth. The defendant came into Newaygo County District Court, got arraigned and instead of having a preliminary examination, which is when Rachel Timmerman would have had her side of the story placed under oath, instead of doing that, the defendant waived that and it went over to circuit court.

"What happened then? Chrystal Roach told you that rather than staying in circuit court where it was supposed to go to trial, the defendant went through a lawyer and then flip-flopped the case back into district court and wanted a preliminary examination.

"Then she told you that when the preliminary examination was supposed to come up the second time, and we're now getting into June of 1997, the defendant waived preliminary examination again and the prosecution hadn't even given permission for that to happen as it was supposed to be asked for. The prosecution was supposed to agree to this if it was going to happen. Chrystal Roach said somehow or another they waived the preliminary examination without permission. She showed up. She had subpoenaed Rachel Timmerman for a preliminary examination that never happened.

"Then the case went over to circuit court for trial the second time. The defendant told you that his lawyer said he should do the preliminary examination. It was his decision, according to him, not to do it. He wanted to go to trial.

"It was all this flip-flopping back and forth on the rape charge that did two things. It delayed the trial and it prevented Prosecutor Roach from getting Rachel Timmerman's sworn testimony in the preliminary examination. Remember, she said that had Rachel Timmerman testified in the preliminary examination, I could have used that testimony even if she never appeared again. She wasn't able to do that. That's why the defendant was doing all this with his rape case. He was trying to delay things until Rachel Timmerman got out May 5, 1997, and he succeeded in doing that. But by May and June he'd run out of options. He was going to have his trial in or after June. There was nothing else that was going to stop it.

"So Rachel Timmerman gets out May 5. She lives with her father, Tim Timmerman, until the time she disappears June 4. So she was out less than a month before she disappeared.

"What did we hear about that period when Rachel Timmerman got out of jail? Remember, she was living with her father up until June 4. The afternoon of June 4, Tim Timmerman's sitting in the backyard. Rachel Timmerman comes up to her father and says, 'I'm going out with a boy, going out to dinner.' She takes baby Shannon, says she loves her father, kisses him, walks away. He never sees either one of them again.

"Because Rachel Timmerman never was seen again and because these letters start appearing written in her handwriting after she disappears, the rape charge was dismissed June 25, 1997. The defendant never had to face the rape charge. When Rachel Timmerman was killed, he's the one who benefited from her death. That piece of evidence all by itself shows you the defendant murdered Rachel Timmerman.

"Is that all that you heard during this case?" VerHey paused and looked intently first at one juror, then another. "No, there's more. What about these letters? What about the letters that started appearing in Rachel Timmerman's handwriting after she disappeared June 4?

"The first one came to Tim Timmerman the very next day, June 4, 1997, Exhibit 65, postmarked June 4, Cedar Springs, Michigan, in her handwriting. 'Dear Dad, I'm sorry I left. I met the man of my dreams. Going on vacation for awhile. Might get married. I'll write you later.' Remember what Tim Timmerman said about that? He didn't know anything about Rachel Timmerman going on vacation. In fact, she told him she'd be back that evening of June 4. This was a surprise to him. She didn't even tell him who this guy was who picked her up. Turns out, according to this letter, it's the man of her dreams and she might marry him.

"What else do we know about Exhibit 65? Well, it came in this envelope with this stamp on it and this is no ordinary stamp. This is not some postage stamp that you stick on with your thumb to an envelope. This stamp is part of the envelope. And what's more, it has a hologram of a space station on it. If you move it around, you can see a planet, you can see a space station. Very unusual stamp.

"What else did Tim Timmerman say? A little while later he gets another letter from his daughter, June 16, postmarked Little Rock, Arkansas. Delbert turns out to be the man of her dreams. Tim Timmerman said, 'I've never heard of anybody named Delbert, certainly never heard of any plans about Rachel Timmerman going to Arkansas.'

"'Me and Shannon are in Arkansas. We're going to stay here for awhile. Delbert's gotten a job. We may settle down here. I'll talk to you later.'

"What else do we know? Here's that stamp again. Little Rock, Arkansas. Same hologram stamp. Now, this letter, Exhibit 64, is written in Rachel Timmerman's handwriting. But we know that by June 16, Rachel Timmerman was not in Arkansas. She was dead and in the bottom of Oxford Lake. Everything in this letter is a lie.

"What other letters did we see? Well, here's one to Chrystal Roach, the prosecutor, Exhibit 62. Rachel's handwriting. Rachel Timmerman writes Chrystal Roach a letter saying, 'I'm very sorry. Please don't prosecute me for filing a false police report. Marvin Gabrion did not rape me.' And what she goes on to write in this letter is 180 degrees different, is a completely different story than what she was saying before she disappeared on June 4.

"In fact, look at this letter and compare it to the defendant's version of what happened on the night of the rape. Rachel Timmerman has all of a sudden come around exactly to the defendant's way of thinking in this letter. 'I wanted to have oral sex with the defendant and I did have oral sex with him. When he ejaculated, I placed his semen in my vagina with my hand. He refused to have intercourse with me when I asked him to have intercourse with me. That made me mad,' she says in this letter. 'His dog bit me on the nose.'

"Why on earth did Rachel Timmerman, in one of the last things she ever wrote, spend her time exonerating the defendant, saying he didn't do it and following the script word for word of what the defendant had said in his statement? Well, Exhibit 62, which is that letter, came in an envelope with a hologram stamp on it of a space station. Exactly the same as the others.

"Judge Drake, district court judge, Newaygo County, had handled some proceedings on the rape case that Rachel Timmerman brought against Marvin Gabrion. Exhibit 66. 'Judge Drake: I'm writing you in hopes that you will not press charges on me for falsifying a police report. Marvin Gabrion did not rape me.' And then the letter goes on to follow the script. 'I wanted oral sex; we had oral sex. I wanted to have sexual intercourse after that. He refused, made me mad. I put his semen in my vagina with my hand. His dog bit me.' Exactly according to script.

"This letter, postmarked Little Rock, Arkansas, June 15, comes to Judge Drake. It has the same hologram stamp on it as the other ones. The last written statement we ever see from Rachel Timmerman.

"Why do these hologram stamps matter? Well, because the defendant was writing letters himself. He wrote his brother, Exhibit 68, tells him a bunch of stuff, none of which is really that relevant to this case. Exhibit 67, another letter to his brother. Look at the stamps. Same stamps, same hologram.

"He even wrote a letter to his realtor, who was going to help him sell the Altona store. Here's the letter. Read it if you want and I'm not sure it tells you one thing over another, but look at the envelope. Exhibit 69: same hologram stamp, space station on it. The defendant on Friday told you, 'Yeah, I got—I got letter—I got envelopes like that down in Big Rapids. You can get them there.'

"These letters in Rachel Timmerman's handwriting and the letters that the defendant wrote himself for his own purposes show you all by themselves that the defendant killed Rachel Timmerman. That hologram stamp shows that they came from the defendant. The fact that she followed the script that the defendant gave her of what happened on the rape night shows you that he had her in his clutches. All by themselves these letters show you that he's the killer.

"And one final thing about those letters. Remember, post-marked Little Rock, Arkansas. The poor guy who just wanted to sell his car and the defendant wanted to buy it and ends up taking the door handle off it and disappearing with it? He remembers the defendant and then he remembers the defendant wanted to know if this car would go to Arkansas. So the defendant has a connection to Arkansas. All of that with the letters all by itself tells you the defendant is the killer.

"Is that all? No. What else did you hear? Well, we've seen Oxford Lake. We've seen the video of how you get to Oxford Lake and you know if you know anything by now that it's in the middle of nowhere. You go down unplowed roads in the wintertime on Forest Service property. Then you go on a two-track and you wind through rye fields and brush and trees and undergrowth and you finally get to Oxford Lake. This is not a lake very many people know.

"But the defendant knows it. He knows all about it. Look at— look at what he drew. Look at this map that he drew of Oxford Lake."

The courtroom was pin-drop quiet, as if the spectators were engrossed in absorbing what they were learning.

"Detective Miller, who's been there several times, but only in connection with this case, he had never heard of this lake before he started investigating this case, told you that this is a pretty darn good map. Shows you every two-track, shows you the parking area, shows you where there's a hill, shows you where there's a creek, shows you two-tracks over here, shows you where this one dead-ends, shows you where the outlet is and then shows you where there are cabins way down here.

"The defendant knows where Oxford Lake is. We know that he drew this map because the trustee from the jail told you he got a

bunch of information from the defendant in some scheme where the
trustee was supposed to go try and buy federal property around this
lake so that the case would go away. But when he saw what was on
here, 'Body found, one of three,' he decided he didn't want any part
of that scheme and he gave it to Detective Miller.

"The defendant admitted drawing this map. Remember?" The
jurors leaned forward, intent on what was being said. "He talked to
a reporter who went down to the Calhoun County Jail and interviewed him at his request and he told her, 'Yeah, I drew that map. I
drew that map because I wanted the police to search the lake and satisfy themselves that there aren't any other bodies there because I know
this.' Somehow he knows this.

"So there's no dispute he drew this map. The only thing that's
wrong with this map, and you heard Detective Miller tell you, is he
put the line in the wrong spot in relation to where the body was found
and he wants us to think that there's a boat landing here. Well, you
can easily see why he'd do something like that. But everything else:
dead-on accurate. The fact that he knows Oxford Lake so well, not
to mention the fact that he's been seen there, which we'll get to a
little bit later, tells you all by itself that the defendant murdered Rachel
Timmerman."

VerHey paused briefly. The silence in the courtroom was heavy;
no one dared break it. Then, one voice muttering undistinguishable
words—Gabrion's. VerHey used the pause to change his course
slightly.

"Is that all you heard in this case? No, there's more. What
about the boat? What about the defendant and his boat?

"Now, when you heard Detective Miller testify at the beginning
of this case and saw where this body was found in Oxford Lake, it
became clear right away that the murderer had to have a boat. Sixty
pounds of block on Rachel Timmerman, she's out in the middle of the
lower half of this lake. The whole thing's nothing more than a glorified
swamp with a foot or two of water over it and ninety feet of muck.
There's no way you could have gotten that body there without a boat.

"Did we hear anything about the defendant with a boat? We

heard all kinds of things, didn't we? Starting with Sam Franklin, the guy who lived across the street from the defendant's house in Altona, who told you that on June 4 at 4:00 in the morning when he was trying to sleep, he woke up all of a sudden because he heard a bang and leaned over, peeked out the blinds and he saw the defendant had just dragged a boat out of the back of his pickup and was dragging it towards his garage.

"He told you he also saw the defendant take out some chain and three cement blocks. Also he told you, 'Well, I thought the guy had been fishing and he was just getting back from fishing.' After he saw the defendant hose out the boat, he kind of quit paying attention, rolled back over and tried to go back to sleep.

"That's when the defendant fired up his grinder. Mr. Franklin shot back up in bed. He said he leaned out the window and said some unkind things to the defendant about why he didn't get a job like everybody else and let everybody else sleep and then he called the police because he couldn't sleep. The guy was grinding on a boat in his garage at four o'clock in the morning.

"Fast-forward a few hours to Oxford Lake. Kay Haveman and Roseanne Schuette saw the defendant with a boat, same description, Rachel Timmerman, pickup truck on the shores of Oxford Lake, right where the parking area is.

"Fast-forward, June 6, the evening now. The Fultons and Jenny Bingham are on a campsite on the Little Muskegon River. They already ran into the defendant earlier because he came out with a motorcycle and said, 'Will you watch my motorcycle?' and he chained it there. They said, 'Fine.' Came back that evening, nighttime of June 6. Now he had a boat and he gave them some fairy tale again about how he was from Ohio. He'd already told them he was from Ohio, that he was married, his wife and kids were down in Ohio, he was up there camping, but the place that he was camping wouldn't allow him to have a boat there unless he paid more money. He didn't want to do that, so he said, 'Will you watch my boat, too? And by the way, you can use it.' They said, 'Fine.' He left the boat there.

"Interestingly, Jenny Bingham noticed that the defendant

looked different on the evening of June 6. He had a hunk of hair torn out of his head and he had scratches on his face and she even asked him about it. 'What happened to you?'

"'Oh, I got in a fight with a friend.'

"She also told you that he was wearing gloves all the time, new-looking gloves. Apparently he told them, 'Well, I'm cutting wood. That's why I wear my gloves.' The gloves were new-looking. And then they found out, of course, that he was not staying at some public campsite where anybody would charge you anything for a boat or otherwise. He was staying a little ways down the Muskegon River, same area they were, with exactly the same kind of room that they would have to store a boat and motorcycle.

"So you have to ask yourself: Why is he doing that? Well, he had just used the boat to kill Rachel Timmerman and he didn't want to be anywhere near the boat until he was sure he had gotten away with it. He left it there with them for awhile.

"Franklin's testimony about the defendant grinding on the front portion of this aluminum boat was confirmed, in case you need it confirmed, by Mr. and Mrs. Kwiat who later on saw a boat with grind marks on it out in front of the defendant's store in Altona. They thought about buying it, thought again when they saw that the numbers were ground off the boat, didn't buy it. But they remember the defendant and his boat. It was also confirmed by Randy Young, one of the several Youngs who live in Altona, who said he was interested in the boat and went and looked at it and then stopped being interested when he saw the numbers had been ground off. He remembers it, too.

"The fact that the defendant was doing these things with this boat, grinding numbers off, putting cement blocks in, putting chains in, that tells you all by itself the defendant's the murderer. Is that all you heard? No, there's more.

"Part of the jury instructions you'll get from Judge Bell include an instruction that says if you think the defendant ran and hid after he knew he was wanted for questioning on this case, you can consider that as proof that he knew he was guilty. What did we hear about that?

Did the defendant run and hide? Sure, he did.

"John Cornelius again, the man who has known the defendant since they were both kids, got a phone call from the defendant saying, 'Hey, I'd like to have you do some work on the Altona store for me. I'm thinking about fixing it up. Would you do some construction and repair work for me?' We even played the tape for you of the message that he got.

"Part of that tape that you heard, Exhibit 72, says, 'I appreciate you doing this and would you also tell my parents that I'm okay and that they can't get in trouble and you can't get in trouble for helping me, because I'm only wanted for questioning.' So he knew he was wanted for questioning. This is after Rachel Timmerman's body floated to the surface of Oxford Lake and after the police figured out who it was and after they made some inquiries about where the defendant was. Remember Detective Miller said he went and talked to the defendant's father trying to find the defendant. So he knew. He knew he was wanted for questioning.

"Did they ever find the defendant in Michigan? No. When did they find the defendant? Again, looking at this timeline, he wasn't found until months later, October 14, 1997. And he sure wasn't found in Michigan. He was found in upstate New York. Sherman, New York.

"Detective Ferri told you that as an FBI agent in New York, he learned during the investigation that the defendant might be there. He went to the post office, showed some photographs of the defendant to the postal workers, learned the defendant was there and had a P.O. Box not in his own name, but in the name of Robert Allen. Agent Ferri decided to get the SWAT team, stake out the area and they arrested the defendant.

"What else? Agent Ferri saw the defendant go through his wallet. He found Exhibit 74, a picture of the defendant on a Virginia driver's license with the name Ed Lee White, a Virginia address and a social security number on it. And you heard from Agent Rutzinski, who's the FBI agent from Virginia who has a driver's license from Virginia of his very own, testify that this is indeed a real Virginia driver's license.

"So the defendant was running and he was hiding. He ran to New York, who knows where else. We've heard West Virginia, we've heard Virginia, we've heard Indiana—all over the place. And he was using one of two aliases: Robert Allen or Ed White.

"Along those lines we heard Mr. White himself testify, the unfortunate guy who answered an ad the defendant put in the paper pretending to be a construction supervisor saying, 'I'm going to start some construction' and put an ad in the paper looking for workers. Ed White met him at a truck stop and you can just picture this. The defendant had the whole thing. He had his little clipboard, he had his forms, he did a job interview of Mr. White and he said, 'Oh, by the way, because of state regulations and all these licensing things, I'm going to have to copy your driver's license and social security card.' White gave it to him, you know, thought, 'Well, this is unusual, but all right. I want the job.'

"The defendant went over to a copy machine, copied them and gave them back and then went through the rest of the charade. 'Oh, this looks good. Why don't you start work when the weekend's over? I'll meet you back here.' Poof, he's gone. Last time White ever saw the defendant. But we know the defendant was looking for a new identity and he got one.

"We know he was using it. Remember Jon Sanchez? The defendant approached Jon Sanchez about buying some property. You'd need a four-wheel-drive to get to it. It's out in the middle of nowhere. The defendant said, 'Hi, I'm Ed White. I'd like to buy that five-acre piece of property. Why? Well, my wife was murdered and I want to get away from it all.'

"So he did want to get away from it all. He was running, he was hiding, because he knows he's guilty. And we know he's guilty because this piece of proof all by itself shows you he's the killer.

"Is that all? No. What else? The defendant said he would kill Rachel Timmerman. He told Rachel Timmerman that on the night he raped her. He told her, 'If you tell anybody, I'll kill you.' Well, she's dead. How do we know that? Well, we heard what she had to say from beyond the grave, if you will, because she told everybody, practically, she came into contact with how frightened she was of this man and about the fact that he said he'd kill her.

"Whom did we hear that from? Her brother. He was at the house after she came back, after she ran in, had this argument with the defendant with a claw hammer. He was on the other side of the door banging on it. Her sister remembers that and he threatened her right through the door. Her brother said, 'You know, she was hysterical, upset. I got her calmed down. I told her she should go to the police. She said she didn't want to do it.' This is what her brother said. And the reason she didn't want to do it is because she said, 'You don't understand. He said he's gonna kill me.' They talked her into it.

"The social worker for Newaygo County who had known Rachel a long time, considered her a friend, known her through her difficulties of her teenage years, knew her with her problems trying to get started with a newborn, talked to Rachel Timmerman right after this rape because Rachel Timmerman wanted to know about a morning-after pill, wanted to know what could be done. Nikki Wilson said Rachel Timmerman told her the defendant said he'd kill her if she told anybody. And what's more, she told the social worker that Marvin Gabrion said, 'Not only will I kill you, I'll kill Shannon first and I'll make you watch.'

"Helen Baker. Memorial Day weekend, 1997, Rachel Timmerman went over to Helen Baker's trailer. Their kids played together. She said Rachel Timmerman was acting really strange. She wanted to shut the drapes and then she kept peeking out to the point where Helen Baker asked, 'What's the matter with you? Why are you acting so weird?' And she said Rachel Timmerman told her, 'Marvin Gabrion's gonna kill me.' No fewer than seven times did Rachel Timmerman say that to Helen Baker that day before Rachel Timmerman finally left and Helen Baker never saw her again.

"What about Juliet O'Neil, who was the Newaygo County sheriff's dispatcher? She reported two calls from Rachel Timmerman about Marvin Gabrion. One was—you remember the first one she was hysterical. She couldn't even calm down enough to tell a coherent story until she finally got her wits together. She said, 'I just saw Marvin Gabrion. Something has to be done. Can you help?' Juliet O'Neil did what she could do and that was the end of that call.

"The last call Juliet O'Neil got was perhaps the saddest one of all. Remember that one? Rachel Timmerman called, she was calm, she was not hysterical and she said, 'I just want there to be a record. Marvin Gabrion's gonna kill me.' You can almost hear the despair in her voice. She knew this guy was going to kill her and there was nothing that could stop it.

"Those calls, Rachel Timmerman's statements, the defendant's threats to kill her, all by themselves prove to you that he's the murderer, that he killed her with deliberation and in cold blood. Is that all? No. No.

"John Cornelius has known the defendant nearly all his life. He went to the local store where you can buy cigarettes and pop and things like that. John Cornelius had been in the store, he was leaving, he saw Marvin Gabrion walking towards him in the parking lot. He told you, 'When I see Marvin Gabrion, I say hi to him.' So he went up to him and said, 'Hi, Marv. How you doing?' They had a conversation. He told Marvin Gabrion an innocent remark, 'Well, I just got rid of my girlfriend. We broke up.' And then Marvin Gabrion told him something that made his hair stand up on end. He told John Cornelius, 'I got rid of my girlfriend, too—permanently. I bound her with chains, locks and blocks and threw her into a lake.'

"What did John Cornelius do? Well, he went home. Within two hours he told his mother what happened and both of them have told you that that was before they knew anything about any body being found in Oxford Lake.

"What else do we know? Well, we know that the defendant apparently fancies himself, or at least did, the boyfriend of Rachel Timmerman. On Friday during his exchange with Mr. Davis he said you could call it a date rape. He thinks Rachel Timmerman was his girlfriend.

"Now, John Cornelius has had a mental breakdown. There's no denying that. And you'll probably hear some things from the defense about him. But when you consider his testimony, consider this.

Within two hours he went and told his mother. She testified, if you remember, by videotape because of her health. She repeated the same story that John Cornelius repeated to you. Both of them have told you it was before anything was on TV or in the media about anybody being killed in Oxford Lake.

"So that piece of evidence all by itself proves to you the defendant is the killer. Is that all? No, there's more. Let me show you— let's talk about the blocks and paint and tar. Now, we heard from Detective Miller that there were two blocks attached to Rachel Timmerman when she was found on July 5. We also heard that they seized some blocks from the defendant's backyard and they also seized some blocks from the sign in Altona, right outside Altona.

"You've seen these blocks. You can tell just by looking at them that there's tar on one side and there's paint on the other and the tar has stripes and it has little curlicues and figures. Just by looking at them and using your common sense and everyday experience, you know that they came from the same place."

Now he turned to the expert opinions:

"But we also know from hearing from the FBI experts that they are the same blocks. For example, Bruce Hall. None of us will probably ever think about blocks the same again, will we? Bruce Hall, who's an expert in blocks, he doesn't want to call them cement or cinder blocks, but on these kind of blocks, said a couple of things.

"First, he told you that you have to recognize that there can be two block manufacturers right across the street from each other or nearby and they're churning out different kinds of blocks because it varies based on what you throw in there. You throw in Portland cement and then you throw in all kinds of other stuff. Some people use sticks, some people use gravel, some people use ash or cinders. They're going to be different. And then the same place might change its blocks over time. Like you might have a big pile of cinders one day or you might have gravel one day or you might have crushed up other hard stuff some other day. The blocks are going to look different.

"What did he tell you about these blocks? These aren't different. The blocks from the sign are just like the blocks attached to Rachel

Timmerman and just like one of the blocks from the defendant's yard. There's one, of course, that we can all see that is a lot different. When you start really looking at them you can tell that one of these blocks from the yard is different. But these other ones, they're all the same. And they're usually all different.

"Mr. Hall also told you he came out here from Washington and looked around West Michigan. He was trying to see if there were blocks like that lying around. He couldn't find any. He couldn't find any that looked like that.

"What else? Well, we know that these blocks had red paint on one side. Ron Menold, another expert, told you, 'I ran this paint through various chemical tests, looked at them, looked at their molecular structure and I can't tell them apart chemically.'"

VerHey was painstakingly placing the jigsaw pieces, completing the tragic picture. It was very hard for the family to hear and watch, especially for Rachel's father.

"Robert Rooney, the tar man, said, 'I looked at the tar on the back, did the same kind of chemical tests to see what they're made out of, what atoms are there. I can't tell them apart.' Well, are all tars the same? No. You heard Agent Gilligan went out shopping and got three different kinds of black adhesive tar and sent them to Mr. Rooney and he looked at those. Those are all different. The ones on these blocks aren't different.

"What about the spray cans? We know that one of the blocks attached to Rachel Timmerman had a little bit of pink spray paint on it and we also know that Detective Miller seized two cans of pink spray paint from the defendant's house in Altona. Now, if you look at these cans back in the jury room, they're both the same brand fluorescent spray paint. They're both red. You look at them—they've both been sprayed. If you look at them, you could look at them all day, they'd look the same.

"But you know from Ron Menold that one of these cans matches the paint on Rachel Timmerman's block and the other one doesn't. That's how different paint can be when you get down to what it's made of chemically. Two cans sitting side by side on the same shelf that look exactly the same are different chemically. But one of the cans is identical chemically to the pink spray paint on one of the blocks attached to Rachel Timmerman.

"Are they the defendant's blocks? Two of them were taken from his backyard. You know those were his blocks because Mr. Young, who used to own that place, used to own that yard, said, 'When the defendant moved in, I moved right next door and I watched him unload a bunch of blocks into the very spot where Detective Miller found them. He brought them there. The defendant brought them there.'

"The defendant even told you the blocks on the sign were his. He just says somebody else took them and framed him with them or something. But he admitted those are his blocks on the Altona sign, the one that reads 'Please slow down...' Randy Young told you, 'I watched him put the blocks on that sign.' There's no doubt that these are his blocks.

"So everything about these blocks, the way they're made, the paint on them and the tar on them, all tell you again the defendant is the murderer. Is that all? No.

"What about the keys? Detective Miller told you when he searched the Altona store he found a couple of keys. He found a lot of keys, but he told you about these two, Exhibits 36 and 39. Padlock lock keys. He told you that he didn't find a single lock at that store or anywhere else associated with the defendant that these keys would open. Found keys, didn't find locks. But on a hunch he took these keys, tried them on the locks that were used to attach the cement blocks to Rachel Timmerman when she was killed. They opened the locks. These keys open the locks.

"How do you know they're his keys? They were in a bowl—at least one of them was in a bowl with change in it. Remember that? In the bowl was a prescription medicine vial, Exhibit 42. The vial has Marvin Gabrion's name on it. It's his medicine in the bowl.

"Another key in the bowl, Exhibit 37, was found there. And what lock did that key fit? Well, it fit this one that the FBI got from Eve Butler out in Virginia. Remember Agent Rutzinski went out

there, showed a photograph of the defendant to Eve Butler out in
Virginia, got the stuff that the defendant left with Eve Butler. This
key opens that lock. They're his keys and they open the locks that
were used to kill Rachel Timmerman. That evidence shows you all by
itself the defendant is the killer."

Another piece and then another. For Tim, this dialogue was agonizing. But when he glanced over at Gabrion he heard the oft-
repeated refrain "lies, lies" and gasped at the brazenness of the man
whom he was sure killed his daughter.

"Is that all? One final thing I'll talk about to show why you know
he's guilty. The defendant brought Rachel Timmerman to Oxford
Lake when she was killed. How do we know that? Kay Haveman and
Roseanne Schuette were at Oxford Lake in June of 1997. Roseanne
Schuette drove her mother, Kay Haveman. They both lived nearby
Oxford Lake. It was getting towards evening. They drove there in
their pickup. Roseanne Schuette parked in the parking area that we've
heard about and saw on the video. She stayed in the truck, her mother
got out, went down the hill for a few minutes, came back up, got back
in the truck.

"And then came a black pickup, three people in it, parked four
feet away from their truck. Two men and a woman in the truck. The
passenger, she identified, both of them identified, is Marvin Gabrion.
He got out, walked over and said something. Roseanne Schuette
remembers him saying, 'Hi, how's the fishing?' Kay Haveman remembers, 'Hi.' Roseanne Schuette said Kay Haveman said, 'It's okay. The
fishing's okay.' And that's all they said.

"Both of them told you that there was a blonde woman sitting
next to the defendant in the middle of that pickup truck. Both of
them identified Rachel Timmerman as that person. No duct tape on
her. She didn't say anything. Roseanne Schuette remembers her
looking, looking over once at Roseanne Schuette and then looking
down. Neither one of them could see below her torso because the
door was closed of the pickup truck she was in. They couldn't see
what was in her lap and they couldn't hear anything like a baby or
anything like that. But they saw her.

"What else? Well, after that short exchange, Roseanne Schuette and Kay Haveman drove off. Now, this question has probably occurred to you: Why would the defendant let them drive off? Right then? Well, he must have thought about not letting them drive off. He walked over, got close enough to them, but he had a problem. There was two of them and he only had one helper and they were already in their truck. They were ready to drive away.

"Plus they hadn't seen anything. They didn't think they'd seen anything then. They'd just seen two men and a woman at a lake with a boat, an aluminum boat in the back. That didn't strike them as unusual. So they drove off. They didn't think they saw anything. Had everything gone according to plan, they would have never known they saw anything. Remember? The defendant had already taken care of that. He had all these letters that went on about how she was moving to Arkansas with the love of her life, Delbert. Just another crazy nineteen-year-old who ran off with some man. So he let them go.

"Do they know now that they saw something? They sure do. You heard them say how scared they were, how scared they are; how they didn't say anything to the police, had to be dragged in here.

"Compare them to, for example, Amy Kwiat. All she saw was the defendant driving a dark pickup truck with a boat in the back away from Oxford Lake. Looked like the boat was about ready to come out of the back of the truck, it was going so fast. Did you see her up on the witness stand when she testified? She didn't see Rachel Timmerman, but she was about ready to quiver right out of that chair because she was so scared.

"Kay Haveman and Roseanne Schuette saw the defendant and Rachel Timmerman at Oxford Lake right before he killed her. That also tells you that he's the killer."

VerHey stepped away from the podium. His voice carried clearly and forcefully through the courtroom. There was no need for flourishes or theatrics here. Fact by relentless fact he had structured the case against the defendant.

"Each of these pieces of evidence that I've gone through with you point to one and only one person: Marvin Charles Gabrion. Each of them all by themselves, each by itself, shows you, should convince you that he's the killer. Taken together, they leave no doubt that the defendant murdered Rachel Timmerman; that he did it on purpose with malice, with premeditation and only because she was going to try and put him in jail for raping her. There's no doubt about that.

"Is that the end of this case? Is that the end of what you have to do as jurors? One final thing. Even though you know he's the murderer, you have to go to the next step and be sure you know where he killed her. The jury instruction tells you it has to be on our property, has to be on federal property, on land or on water. So you have to be sure that that's what happened here. So let's take that a step at a time.

"Here's a drawing of Oxford Lake and all the property around it. The U.S. Forest Service surveyor prepared this before she testified. When you look at this, you can see everything around this lake belongs to the Manistee National Forest. It's federal property except for this little square right here on the north end of the lake. So to do your job conscientiously, as I know you will, you're going to have to be satisfied that Rachel Timmerman was killed on federal property.

"So one thing you have to ask yourself is did her body float once it went in the water? After he threw her in, after she died, could her body have gone around this lake when it was underwater, first of all? Let's do it this way. The answer to that is no.

"How do you know that? Well, remember what Agent Gilligan told you. She weighed all of the blocks and chains and locks and everything that was attached to Rachel Timmerman. It was over sixty pounds. The Army Corps of Engineers diver who was on the witness stand for probably, I don't know, three minutes, told you that he went to Oxford Lake, was taken to the spot where Rachel Timmerman's body was found. He made his own diving suit—remember he had one of these surface air setups where you get your air on the surface, but he made his suit neutrally buoyant. That means he didn't sink on his own and he wasn't going to stay up on his own. He was neutral as to weight in the water. Then he was handed sixty pounds of weight.

"Agent Gilligan told you that she timed it and measured it. At this point she told you there was just over two feet of water on the surface and then you hit the muck. And you know from Detective Miller you've got ninety feet of muck under the water.

"In a matter of seconds the Army Corps of Engineers diver sank to the depth of twelve and half feet before he finally stopped. He told you he was completely encased in the muck. Agent Gilligan told you the same thing. He had gone all the way down below the water into the muck.

"She also told you that some time later in this spot they put a cofferdam, one of these empty coffee can type things they put in the lake. It's a big cylinder and they sucked off the foot or two of water and then took off a few feet of the muck and then they started looking for evidence. The thing that she told you about that was at that depth, around ten feet, it was really thick. It was hard to rake.

"Why does any of that matter? Well, you know Rachel Timmerman was stuck in the muck. When she went in, she stuck down there. It wasn't possible to drift around at all, let alone 227 feet, let alone way up on this end of the lake, when she was at the bottom."

The collective gasp in the courtroom was audible.

"What else? We know that Rachel Timmerman's body floated to the surface. So you have to ask yourself, 'What about that? Could her body have moved around in the lake after it floated to the surface?'

"The forensic entomologist, the guy who studies bugs, told you that after looking at the fly larvae on the body when he got it, he was able to say that her body floated perhaps as early as July 1 but for sure by July 2, 1997. The body was found July 5. Is it possible that her body floated around Oxford Lake after it surfaced? The answer to that is no. How do we know that? Well, a few different ways.

"First of all, remember what Detective Miller told you. When they found this body on July 5, he was able to make a reference point, do a measurement so he could remember where this body was in the lake. They couldn't get the body out that night when they got to the lake. It was getting dark and it was going to be difficult. He told you, looking at Exhibit 10, that when he saw the body, he could see one of the cinder blocks or cement blocks suspended below her and it was stuck in the muck. The block was—a couple inches of it was in the muck.

"They had to come back the next day. When they came back the next day, the body was in the same spot. It hadn't moved overnight. That's one thing.

"Remember they had to get a trampoline cover to scoop this body out of the muck. They had to push it down into the mucky bottom of Oxford Lake to scoop up the blocks and everything else and they wrapped it up at the top, attached it to the bumper of a pickup truck on shore and dragged it out. That also shows you that this body was anchored in the muck right where it surfaced.

"What else do you know from the crime scene itself that shows you this body did not move around?" He looked intently at the jurors, who did not look away. "Well, remember Detective Miller said that they found skin fragments, which turned out to be important skin fragments because many of them were the finger pads and toe pads of Rachel Timmerman where the fingerprints were and they needed that to find out who this person was. He said he found that in the muck under the body. Had her body been floating all over the place during these few days, those fragments would not have been right under the body in the muck. So there's that.

"Well, what about this? Detective Miller discussed Exhibit 4. He told you that this is the south end; this is the north end. He told you that this is a fairly accurate photograph of what Oxford Lake looked like in July of 1997, but it wasn't altogether accurate. Why wasn't it accurate? He said thick as this stuff is that you can see here, this picture was taken in May the next year and this doesn't show how thick this stuff was by July when he saw it.

"So he said it's accurate, but just keep in mind that this mat of weeds is thicker or was thicker in July. And he told you this wasn't here, this channel. And he told you that in July, on July 5 when they found the body, here's the boat launch, they tried to get a boat to the body which is right in this area and couldn't do it. It was too thick. They couldn't force a boat through there. They had to go all the way around here until they found a little channel in this weed mat and then they were able to get to it. And you can see right here that the weed mat continues around the north end, which relates to this line right here.

"What else do we know about that area? We know that right here where the lake pinches together, that the water depth is only inches deep. Detective Miller told you it's inches deep, perhaps as much as a foot deep right in the middle of this channel area, but the water's inches deep and then there's this weed mat here.

"Could anything have gotten over this weed mat? Could a body attached to a cement block have gone from this area to this area? No way. George Vande Velde, the guy who was there and first discovered the body, told you he's broken oars trying to get through this stuff in a boat. There's no way her body floated across the boundary from private to the national forest property. Where her body was found on July 5 is exactly where it was on June 6: 227 feet—seventy-five yards—south of the boundary line.

"That leaves us with the last question about whether Rachel Timmerman was killed on federal property. Was she alive when she was put in Oxford Lake, when the defendant put her there? And the answer to that question is yes."

For a moment Tim felt sick to his stomach, but he knew he had to hear it all.

"Dr. Cohle came into court last Tuesday and told you his opinion. His opinion when he came into court as a forensic pathologist was that she drowned. He told you how he got to that opinion. He ruled out every other possible manner of death. Looked at whether she was poisoned, whether she was shot, whether she was stabbed, whether there was a drug overdose, all these things. No evidence of any of them.

"He said, 'I'm a forensic pathologist, so not only do I help determine the way people die, I do it when it's a legal matter.' So he looked at the surrounding circumstances and he told you, 'What I knew about this homicide was that this woman was found in a lake and was taken from a lake attached to weights and she had duct tape around her and she was handcuffed.' He said, 'That's why my opinion strengthened that she drowned.'

"His opinion improved, it got stronger, after he learned about the things that we know about now. He didn't know until he got into court and was asked, 'Well, did you factor in the fact that she was seen on the shores of this lake in June'—which is when he put the time of death, remember. He said two to four weeks before he saw the body on July 5. 'Did you factor in, doctor, evidence that this young lady was on the shore of the lake with a guy who had threatened to kill her who had a boat?' No, he didn't. 'Well, would that change your opinion?' He replied, 'Yes, it would.' That became even more his opinion.

"Okay, what about asphyxia? The defense asked him a lot of questions about asphyxia, didn't they? Asphyxia, remember, is when somebody chokes, suffocates. Could he rule that out? Well, he's a scientist. He's a man of science. They don't rule anything out. Just like men of science can't rule out, for example, if it's possible that a state police helicopter picked up a body on the north end and put it on the south end? Could they rule that out? No. It's possible.

"But listen to what he was asked specifically about asphyxia. Was he asked if he looked for all the hallmarks of somebody who's suffocated or is asphyxiated? He did look.

"He looked for nail marks on the neck. There weren't any. He looked for bruises on the neck. There weren't any. He looked for scratches on the neck. There weren't any. He looked at this little bone that we apparently have in our throats called the hyoid bone that can be broken if one is strangled or asphyxiated. He looked at that. Was it broken? No. He looked at the cartilage in the throat to see if that had been cracked or broken, traumatized. Yes, he looked. No, it wasn't. He looked for tears in the lining of the cheeks, the mucosa, I think he called it, to see if there was anything like that, any trauma like that, because that's an indicator. That's a hallmark. He looked. No, nothing like that.

"He looked for petechia, I think it's called, burst blood vessels in the eyes or in the lining around the eyes because that happens when a person is suffocated or asphyxiated. 'Look for that?' 'Yes, I did,' he said. 'Did you find it?' he was asked. 'No. Nothing. No evidence of that.' No proof of any sort that the defendant asphyxiated Rachel Timmerman before he threw her into the lake.

"Is that all you have about that? No." VerHey shook his head but his gaze did not waver. "Remember, we're counting on you to use your common sense and everyday experience in evaluating this evidence. So what do you know about this crime that tells you that she was alive when she went in the water?

"You know she was handcuffed, had her hands cuffed actually behind her when she went in. Why would somebody be handcuffed? To keep her from pulling chains off, to keep her from trying to get the weights off that are holding her underwater. Do you put handcuffs on a corpse? No. Why would you? A corpse isn't going to try and get the weights off.

"We know that this body, by the time we found it, Rachel Timmerman had tape on her eyes and mouth. Why would you do such a thing? Why would the defendant do such a thing? Well, you put tape on somebody's eyes to keep them from seeing what's about to happen. You put tape on her mouth to keep her from screaming when she sees what's about to happen. Would you want to do something like that, would you have to do something like that to a dead body? No. Dead bodies can't see. Dead bodies can't scream."

How many times would the awful reality of this scene be replayed in the minds of Rachel's family? Perhaps forever...

"Rachel Timmerman's body had padlocks to hold the chains and the blocks to her with locks and they were locked. Why would you do such a thing? To keep somebody from possibly trying to slip the weights off. She didn't have a key. Would you do that to a dead body when you threw it in the lake? Dead body's not going to try and get those weights off. You don't need locks. Use the clips that he used. He had clips attached to these chains. You can look at them when you examine the evidence.

"Well, it is possible the defendant just was being sloppy, wasn't being careful, didn't care. One thing we know about this man after listening to this evidence is that he is a cunning, smart man. This is the same guy who can make a false ID out of thin air after an interview with some poor guy in Indiana and turn it into a valid driver's license in Virginia. This is the same guy who can manipulate the justice system in Newaygo County to stall for time until he can get his hands on his victim.

"Marvin Gabrion would not leave clues like that behind unless he had to. He wouldn't leave duct tape when there's a chance that somebody might find out that he's the kind of guy who tapes curtains up in his house, when he's the kind of guy who leaves rolls and packages of duct tape at his campsite at Hungerford Lake. He wouldn't leave locks when there's a chance that somebody might find the keys to those locks in his house. He wouldn't use his cement blocks unless he had to, because there was a chance somebody could match them. He had to do it, because she was alive when she went into the water.

"Is that all you know about why she was alive? No. That's how the defendant said he killed her. John Cornelius: Remember he had this bizarre conversation with the defendant when he was dropping by? He ran into the defendant and said, 'Have a beer with me.' And then the defendant launched into some conversation about how 'It's not hard to get rid of people. You just weight 'em down and throw 'em into a lake.'"

The savagery of it hung in the air.

"Now, if you're going to bring that up and talk about it and use details about how you get rid of somebody, kill somebody, you have to listen to what he says. He didn't say, 'Here's how you get rid of somebody. First you suffocate 'em and then you weight 'em down and throw 'em in a lake.' When he talked to John Cornelius and said, 'I got rid of my girlfriend permanently,' he was implying, 'I weighted her down, threw her overboard into a lake.' He didn't say, 'First I suffocated her then weighted her down and threw her into a lake.'

"What else did he say? Well, he told Tim Timmerman—remember when he testified on Friday he was asked about a letter he wrote to Tim Timmerman, Rachel Timmerman's father, and he agreed that he had said this to Tim Timmerman. He said to Rachel Timmerman's father, 'You will spend eternity reliving Rachel's last few seconds gasping for air on a muddy lake bottom.' He said that and he told you he said it to Rachel Timmerman's father after he killed her.

"There is no doubt about how he killed Rachel Timmerman. There's no doubt about any of this. You've heard all the evidence in this case. You know the defendant murdered Rachel Timmerman because she dared to try and bring him to justice for what he did. He murdered her after planning to do it, scheming to do it, plotting to do it and after saying to her and to others he would do it. You know he's guilty of this terrible crime, ladies and gentlemen. And you've taken an oath to apply the law to what you know to be the facts and now that you know what the facts are, we ask you to return a sentence of death in this case. Thank you."

VerHey returned to his seat.

Judge Bell responded, "Thank you. I note here it's 11:30, ladies and gentlemen. We've been sitting here quite a while and I think we'll have some further arguments. Let's take a break at this time. I think they're bringing lunch in to you today. Let's break for now and then let's start up at 12:45. We'll take that hour and a quarter break early, and at 12:45 the defense will proceed with its closing arguments. You may stand recessed at this time."

Tim relaxed his muscles and, for the first time that morning, leaned back in his seat.

Chapter 24

The Closers

After the lunch break, Judge Bell cued defense attorney Paul Mitchell to provide his closing argument for the defendant. Mitchell quickly glanced at the judge then the jury and began. "Thank you, Your Honor.

"Good afternoon, ladies and gentlemen. This has been shorter than we all supposed, but I'm sure it's been longer than you would have liked. But we're now a week away from having started this trial.

"I have this opportunity to speak to you and it's the only one I have in the closing argument area, because I don't carry the burden of proof in this case. Mr. VerHey and Mr. Davis must carry that burden, so they get the opportunity to answer what I have to say in rebuttal. In other words, you'll hear from them again this afternoon. I don't have that opportunity. So I would ask that you pay attention, please, to what I have to say, because that essentially is my answer to what they would come up next with.

"When I spoke to you a week ago I mentioned three main areas that I would be looking at in defense in this case. I believe those three areas generally were the lack of direct evidence linking my client with this offense; the gaps, if you will, in the scientific evidence and areas in the scientific evidence that would point otherwise than this case would point according to the prosecution; and lastly, I told you that we'd be—I would be concentrating in certain parts on no evidence beyond a reasonable doubt about how or where this offense occurred. Those three areas I will be discussing this afternoon.

"Let's begin with no credible direct evidence." He peered, for a moment, at his notes; then continued. "The closest, I suppose, the government comes to in this case to direct evidence, evidence someone saw something that might bear upon what happened here, is when we have a collection of people who were all around the Oxford Lake area at various times and at various dates.

"We began essentially, I suppose, with the testimony of Amy Kwiat and Chad Kwiat. If you recall, Amy Kwiat came into court and told you that she saw my client, she said, driving a full-sized pickup truck at a high rate of speed the way—coming the way out on the two-track from Oxford Lake. She said it was a little smaller, but then she agreed that she had said it was a full-size earlier. But she said it was coming out and she said she could see who it was, because the person had a glazed look in his eyes and that there was only one person in the truck and that she had two or three minutes to see in this truck.

"Mr. Kwiat, Chad Kwiat, said it was almost instantaneous. It was not two or three minutes. It was right on him. He had to get off the road quickly and the truck went by. That indicates, in my opinion, that if it happened, if it happened and my client or someone who looked like my client was driving that truck, that Mrs. Kwiat really did not have a good chance to see what she said she saw. The timing is off and, frankly, if Chad Kwiat is to be believed, he said he never saw the person in the truck because he got off the road quickly.

"But you have to understand when this information came out. It didn't come out right away. It didn't come out when the body of Ms. Timmerman was found in the lake." Mitchell scanned the jury box and nodded sadly. "It came out some time after that. And you recall Mrs. Kwiat said she saw my client walking after his arrest in Buffalo and that's when she decided that that's who it was. It was obvious from the questioning of Mr. VerHey that my client, when he was arrested, was walking with his overcoat over his head and his head was not visible. So she changed it to say, 'Oh, I saw a photograph' and that was when she said that she decided that was the same person.

"Her evidence, her testimony, is somewhat incredible. Couple that with the fact that before she came forward with this evidence—the only part of the evidence, incidentally, that Chad Kwiat went along with was that a dark truck pushed him off the road because it was coming out. But this evidence does not come to light until sometime afterwards when Mrs. Kwiat talked to her lawyer and the lawyer came forward with the evidence.

"If that evidence was to be believed in its entirety, one would assume that the evidence would have come to the—come forward. They would have come forward with the evidence sometime before that. So again we have a situation where we have what the government would describe as direct evidence and yet that direct evidence has a credibility problem. Credibility in when it came forward, when they came forward with the evidence and whether the evidence itself can be believed between the two people.

"And then we have a wholly incredible evidence, a wholly incredible testimony from Kay Haveman. You were able to watch the videotape of her testimony taken at a previous date and played for all of us in this court. Ms. Haveman can be completely disregarded as a witness if you listen carefully to what she had to say.

"First of all, she agreed that she didn't talk to the police until long after this case was a case. In other words, my client had already been arrested. The body had surfaced some months previously in the lake. July, the body; October, my client's arrest. November the 27 was the first day that my—that Ms. Haveman was interviewed by the police.

"And what did she tell the police? You remember what she agreed she told the police when I asked her? 'Did you tell the police you saw a car?' She replied, 'Yes.' 'Did you tell the police that which you are telling this jury today or in this videotape, essentially, today?' 'No, I did not,' she responded. 'I was afraid.'

"So then she tells you what she saw. She said, for instance, that she arrived at the lake and wouldn't tell you who she was with. She arrived at the lake to look around, just for a break of fresh air. She told you that she arrived and then got mixed up as to who arrived first, her or the vehicle that showed up. Again, we have a black pickup truck, a full-sized black pickup truck.

"I asked Ms. Haveman, 'Now, what were you driving? What car were you driving?' I asked her. 'My economy car,' she had said. And then I asked her about a previous statement she had made. 'What were you driving?' 'Oh, I was driving my truck,' she said. She was still confused over what she was driving and what time in the sequence of events she arrived at the lake.

"It is her belief that she was actually walking back from a trip down to the end of the lake and I'll point that out on here. She specifically stated that she was down near the channel here and walked back. The only way to walk back, according to Detective Miller's testimony, is through this area here. This is all weed, the soggy weed area. You can't walk on that. She said that she walked back to this point, looked out and then walked back to the car after about fifteen minutes. And the bugs weren't bothering her, she said. There were bugs out, but they weren't bothering her.

"I then asked her, 'Didn't you also tell the police that you had seen Marvin Gabrion later than that, later, even, after the body had surfaced in the lake?' 'Yes,' she said. 'I did. I saw him on two occasions.' On both of those occasions he was over on the road near where she lives. And on one occasion she said he had, about a month after the body had surfaced, he had binoculars in his hand. That is too incredible for words.

"But at the last minute we got another witness who bolstered her testimony who came in. Her daughter, the one she would not tell who she was with—that she was with at that—on that day. That person came into court, the very last witness you heard by the prosecution, the very last minute, and she popped. 'Oh, I'm the person,' said she, 'who was with my mother on that day. You don't believe my mother, but I'm helping her credibility here.'"

Mitchell's somber face gazed at the jurors and he shook his head.

"What does she say? She says that she heard nothing—she lives, incidentally, in the same area as her mother, which is just to the west of Oxford Lake a couple of miles. She said, 'I heard nothing of any of this stuff. I heard nothing about a body surfacing. I heard nothing about them looking for Marvin Gabrion. I knew none of this. None of this. When the police came, I told them, gee, I'd seen someone around, I think, on 13 Mile or Evergreen and Lincoln.' Said nothing to the police then about what she told you. Nothing.

"And when she came in, she said, 'Yeah, I was driving. My mother was riding with me. And it was just a couple of minutes when my mother was walking back to the car when we saw this thing.'

"Now, Mr. VerHey would have you believe that somehow these are two independent testimonies gelling as one when in reality, ladies and gentlemen, you can believe that Ms. Schuette, Roseanne Schuette, was simply parroting what her mother had told her afterwards with the exception that she got it wrong as to how long her mother was out. Her mother was not out for fifteen minutes, according to her. She was just a couple of minutes and back in the car and back they went.

"That is unbelievable, too, that someone would actually hold back that kind of information and give it out as though there was nothing wrong with that, as though somehow that's all—no problem in the world with that."

Mitchell frowned, pausing for a moment, then went on.

"What is her explanation as to why she did that? Her explanation is, quite simply, quite bluntly, that she was afraid. 'Afraid of what?' I asked. 'Oh, him and his family,' said she. 'But,' I said, 'well, but you didn't even know who this family was or anything about this case.' 'No,' she said. 'I didn't.' So that fear is out of nowhere, comes out of thin air. And you're supposed to consider that as valuable, vital information in a capital murder case. That is what they would have you believe beyond a reasonable doubt is correct.

"Reasonable doubt is the type of doubt you would have in a situation where you were buying a house, for instance, or making other decisions in your life, important decisions. Would you rely upon the word of Kay Haveman and Roseanne Schuette, her daughter, in spending that kind of money? I would suggest you would not. Would you therefore rely upon their word when you decide whether or not this case has been proven beyond a reasonable doubt? And I would suggest again that you would not.

"There is an interesting thing that all these people have in common who were by the lake, the four people you've heard from: Amy Kwiat, Chad Kwiat, Kay Haveman and Roseanne Schuette. They all say this vehicle that they saw was a black full-sized pickup truck. And one other person says that too. She says she saw a pickup truck with three people in it on 12 Mile Road. 12 Mile Road, ladies and gentlemen, has been alluded to as being this area here.

"Who else up there has a black pickup truck? Do you recall that? Do you remember Mr. Vande Velde telling you that he drove a full-sized black pickup truck? So if anybody remembers a black pickup truck in that area, it is likely Mr. Vande Velde's.

"I'm not suggesting Mr. Vande Velde's done anything wrong. I'm simply suggesting that if one is transposing memories onto a now fabricated testimony, one can just as easily use a black pickup truck that one has seen around, especially one that you heard from Mr. Vande Velde would carry on occasion a boat. In fact, the day that he found Ms. Timmerman, he went—he didn't have a boat in his black pickup truck, but he drove back with a boat because that's what he used to get onto the lake to check out what he thought he had seen.

"Nowhere else in the testimony that you've heard puts my client, Mr. Gabrion, in a black pickup truck. The pickup truck that you hear time and time again in this case is a red SUV, a red SUV; not a full-sized pickup truck, sort of a mini-truck, if that's the right word.

"There are other witnesses that the prosecution would have you rely upon as evidence in this case whom I believe have problems. One is Sam Franklin. You remember Sam Franklin, the person who saw—whose vision of, whose view of my client's place in Altona is represented in Exhibit 29."

Raising his arm Mitchell pointed to the exhibit.

"If you would look at Exhibit 29, please, ladies and gentlemen. Exhibit 29 purports, according to Mr. Franklin and according to Detective Sergeant Miller, to be the view one would have of the Altona store from the property, the neighbor's property that Mr.

Franklin was staying at during 1997, the morning that he told you that he was awakened by some noises. He told the first people who came to the scene, those being the Mecosta County sheriff's department, that he was—that he was awakened by the grinding, then amends it to say he heard the bump of a boat and heard the grinding after that. He yelled out, et cetera. Nowhere in that first report does it say or does he admit that he said that he saw blocks, chain and all the other items.

"Now, look at the view he has. That's a very limited view of that area. The garage is actually tucked away in that dark area behind the house, to the left of the house, to the left of the store.

"Mr. Franklin was given another opportunity to tell them all he knew and he was then interviewed at some later date by the—not the Mecosta County sheriffs, the first ones, but the Newaygo County Sheriff's Department. They said—they—he told them and he admitted that he told them that he saw oars on the boat, but he said nothing else. He said nothing else about any other items. Not until he went to the grand jury and not until he came to this court and testified did you hear all of the other things."

Mitchell had been speaking in a rush, compounding his feints at the government's case. He slowed now as he addressed the jury.

"Ask yourselves, ladies and gentlemen, at 4:30 in the morning, could you determine that there were three blocks, some chain, a life jacket or two, all being taken out of a boat, being put back in a boat, in the darkness of the night? Even with some light shining upon that area, even with the garage light on, would you see from that distance those items? I suggest to you no.

"I'm not saying that Sam Franklin is lying to you. I'm saying he's mistaken. And he embellished his testimony for whatever purpose he has, for whatever reason he has. What people tell for the first time is usually what they saw. It is rare that they come up with the kind of detail afterwards that he came up with in this case. Use your common sense, ladies and gentlemen. Mr. VerHey would have you use your common sense. Please do."

Mitchell rubbed his chin thoughtfully.

"One other tandem, if you will, of allegedly direct evidence is the Cornelius family, John and Kathryn. You all were treated to John when he came into court. John is a sad person. He is, as he told you, a paranoid schizophrenic. He is—as he told you, so honestly told you, 'I hear voices. I see things. You know, that's my problem.' And then he went on to tell you the most outrageous statement you can hear.

"Why would Marvin Gabrion come out of the store and tell him what he claims he told him with other people around? That makes no sense at all. But John, the paranoid schizophrenic, wants you to believe that that's what happened. John, who can't get anything right.

"Do you recall the cross-examination of John? It was painful. It was labored. Because John sort of agreed with whatever was said and just rambled on. You had to get him on task to keep him where you were. Again, is that the type of witness that you want to hang your hat on in a case involving capital murder? And my response is I don't believe you do.

"Now, they'll say Ms. Cornelius said that he came home and told her and that proves that it happened. That proves nothing. He may have come home and told her something, but it proves nothing. It proves nothing other than John Cornelius may have said it. But remember the testimony of Kathryn Cornelius when you decide whether or not this occurred.

"If you recall, John told you he was staying with his friends the Meyers, Gail and Benjamin, who live near Jugville. Jugville, according to Ms. Cornelius, is about five miles to the west of White Cloud. He told you that's where he went for a pack of cigarettes and that's where he went when he went afterwards. About two hours later he went home to see his mom. Maybe the day after, but about then.

"Remember also parenthetically that during the interview of Mr. Cornelius, the police stopped the tape, restarted it and Mr. Cornelius had a different memory of what he remembered. He had a whole different memory. 'Yes, in fact, I did tell my mother right away after I saw this.' And yet when he was being interviewed earlier, if you recall, he said, 'Oh, I told my mother right about the time I saw it on the news.'

"Again, is this what we want to hear for evidence? Is that the kind of evidence you want to believe in a direct testimony aspect? I would suggest not." He grimaced.

"But Mommy says other things. Kathryn says that he was home that morning. He wasn't at Benjamin Meyer's. And he was living in White Cloud in the trailer park in the middle of White Cloud within easy walking distance of any number of places to buy cigarettes and any number of places to have coffee.

"You remember I asked her about that. 'Couldn't he have gone to the gas station?' 'Yes, he could have.' 'Could he have gone to the convenience store?' 'Yes he could.' 'Could he have gone to the grocery store which is within hailing distance of your house?' 'Yes, he could,' she said. But instead she told us in that videotape that John was picked up by Benjamin Meyer to buy a pack of cigarettes and they drove to Jugville, five miles out of town, to purchase a pack of cigarettes and then within the hour he came home and she said, 'Well, then that's when he told me.'

"That's in direct contradiction to what John said and it is the direct contradiction to logic. Why would anyone drive five miles for a pack of cigarettes to go to the Jugville store when one could purchase cigarettes from any number of places in White Cloud? That's the challenge here: to look at this evidence with a jaundiced eye to determine whether or not those people are sufficiently credible or you to decide that is the kind of direct evidence you want to believe.

"One other witness in that regard was Ms. Baker. Ms. Baker was the friend of Mr. Timmerman who told you that she didn't know anything about a rape until much later, the next year, the same day she said that Rachel came to her house and began looking out of the window of the trailer of the house. Interestingly enough, she was dropped off by her stepmother, with whom one can assume she was quite safe, and dropped off where? She was living at the time in Cedar Springs, but she was dropped off where? Newaygo, where this supposed harm was awaiting her at that point.

"She went into Ms. Baker's house, spent a good fifteen minutes being fine and then started to look out the window as though something was wrong. Ms. Baker was being a little melodramatic, I fear, in this case, and that's what I would argue Ms. Baker's testimony was. Somewhat melodramatic and not very consistent.

"The government made a great deal over the boat involved in this case." Mitchell waded in. "But how many boats are there in this case? We have a situation where Mr. Young, Randy Young, said he purchased—or no, didn't purchase—he was looking at a boat in Mr. Gabrion's yard in May and the numbers were ground off that boat then and then it was no longer there.

"We had the Kwiats say they saw a boat, and I believe they were termed flat-bottom boats, in the yard of Mr. Gabrion's house or place of business in Altona after Ms. Timmerman surfaced or at least after it was alleged that she was no longer seen. We had Mr. Franklin tell you that this boat, which is described by nobody else as being brown or medium to dark brown, was also having the numbers being ground off of it. And yet we had Mr. Young who said the numbers were already ground off of that boat that was out there in May.

"We had Mr. Franklin tell you this was a V-bottom boat. We had everyone at the lake whom you've heard from who claim to have seen things tell you that it was a V-bottom boat and it was silver in color." Mitchell raised another question. "It's a normal boat. And yet that's in contradiction to what is seen at the store in Altona.

"It's also in contradiction to that which occurred in the campground in Montcalm County, the one where Jenny Bingham and the Fultons claim that my client came with a motorcycle and later a boat. That too is described as a flat-bottom boat, not a V-hull, as described by Mr. Franklin and as described by the people who allegedly saw something at the lake.

"All of those things are inconsistent and that's part of the problem with this case. The government wants to wrap it all neatly up, but there are problems. There are clear problems with the proofs in this case and that's just one indication of those problems.

'I told you we'd talk about the second area and that would be the physical evidence. We have many, many, many items sent to first the lab here in Michigan and then sent on to the FBI. Things like duct tape, duct tape holders from Hungerford Lake, from my client's residence, from his car in Buffalo, from various other things, items. All of them were tested for fingerprints. None returned with anything usable."

Mitchell made his plea to the jurors in case they found his version believable. They appeared skeptical but he went on.

"Now, we have already been told that my client used gloves, so you wouldn't find his prints necessarily. But we do know that Ms. Timmerman would have left fingerprints, likely left fingerprints, because she left a ton of them on the ten pieces of paper sent to the lab for testing, the ten pieces of paper that were known writings of Rachel Timmerman. There were sixty-two latent fingerprints and three latent palm prints of value developed on those nine sheets of paper, K-27.1 through K-27.9. A significant number of latent prints and a significant number of those latent prints were Rachel Timmerman's. So you can assume that if she was any of the places they believe she was, then it's likely she left some fingerprints. And yet we find none in this case.

"But it doesn't end with fingerprints. The prosecution would have you believe that many people don't leave fingerprints and it's true they don't and I must concede that. But we do know that Rachel Timmerman does because there were tons of them on those ten sheets of—nine sheets of paper.

"But we don't have to end the inquiry there. We have any number of lifts of fiber and hair from various items. We have almost the entire Hungerford Lake camp, that which remained there. We have the mattress in Hungerford Lake had latent—not latent, sorry, pulled fibers and hair taken from them. My client's house from stairwell to stairwell, pieces of carpet, my client's cars, taken lifts from each one. And not one, not one of those lifts produced a hair even grossly similar to that of Ms. Timmerman's.

"The only the thing the prosecution has from that perspective is the hair on the side of the road, the hair attached to the one piece of duct tape that was found by the side of the road at Oxford Lake. That hair, ladies and gentlemen, or those hairs were grossly similar under a microscope, they said, to Rachel Timmerman's. But did they take it a step farther? They did not.

"Remember I asked Mr. Deedrick if a better way, a more conclusive way to determine whether something is someone's hair, for instance, is through DNA testing? He agreed that would be true. We didn't have the DNA testing here. So all we have is grossly similar hair.

"And we don't have one other thing here that's of interest. We don't have a single piece of duct tape that was around Ms. Timmerman's head that matches with any duct tape found in this case, including the piece of duct tape by the side of the road at Oxford Lake that allegedly contained Rachel Timmerman's hair. It doesn't match.

"Remember Mr. Menold telling you, ladies and gentlemen, 'Well, I test first of all for the tear to see if it can fit, two pieces coming together. It didn't fit. I look then to the makeup, the biological— sorry not biological—microscopic makeup of the tape. It didn't match. They didn't match. I even look at the yarns that go into the matrix that holds it—not holds it, but provides strength to it. Found none of those matching any.' So the trace evidence in this case comes up to nil.

"We had a great dramatic moment last week when I think it was Detective Sergeant Miller who opened those locks with those keys. Boy, that looked like pretty conclusive proof, didn't it, ladies and gentlemen? Except that we brought in Mr. Fields this morning who told you there were something like 300,000 of those locks sold in a few-year span between 1991 and 1997. The possibility of having the same keys for the same locks is out there. And that in and of itself is the kind of thing that can produce in your minds the reasonable doubt that is throughout this case. That in and of itself.

"The paint, the paint on the blocks. I'm not arguing about the blocks too much. The blocks are the blocks. We understand that. But the paint is only similar in that it could have come from the same source. Remember Mr. Menold again, the guy who testified about the duct tape also testified about the paint, and his conclusion was they could have come from the same manufacturer, the same source.

Could have. I also asked him, 'Don't manufacturers make a lot of paint and then ship it out in various cans, et cetera, so the same batch can hit various marketers, if you will, of the paint?' 'Yes, that's true,' he said.

"But perhaps the most telling of all the evidence in terms of physical evidence that was sent to Washington was the hair, the hair that came up where Mr. Deedrick found it in the FBI lab and shipped it on to the DNA person, Mr. Stewart. Mr. Stewart told you in no uncertain terms, to an absolute scientific certainty that the hair does not belong to Marvin Gabrion. That's pretty significant.

"Now, lastly I said we'd talk about the issue of where and how this death occurred. There was a death here, there's no doubt about it. And Dr. Cohle said, 'Oh, she was likely drowned.' I wonder if in your minds likely is the same as beyond a reasonable doubt. I suspect it's not.

"What else did he say? The prosecution said, 'Oh, he checked everything to determine whether or not she was strangled or asphyxiated.' Yes, he did. He's a very thorough man. He is a man of science. He checked the neck bones, the various parts of the neck to determine any damage, found none. 'But,' I asked him, 'would that be—would that result from ligature or—is that the right word? I think it's the right word—ligature or strangling with hands?' 'Yes, you might see that there,' he responded. 'But would,' I asked, 'that be the result of asphyxiation if you simply covered the only airway available?' He said not necessarily. He didn't think that would actually happen.

"The prosecution makes great argument that you do not see the little blood vessels, damage to blood vessels in the eye which you normally see when there's a strangulation of asphyxiation. Dr. Cohle said, 'It may have been too late. I did not see that, but it may have been too late to see that in the eye. This body had been there for some time. The eye becomes more opaque, at least parts of the eye become more opaque and you're not likely to see it anymore.'

"You don't have to accept asphyxiation as the only cause of death, obviously, but you have to consider it because it is possible. And its possibility alone creates reasonable doubt in this case as to where, where this matter happened. If you were to believe, for instance, that Marvin Gabrion killed Rachel Timmerman, you would still have to determine whether or not it occurred on federal land.

"Now, there are indications of drowning, sure. Perhaps several of them. Mr. VerHey said the hands were bound behind the back. That's not an indication of anything other than the hands being bound behind the back. 'You don't bind a corpse,' said he. No, perhaps you don't. But you may leave a corpse bound with the same binding that occurred before death as after death. You leave it on. Why would you want the arms flopping around? There's a good reason to do that.

"'Why,' said he, 'do we use locks on the body if the body was dead?' Well, take that a step farther, ladies and gentlemen." One juror whose face was inscrutable leaned forward. Mitchell glanced his way and quickly went on. "Ask yourselves this question. Why would you put locks on there if the body was alive? What difference does it make as long as those hands are bound behind the back? So that's no indication of anything. The locks are, for want of a better word, a red herring. They're there, but they don't create a determination of drowning or otherwise or asphyxia. None of that.

"We do know that Rachel Timmerman disappeared in Michigan and we know that she presented dead in Michigan. But we don't know where that occurred.

"Oh, says the prosecution, well, you know, this whole area is surrounded by national forest. And if you look at this map here, you'll see that there is a portion of this lake that is not national forest. It's white. The rest of it is this pink and that is national forest. But one is not confined by these boundaries. The prosecution wants you to believe that if it didn't occur here, then it occurred here. There's no evidence that it occurred—there is perhaps only evidence that it occurred in Michigan, not necessarily part of the federal government.

"'Ah, she was stuck in the muck,' they say. Perhaps. Perhaps not. She looked pretty well floating to me in that picture you see. But if she was in fact drowned in the muck, why is there no mud in the body at all? None in the esophagus, none in the lungs, none, according to Dr. Cohle, in the nasal passages. And that was the only air—according to the way the body looked, the only airway available was the nose. No mud. And yet that body would have sunk fairly quickly into that muck, according to the diver who went down at that point. If it's only two feet deep, you're in the muck pretty quickly. And while the muck is viscous at the top, perhaps, it gets less so as time goes on. And as you sink lower, you will ingest mud into the system. There's no mud in that body. None, according to Dr. Cohle.

"So in summation, there is no proof beyond a reasonable doubt that this person died on federal property. Only the likelihood. And I leave it with you, ladies and gentlemen, whether likelihood equates with proof beyond a reasonable doubt. Thank you very much."

Mitchell had presented an effective close, the sole aim of which was to get his client a life sentence rather than the death penalty. Step by step he had attacked the prosecution's case, at every step calling into question the validity of testimony. In some courtrooms this is called the "confusion defense." If enough confusion or even doubt can be cast about parts, then perhaps it might affect judgment of the whole. He had played his role well.

In the closing arguments, however, the prosecution gets the final word with a rebuttal. Tim VerHey walked back toward the podium. In spite of the demands of this wearying trial, he still appeared fresh and confident. He thanked the judge and addressed the jury.

"We're hearing echoes today when we hear that this killing didn't occur in Oxford Lake. But we know it did. Why? We went through this already before lunch. Look at how she was bound. Look at the fact that she was taped. Look at the absolute absence of asphyxiation, no proof of that. Look at the fact that she was seen with Marvin Gabrion at this parking area in June when he had a boat in the back. Right here. Right in this boat landing area.

"What are we supposed to believe, that he just went here for a little while and then drove her somewhere else, killed her and brought her back again? Does that give you any reason based on your common sense and everyday experience to doubt where he did it?

"What else?" Quickly he outlined the objections to testimony and refocused the witnesses' statements. Twice Mitchell interrupted the rebuttal with objections, which the judge quickly set aside. Ver-Hey began to turn his rebuttal to a conclusion.

"We have the fact that there was a wadded up piece of duct tape about a hundred yards from this boat landing area with Rachel Timmerman's hair on it. Anybody that's ever used duct tape knows that it's very easy to wad it up. Once you get it wadded and the two sticky sides together, you might as well forget it. You've got to throw it away, start over.

"This piece of duct tape with Rachel Timmerman's hair on it is down here. It's not in Mexico or New York or at some other spot in Michigan. The duct tape was put on Rachel Timmerman on the south end of Oxford Lake where the defendant was seen with her in June when she died."

VerHey quickly but systematically rebutted similar defense objections. Then, letting his deep-held convictions show, he passionately closed with his key point—the nature of the murderer himself.

"And we heard this disgusting tale on Friday from the defendant, didn't we? This fairy tale that he told us about how somebody else killed Rachel Timmerman. Even when it would save his own skin, he couldn't bear the thought of giving the credit to somebody else. Even that story with Ian and Eddie helping Rachel commit suicide, which would, if he's going to pull this off, would put him out of the picture, he can't even bear doing it, because the story is that they all come to him. They bring him the suicide note, they bring him this baby and then he, Ian and Eddie drive to Philadelphia and put the baby up for adoption. That's his story to you.

"Even Friday, even today, when it would save his skin to tell you somebody else did it, he can't bear to do it. And even Friday he's taunting the family of Rachel Timmerman. Remember what he said? You know, if Tim Timmerman and Mrs. VerHage, the lady who's the paternal grandmother of Shannon VerHage, if they go get counseling, maybe, maybe they'll get their baby back. Maybe they'll get their granddaughter back. He sat there and said that on Friday to these people who have for five years been wondering what happened to Shannon VerHage. He told you under oath he knows what happened to Shannon VerHage and even today he won't tell you. He won't tell them. He won't give them any peace of mind, because he's enjoying himself.

"And perhaps the only true thing you heard on Friday that came out of the defendant's mouth was when he was asked by Mr. Davis, 'Do you think what you did to Rachel Timmerman is justified and not murder?' The defendant answered, 'No, I don't think what you did to her is justifiable at all. I think what you did is you forced her to testify in a case against a person lying in a case which forced her to become a victim to a crime, you and these prosecutors and the police. You know what you did.' He told all of you on Friday that the prosecution and the police killed Rachel Timmerman by forcing her to testify."

Tensions visibly heightened in the courtroom as VerHey moved on.

"Ladies and gentlemen, to wrap up, in this country, in our system of justice, if someone's charged with a crime and they come into court and say, prove it, there's nobody in the world who can apply the law, our law, except a jury like you. I can't do it, the Court can't do it, the FBI can't do it, Michigan state police can't do it. Only a jury like you.

"We have a law in this country that makes it illegal to take somebody's life intentionally with premeditation on federal property. What the defendant did in this case by killing Rachel Timmerman was sadistic, cruel, intentional and done in cold blood. And what he did was also against our law."

VerHey's eyes regarded each juror separately as he edged toward the end of his argument and as he did, Tim felt a weight being lifted from his shoulders for he had to believe the jury would now know the truth.

"You know he committed this crime. You know he's guilty. What I'm asking you to do now is follow the oath that you took when you became jurors and apply what you know to be the truth to the law.

"Ladies and gentlemen of the jury, if you let Mr. Gabrion walk out of here with his life that will not be justice.

"Thank you very much for what I know is your careful attention
to this case."

Chapter 25

The Ultimate Verdict

With the hearing's conclusion, Judge Bell delivered his somber instructions to the jury, carefully providing definitions for unfamiliar terms. The words echoed in the hushed courtroom.

"The burden of proving a sentence of death beyond a reasonable doubt is the government's. The burden is doubt for a reason, not an abstract mathematical possibility.

"Mitigating factors fall under a lesser standard of proof. Mitigating factors are proven by a preponderance of the evidence; that is, if they produce in your mind a belief that it is more likely that they are true.

"You may use any information and evidence from the guilt phase to help you make your decision.

"The gateway, intent factor has already been established beyond any reasonable doubt. Mr. Gabrion was found guilty of murder; you need not discuss it further. There are statutory factors."

Marvin Gabrion paid very close attention as Judge Bell gave more definitions. The spectators knew what *heinous* and *depraved* mean. Gabrion occasionally turned toward the courtroom, appearing agitated.

"There are four non-statutory factors. You, the jury, unanimously need to find that the government has established beyond a reasonable doubt one of these factors.

285

"One, that the defendant is likely to commit criminal acts of violence in the future which would be a continuing and serious threat to the lives and safety of others and that such future dangerousness is an aggravating factor. Two, that the personal characteristics of Rachel Timmerman and her uniqueness as an individual human being were such that her death has resulted in a loss to society, has caused injury and loss to her family and that such victim impact evidence is an aggravating factor. Three, that in committing the offense, the defendant caused the death or disappearance of Rachel Timmerman's infant daughter Shannon VerHage and that such death or disappearance is an aggravating factor. Four, that the defendant obstructed justice by murdering Rachel Timmerman because she was the complaining witness in a criminal sexual conduct charge against him and that such obstruction of justice is an aggravating factor.

"There are mitigating factors. A mitigating factor is an extenuating circumstance. It need only be proven by a preponderance of evidence. You will be asked, but are not required to report your findings. I'm going to read to you the mitigating circumstances.

1) Defendant grew up in an impoverished and violent environment and was the victim of abandonment, neglect and emotional, psychological and physical abuse as a child.

2) Defendant was not provided with the necessary parental guidance as an adolescent which prevented him from acquiring the necessary social skills and maturity to deal with adult situations and traumas.

3) Defendant's early family life and childhood contributed to his adult psychological deficits and criminal conduct.

4) Defendant was not a disciplinary problem in school and does not have any history of criminal conduct before the age of twenty-three.

5) Defendant's abuse of drugs, alcohol and chemical inhalants contributed to his criminal conduct.

6) Defendant suffers from an organically acquired personality disorder.

7) Defendant has features of several personality disorders, including histrionic personality disorder, narcissistic personality disorder and borderline personality disorder.

8) Defendant has suffered traumatic brain injuries which have led to neurological impairments, including Geschwind syndrome.

9) Defendant suffers from brain dysfunction which has impaired his ability to control his conduct and to function in the absence of strong support and guidance.

10) Defendant committed the offense under severe mental or emotional disturbance.

11) Defendant's capacity to appreciate the wrongfulness of his conduct or to conform his conduct to the requirements of law was impaired, regardless of whether his capacity was so impaired as to constitute a defense to the charge.

12) Defendant will not be a danger in the future if he is confined in a highly structured and secure federal prison."

Each jury member also received written statements of these guidelines to direct their discussion. One final charge from the judge:

"The defendant has already received a sentence of life in prison without the possibility of parole. You, the jury, may find that is a just sentence. The government is asking you to look at and weigh the aggravating and the mitigating factors, using your ordinary everyday life experience as a guide. To weigh whether the aggravating factors sufficiently outweigh the mitigating factors to justify the penalty of death. I would caution the jury to avoid passion, prejudice or undue sympathy."

The bailiffs were sworn to protect the jury and they left the court.

It is nearly a tradition in high profile court cases to try to blow off some steam by talking and speculating with people involved. Tim and Lyn always found the defense attorneys, Paul Mitchell and David

288   The Ultimate Verdict

Stebbins, to be very polite and courteous. In fact, after the trial Tim VerHey, talking with Tim and Don Davis together, put his feelings about the defense into words: "They busted their butts for his defense, just to see Gabrion blow all of their hard work."

The post-trial lull also provided an opportunity for Tim to ask some questions of his own particularly to Sergeant Dick Miller:

Sergeant Miller did give me a very thorough run down on the search of Oxford Lake. It started with the cadaver dogs. Two sets of dogs hit three spots. The dog handlers assured him that there were human remains at those three spots. These hits were followed up with ground penetrating radar. The radar confirmed the hits and locations. Additional follow-up was done with a magnetron, very sensitive magnetic imaging equipment. Top notch equipment, used to locate shipwrecks, etc.

Sergeant Miller performed the initial test with a very long pole. He was able to push it down thirty-six feet, no farther. Sea wall building companies submitted bids, planning on going down forty feet. They found the ground to be totally unusable at forty feet and had to go deeper.

The initial bids were for $140,000. The greater depth requirement created funding problems. The MSP kicked in some money. The local US Attorneys found some money. The access road was widened very cheaply, using prison labor. The size of the coffer dams was reduced from twenty feet square to fifteen feet, on a side.

The construction company determined that they could go down ninety feet, but they still had problems. The sheet pilings were very susceptible to water coming back up, through splits, pressure, etc. At one time officers had to jump out fast, due to possible collapse.

The welders had thrown their spent weld rods into the wrong side of the pilings. The rods inside of the hole ruined the pumps, just numerous problems.

There is considerable paperwork during jury deliberations. The Special Verdict Form itself extends to ten pages that weigh the statutory aggravating factors. Not surprisingly, the jury asked to be dismissed at 8 P.M.

It is very unusual for a federal court to work on Saturday, but this one was in session on March 16. Apparently, the jurors were very close to the sentencing verdict. And indeed, shortly after an hour elapsed, the jury entered.

By this point, Tim and Lyn were both exhausted. Tim had worked on his feet all his life and was an avid outdoorsman. The long hours of sitting on the hard bench in a cramped courtroom reliving the awful truth about his daughter's death had taken their toll both physically and psychologically. In fact, Lyn was now holding tight to his arm, afraid that he might jump up and shout "Yes!" as the sentence was read. Or worse. This despite the fact that Judge Bell had warned the courtroom very strongly about showing any visible or verbal reaction to the verdict.

But the guilt phase of the trial had been perhaps the most important to Tim and Lyn. As Tim wrote, "For me, it all goes back to the boat ride. I do know that I taught my little girl how to pray. I don't know how much comfort she got from it. As she sat in her handcuffs, chains and duct tape, Rachel knew all the way out she was going to be murdered, in that muddy lake. I kind of wanted Gabrion to have that same feeling.

The courtroom became very somber, very quiet as the jury announced its decision: the death penalty.

Judge Bell gave the necessary legal words for the transcript— that the jury had pronounced the sentence and that it would be enforced. Marvin Gabrion murmured something over his shoulder to his mother and was led out of the courtroom.

Immediately the furor started in newspapers and Internet media. Marvin Gabrion started his appeals process also.

Shortly after the trial Wayne Davis' remains were discovered in a lake near where Rachel's body was found.

For Tim, the close of a long torment had a different effect. For the first time he had the opportunity to reflect on the events as a whole. He entered his reflections in his last notebook:

There have been questions and commentary aplenty about West Michigan's first death penalty. Marvin Gabrion was convicted and sentenced to die for murdering my daughter Rachel Helena Timmerman.

Life, murder, death. Most of us sit in our homes, with our comfortable lifestyles, much as I did five years ago. Middle-aged, decent job, life is pretty good. Maybe the youthful goals of making the world a better place have abated a bit, toward a more practical grasp of what we can do with our time on earth. Maybe you're still going strong, making your days count for all you can.

Some people have said the death penalty is wrong, just because they say so. Others offer a more reasoned opposition. They ask, "How can a cycle of killing help anyone? We must forgive criminals for their sins and everything will be all right." Others seek to analyze and explain criminal behavior. This really doesn't help.

The trouble is that life, murder, dying and the death penalty are not intellectual issues. They are subjective, emotional issues. They arise unbidden, yet undeniable; so deeply felt that they affect physiological changes in your entire body.

We like to think we are a cultured and compassionate nation of people. The death penalty is not given to cultured, rational individuals. The United States government, through its laws, has a death penalty for criminals. I have found the structure of the statute to be a complex procedure. A well thought-out device designed by educated, intelligent people who have confronted and learned the emotions of homicide.

It is easy for the casual observer to say that the family wants revenge. Gosh, if it happened to my child (but I know it won't), I'd want revenge, too. I can't deny that is part of the picture, but there's much more. It denies the entire judiciary procedure. There is the indictment, a written statement, *The United States of America v. Marvin Gabrion*. This is followed by the arraignment, a call to court to verbally answer the charges.

Before the trial began, Judge Bell instructed the jury that Mr. Gabrion was clothed in a shroud of innocence. He needed to make no defense. It was purely up to the government to prove beyond any reasonable doubt that he was guilty as charged.

I would chastise anyone who makes judgment on this case who wasn't there in the courtroom. If you weren't there, you have little factual basis for making your decision. The jury heard and saw much. The prosecutors had a lot to work with.

Can I ask how much money would it take for you to be a correctional officer? How about for just one day? Correctional officers testified about Mr. Gabrion's ingenuity, deviousness and regularity at being a ferocious prisoner. After being securely locked down for contraband and misbehavior, Gabrion lashed out with the only weapon he had, throwing his own hepatitis-tainted feces at an innocent prison guard.

Many of Mr. Gabrion's scams were quite devious, such as calling up the clerk of the court and trying to arrange his own transfer to Milan, where he liked it better. Ever since Mr. Gabrion had been incarcerated, we had asked that his calls to our home be blocked. Four or five times now he managed to get around the blockage. Would you like to discuss your daughter's heinous demise with her murderer?

Speaking of heinous, how long did it take for Mr. Gabrion to build his apparatus of death? No quick shot to the head for my little girl. No, we had to have handcuffs, then over sixty pounds of metal and concrete. We're still not done, we need duct tape. One of Rachel's mannerisms was to say, "Please, please, please" when she wanted something. Gabrion said on the witness stand that Rachel kept talking and talking and talking. I have no trouble at all hearing her say, "Please, please, please don't kill me."

How long did Rachel know that Gabrion was going to kill her? Didn't he appeal to our senses, our emotions and ask for the same thing with the knowledge that he will be put to death?

What about the innocent neighbor who discovered her in the lake? What about the Michigan state police and Newaygo County sheriff's deputies who had to deal with Rachel's decaying body? Are their lives any better or worse for Mr. Gabrion's actions? I have heard exactly no one in law enforcement or American government step up and say we must let this man live.

Finally, Mr. Gabrion had a chance to make some amends to my family. Life in prison in exchange for telling the location of Shannon VerHage. He refused to give her back.

Yes, we feel good, almost elated at the guilty verdict. We know that America will be a safer place without Mr. Gabrion on the streets. The imposing of the death penalty at the sentencing was, we believe, a job that needed to be done.

Part V

Epilogue

"Down must we go, to that dark world and blind,"
The poet said, turning on me a bleak
Blanched face; "I will go first—come thou behind."

Dante
The Divine Comedy, The Inferno, "Canto IV"

Moody: "The Greenville County Jail is not hell.
These July days it's worser than hell and hotter. It's
so hot you have to lay still on a bunk just to keep
your hed from swimming. I reckon if you moved
around you'd just lose your breth."

Robert Morgan
This Rock

The buildings of the Terre Haute Federal Correctional Complex rise above the flatlands like warty growths on desiccated flesh. The high sky, reaching forever on these Indiana plains, is interrupted only here and there by lone trees.

The penitentiary sprawls across 1,126 acres of land. In its July 2009 census, Terre Haute housed 3,417 inmates. It is at once one of the largest housing projects and largest industries in the state.

The penitentiary began after a long promotional effort by the city of Terre Haute, two miles north, in an effort to stimulate its post-Depression economy. President Franklin D. Roosevelt gave authorization in 1938. The first building opened in 1940. Its intention: to house only non-violent offenders.

As the years passed, the need for varying levels of incarceration changed and also the demand for greater security as those levels changed. The prison expanded. The original building was relisted as a medium-security facility. By 2004 the totally new prison was finished.

One might call it "progressive" in contemporary social/political parlance. It is tobacco free; it has faith-based wards; it has telephone privileges. And it has a booming prison industry where convicts can earn up to $7.50 a day largely making supplies for the military.

Racketeers, wayward politicians, swindlers and general federal criminals of a dozen different stripes have done time in Terre Haute.

But in 1993, a new unit changed the way some people, a very few, did their time. In 1993, Terre Haute became the only federal prison in the United States to house a death row. They meant it, too. It has the only death chamber in the federal system, where the condemned are administered death through lethal injection.

Some of the nation's most notorious prisoners have resided in Terre Haute Death Row. The Oklahoma City bomber, Timothy McVeigh, was executed there in June 2001. He set the record—five years flat on death row, no appeals. Juan Raul Garza, convicted of three drug-related murders, was executed a few days later. Louis Jones Jr., convicted of kidnapping, raping and murdering a nineteen-year-old woman, was executed in 2003.

Current inmates include Seyed Mousavi, Randall Royer, Rafil Dhafir, David Paul Hammer and John Walker Lindh. Many of them have taken advantage of the "progressive" rules and have established multiple Web sites, generally asking for correspondence, soliciting donations or declaring their innocence. David Paul Hammer, who has resided at Terre Haute for over twenty years, even has a site of photos of the prison graveyard. Under one photo appears this caption: "Prison cemetery where I will be buried after my execution. It's called 'Peckerwood Hill' by the inmates."

Several of these men and other individuals on death row have been incarcerated for many years. Legal delays are the primary reason executions are delayed, as appeals filter up the courts. Moreover, the American Civil Liberties Union (ACLU) has been active in bringing lawsuits against Terre Haute, precisely because those suits could forge a legal precedent that would affect State prisons. The ACLU, for example, has filed suit in such cases as Muslim inmates not having sufficient time for the prayer hours required by their religion. In 2008, it filed a suit claiming that "Death row inmates at the federal prison in Terre Haute are routinely denied access to medical, dental and mental health care." The lead attorney cited conditions as "grossly inadequate," failing "to meet constitutional criteria" and jeopardizing "the health and safety" of the over fifty inmates on death row.

By definition, prison is an act of deprivation. That is to say, prisoners are deprived of rights because they have formerly deprived someone of theirs. The deprivation is according to scale. Deprive someone of their lifetime savings by larceny or fraud and you can be given a prison term as punishment and restitution to enact some degree of justice. Blowing up a building in Oklahoma City and causing the death or maiming of hundreds of individuals requires a certain degree of deprivation (in McVeigh's case, his life), but there can be no restitution. Neither of these men can create life; neither can bring the dead back to life. The deprivation they caused is thorough, irremediable and irreparable. Deprivation on Death Row, therefore, includes an additional element—isolation.

Any prison spawns violence. Terre Haute is no exception. On June 11, 2009, a fight broke out in the recreation yard, growing worse by the moment. Unable to quell the uprising, guards fired on the prisoners. One was evacuated to a hospital with gunshot wounds and another was treated for wounds suffered in the melee. The prison went on lockdown. Even the minimal amount of free time was taken away.

Home is a small cell. It stinks. It is hot. One ninety-degree day, David Paul Hammer simply turned on his water tap, plugged all the leaks and wallowed naked in the foot of water that gathered in his cell. As punishment, he was led to the "hole."

In an investigative article about death row in the Texas penitentiary, a liberal and progressive investigative journal, *Mother Jones*, explored conditions similar to many such confinements. With one exception: the Texas legislature passed a bill speeding up the appeals process. The study, done in 1997 by Suzanne Donovan and titled "Shadow Figures: A Portrait of Life on Texas Death Row", is slightly dated, but still gives a fairly accurate portrait. Moreover, the selection of the Huntsville facility is important for several reasons. Texas has overwhelming support for capital punishment, has over 400 individuals on death row and has become so over-crowded that a new facility, Ellis, had to be built several miles north of the old Huntsville prison. Execution is an industry at Ellis; the line has to keep moving. Huntsville itself is the company town. Still, the average length of time between conviction and execution is slightly over three years. On the date of execution, a condemned prisoner is returned to the old unit in Huntsville and enters the death chamber known as "The Walls."

Two statements in the article should be, we believe, reflected upon. First, the author makes a passing observation: "Many men talked about their initial fears in facing Death Row. Once they were convicted and sentenced to die, most believed they would be executed right away. Almost no one anticipates the months or years of waiting, or how living on the Row will change them." This is the first thing we on the outside fail to comprehend. Always, over the heads of those individuals, hangs the sickle of death. Its coming is imminent. Worse, the inmate placed it there himself. Now it hangs by a slender thread, ready at any moment. The very fact that it can be stayed so long by appeals actually makes it worse. More than one inmate wishes he could be wheeled on a gurney into the chamber tomorrow.

The second thing the article reinforces is the unassuageable loneliness of the inmate. Most have few prior relations to call upon. The crimes themselves have severed them from the flow of human society. In the old days, a peculiarly appropriate word was used for them: *outlaws*. They have lived outside the boundaries of decent, civilized life. Their incarceration is a daily and tormenting reminder that they no longer belong within civilized order. They have given up their place. They are now a shirt with a number on its back.

This is deprivation. The name will not be restored to those at Terre Haute until one of them receives the official notice of date of execution from the director of the Federal Bureau of Prisons.

Until then, the legal wheels grind. With a new attorney, Gabrion submitted his first appeal, based on the supposition that his case shouldn't have been tried in federal court because of the property line dispute in Oxford Lake. It would be a lengthy process.

On March 14, 2008, the 6th Circuit Court of Appeals in Cincinnati, Ohio, ruled, in a forty-two page opinion, two to one that the federal government had jurisdiction to prosecute Marvin Gabrion. The lone dissenting vote was based on the philosophy of federal invasion of State's rights.

His attorneys took the final step, appealing to the Supreme Court. On April 11, 2009, the Supreme Court declined to hear the dispute.

So he waits; deprived of the civilized order he has violated. Fearful. Lonely. Begging for pen pals, for photographs, for money. Waiting for the form letter from the director of the Federal Bureau of Prisons:

[Name]
[Reg. No.]
Special Confinement Unit
United States Penitentiary
Terre Haute, Indiana 47802

Dear Mr. [name]
The purpose of this letter is to inform you that a date has been set for implementation of your death sentence, pursuant to the Judgment and Commitment Order issued on [date] by the Honorable [presiding judge] of the United States District Court for [place]. The director of the Federal Bureau of Prisons has set [specific date] as the date of your execution by lethal injection.

To seek clemency under Title 28, Code of Federal Regulations, Sections 1.1 and 1.10, a written request for commutation of sentence or reprieve from the President must be filed with the Office of the Pardon Attorney, 500 First Street N.W., Suite 400, Washington, D.C. 20530. The Office of the Pardon Attorney is responsible for receiving and processing, on behalf of the President, all requests for clemency. The petition must be filed within 30 days of the date you receive this notice.

In near future, I will come to your housing unit to personally discuss with you many of the details surrounding the execution. At that time, I will be available to answer questions you may have regarding the execution procedures.

As the days pass until the letter arrives, prison works its poison into the inmate. On Death Row, the dying starts the day the doors close behind the inmate. It is tangible. One can see its effects. Skin loses its normal luster and turns into a waxy pallor. It lies slack against the bones, like wet crepe paper. The inmate comes outside one hour a day for exercise. Sometimes he exercises in a steel mesh cage, like a dog kennel. Sometimes he is restricted to a narrow area where he paces relentlessly. At Terre Haute, many days are rainy, snowy or frigid. No sun strikes the inmates' skin. So they transform their skin. It becomes an ashen canvas of tattoos—homemade tattoos etched into the skin. They become trapped in their tattoos like scaly armor.

The poison works into the mind of the prisoner. Although the lights are bright and walls the standard off-white enamel (which makes it harder to conceal any chippings), the walls press on the mind. In some prisons, a ward for the psychotic prisoners can be sound-proofed. The screams and shrieks can't be heard in nearby wards. Psychiatric treatment is primitive at best. A favorite prescription is guaranteed to keep the inmate in a near stupor.

The days pass, waiting for the letter.

One can glean the anxiety of waiting from Ernest J. Gaines' *A Lesson Before Dying*: "i just cant sleep no mo cause evertime i shet my eyes i see that door an fore i git ther i wak up an i dont go back to sleep cause i dont want walk to that door no mo cause i dont know what back o ther if its wher they gon put that cher or if it spose to mean def or the grave or heaven i dont know."

Then one day a letter arrives. A specific date set. On Death Row, rumors scatter like grains of rice. Who has the lowest number? Who is next? How long until the next?

Except for one man. It is his time to die. Now it is a ritual, carefully scripted—unless a stay of execution is issued. The guards act as though it never will. They follow the script.

Thirty-six hours prior to the execution time, the inmate gathers a few personal effects and is moved to the death watch cell. He is ordered to write his will.

The steps unfold, each one closer to the chamber. The order for the final meal. His choice of clothing. The preparation of a visitor list for the final twenty-four hours. Whether he chooses to donate his body to medical research, to his family or to interment at "Peckerwood Hill."

The hours narrow. He might have visitors, but he is still alone. No one else can walk this road for him or with him.

He showers, brushes his teeth, puts on clean clothes. The warden and chaplain arrive. They will stay through the execution.

In the anteroom of the death chamber, the prisoner is strapped with restraints to a gurney. He can only raise his head, perhaps to look at the witnesses on the other side of the glass window of the chamber, perhaps to make a final statement. A heart monitor (EKG) is affixed.

At the designated time, the prisoner is wheeled into the chamber. The windows are draped. Both arms are swabbed with alcohol; two intravenous drips are inserted, one in each arm. The IV tubes are threaded through the wall into the anteroom.

The drapes part on the witness room. The prisoner is given the chance to make a statement.

From the anteroom, the fatal drugs are introduced into the IV line. No witness sees the action, nor does the anteroom permit a view of the chamber.

A very fast-acting anesthetic, usually sodium thiopental (pentothal), is injected into the port. This is a powerful barbiturate that puts the prisoner to sleep within thirty seconds.

One of two, or sometimes both, fatal agents are introduced. Both are paralyzing agents. Pancuronium bromide (Pavulon) is a muscle relaxant that paralyzes the diaphragm and lungs. Potassium chloride stops the electrical signals to the heart, inducing cardiac arrest. Somewhere between one and two minutes after the first injection, the prisoner is declared dead.

Marvin Gabrion waits for the day his letter arrives.

Yet juxtaposed with the agony of this scene is the even greater agony of another.

Rachel Timmerman walked from the restored farmhouse, past the garden, along the circling drive to where her date would meet her. Tim looked up from the book he was reading as she passed the garden, struck by the pale gold hair of his daughter and granddaughter.

Their hair wisped like nearly white banners against the blue sky. Shannon's chubby little arms waved, one fist full of Rachel's hair that she swung around like a new toy. From Tim's perspective, sitting in the lawn chair, the two looked like they were dancing in the blue sky.

Just then Rachel caught sight of her father. She detoured around the garden. She wore her new blue jeans and her favorite red plaid shirt, her long hair in a ponytail that Shannon had partially pulled apart. Her smile was as wide as the sun.

"Are you taking Shannon along?"

"He asked me to," Rachel responded. "It's a dinner date so I'll only be gone a couple of hours."

Just then a cream-colored car pulled in the bottom driveway by the barn.

Rachel waved. "Bye, Dad. Love you."

"Bye. I love you too, honey."

The next day Tim received the first envelope with the space hologram stamp.

Dad,

I'm sorry I left without saying good-bye. That guy that picked me up is like the man of my dreams. . . .

Right now we're on vacation.

But she wasn't. Rachel Timmerman, with her daughter Shannon, was on her own death watch. The "date" had delivered her to her most feared person on the face of the earth—Marvin Gabrion.

Exactly what Rachel endured during the following twenty-four to thirty-six hours of her death watch we will never know. Nor do we want to imagine. Somewhere in the perverse twisting of his darkened mind, only Marvin Gabrion will carry those memories with him.

We do know that Rachel fought as hard as she could to live, for both herself and her daughter. Gabrion was next seen with bloody scratch marks, cuts and pulled out hair.

As the handcuffs snapped on her wrists, surely Rachel knew she was in the final hours of the death watch.

She must have struggled powerfully as she walked down the hill, the overhanging trees like a corridor, to the waiting boat. In the boat sixty pounds of cement blocks were attached to long chains wrapped around her body, then padlocked tight. The final hours had turned into minutes.

We don't know whether her baby daughter Shannon was with her. This knowledge will pass with the killer. But authorities suspect so. Which makes one wonder if she too was murdered and thrown into the lake; how was the infant weighted?

Like a person restrained on a gurney, Rachel could hardly move. Duct tape slapped over mouth and wound around her head. Her eyes bulged in terror with the struggle to breathe. A second strip of tape slapped over her eyes and wound around her forehead, forever tangling the light blonde hair. Only her nostrils were free of the tape. Now, in the night, total darkness, the only witness a monster.

Did she stop struggling then, as the boat splashed into the water? When she was a little girl, her father taught her to pray. Was she praying then in the lonely silence, broken by the creak of oars?

The blocks were probably thrown over first. She tumbled after them as the weight carried her down. This was the moment of pure panic. She knew, rationally, that to breathe was death. Then she knew physically, emotionally, that she could no longer hold her breath.

She breathed.